HOW TO BE A

PRODUCTIVITY
NINJA

WORRY LESS → ACHIEVE MORE → LOVE WHAT YOU DO

GRAHAM ALLCOTT

This edition published in the UK in 2016
by Icon Books Ltd, Omnibus Business Centre,
39–41 North Road, London N7 9DP
email: info@iconbooks.com
www.iconbooks.com

First published in the UK in 2014 by Icon Books Ltd

Sold in the UK, Europe and Asia
by Faber & Faber Ltd, Bloomsbury House,
74–77 Great Russell Street,
London WC1B 3DA or their agents

Distributed in the UK, Europe and Asia
by Grantham Book Services, Trent Road, Grantham NG31 7XQ

Distributed in Australia and New Zealand
by Allen & Unwin Pty Ltd, PO Box 8500,
83 Alexander Street, Crows Nest, NSW 2065

Distributed in South Africa by
Jonathan Ball, Office B4, The District,
41 Sir Lowry Road, Woodstock 7925

Distributed in India by Penguin Books India,
7th Floor, Infinity Tower – C, DLF Cyber City,
Gurgaon 122002, Haryana

Distributed in the USA
by Publishers Group West,
1700 Fourth Street, Berkeley, CA 94710

Distributed in Canada
by Publishers Group Canada, 76 Stafford Street, Unit 300
Toronto, Ontario M6J 2S1

ISBN: 978-178578-028-8

Typeset by Bernadette McDonagh and Marie Doherty
Cover logo and illustrations by Burrell Design

Printed and bound in the UK by Clays Ltd, St Ives plc

ABOUT THE AUTHOR

Graham Allcott is a productivity trainer, social entrepreneur and founder of Think Productive. Think Productive run public workshops throughout the UK and also run in-house workshops for staff at a diverse range of organizations including the Cabinet Office (UK government), The National Trust, eBay, Heineken, BT, GlaxoSmithKline and the University of Bristol.

Think Productive workshops include:

Getting Your Inbox to Zero

Email Etiquette

Stress Less, Achieve More

Making Meetings Magic

How to be a Productivity Ninja

Prior to founding Think Productive, Graham's career has primarily focused on social action. He ran community volunteering projects for the University of Birmingham before becoming Chief Executive of the charity Student Volunteering England and then setting up his social enterprise consultancy, Fruitful Consulting.

He was also co-founder of Intervol, the founding Chairman of READ International and has advised Governments, both red and blue, on youth and community issues, most notably The Russell Commission and National Citizen Service. He is a trustee of the youth homelessness charity, Centrepoint.

Despite an intolerance of failure elsewhere in his life, he is an Aston Villa season ticket holder.

Graham lives in Brighton, UK.

For Chaz, my Ninja partner-in-crime

CONTENTS

DEAR HUMAN BEING ...

Do you want to do everything and change the world, yet also find yourself feeling quite lazy from time to time? Yes, me too. We humans are hunting animals that have evolved to such an extent that we no longer need to hunt, so we perhaps have a right and an excuse to be lazy. Yet that doesn't stop us being ambitious and driven either.

I would define productivity as the ability to achieve what you want to achieve, for the least effort. Certainly I don't want to burn myself out and I definitely like still having time for relationships, friendships, passions, hobbies, rest and whatever else floats my boat.

So a few years ago, while juggling a hundred and one things – some paid, some voluntary; some work-related, some not – I developed a new obsession in my quest to change the world: productivity. Creating the most change or impact – whatever that means for you – for the least effort is what this book is all about.

I want to thank you for buying this book. By choosing to read *How to be a Productivity Ninja* you've already shown a desire to make things happen, make an impact and find easier and better ways to do what you do. Over the past few years since I founded Think Productive, we've been working with some of the UK and Europe's biggest companies, government organizations and charities to help them eliminate the information stress that seems so endemic in the modern workplace. So this book is about helping you to do just that.

My approach to productivity is 100 per cent human. Too often, we label those who achieve great things as being somehow separate from us mere mortals. The great figures of our history all undoubtedly had unique talents, charisma and vision. However, none of them were really any different from you or me in a whole host of ways: even the bravest get scared, even the strongest leaders occasionally lack direction and even the greatest human beings suffer from bouts of self-doubt or have other hidden character flaws. And yet there's a common theme running through so many time management books and business books, through the wider personal growth industry and indeed through much of our society: it's the cult of celebrity, the cult of personality.

As we go on to explore the characteristics of the Productivity Ninja in this book, we'll look at how a Ninja creates a mindset of Zen-like Calm, Ruthlessness, Weapon-savviness, Stealth and Camouflage, Unorthodoxy, Agility, Mindfulness and Preparedness. But I hope one of the loudest messages is that in order to be a Productivity Ninja, you don't have to magically become a superhero.

Too many people buy these kinds of books and never even make time to read them. Too many others just indulge in the cult of personality and get lost in the dream of perfection that is presented by the guru figure. They spend time fantasizing about being the person writing the book and buying into the often impossible dreams the guru presents, rather than planning and implementing changes for their own lives.

So just to be ultra-clear, there is no perfect guru specimen to worship here. For all my moments of productive genius there are moments of self-doubt, me screwing it up, procrastinating or doing things less than efficiently. The difference is that now I recognize these bad habits and work at changing them.

Part of what I hope makes my experiences and insights all the more valuable to you is precisely the fact that I don't pretend not to know what failure looks like. Hopefully you'll see that as an assurance of authenticity and an opportunity to learn from some of my mistakes – and not as a reason to ditch this book and go looking for some guru escapism instead. And of course I really hope you're motivated by the idea of boosting your productivity and discovering the way of the Productivity Ninja. This book is in many ways a manual for your work and life. It's also a celebration of achievement. And it's a celebration of the fact that behind every extraordinary achievement lies an ordinary human being, just like you.

1. THE WAY OF THE PRODUCTIVITY NINJA

> *'Being busy does not always mean real work. The object of all work is production or accomplishment and to either of these ends there must be forethought, system, planning, intelligence and honest purpose, as well as perspiration. Seeming to do is not doing.'*
> – Thomas Edison

Ever thought you should get better at managing your time? Have you spent ages wondering how some people seem to be able to get so much more done than you, or how you can learn to cope with the endlessly growing volume of emails and other things that need to be done? Do you wonder why there just never seem to be enough hours in the day?

It's often thought that good 'time management' is the key to productivity, success and happiness. There are hundreds of books on time management, mostly written by 'guru' types who seem to have it all so perfectly and succinctly summarized: prioritize the right things, start the day with a list of what you need to do and then systematically tick them off, from the most important at the start of the day through to the least important at the end. File things away, make short-term, medium-term and long-term goals, organize the clutter around you and manage complex projects with long but perfectly written project plans. It all sounds so easy and so perfect, doesn't it?

Well, let's get one thing clear straight away. I am not writing this book because I'm some kind of time management guru. I'm not one of those naturally organized people. In fact, my natural style of work is quite the opposite: flaky, ideas-based, more comfortable at the strategic level than the 'doing' level, allergic to detail, instinctive, crazy-making and ridiculously unrealistic about what's achievable in any given time period. All of these characteristics are, in their own way, among what you could call my strengths, and have made me successful in things I've done. They're part of who I am. I play to these strengths and also recognize them as the crippling weaknesses that they are. Changing my own bad habits and developing strong, positive new ones gave me the ability to help others do the same. But in grappling with my own unproductive demons and working hard to become more productive and gain more control in my work and in my life, I've come to an important conclusion: time management is dead.

TIME MANAGEMENT IS DEAD

Somewhere along the line, the game changed. We now live in an age of constant connection and information overload. We are bombarded with new information inputs – and from several different sources at the same time – in a way that would have been staggering to comprehend even ten years ago. In the old time management books, dealing with new inputs was simple enough: they came in the form of paper letters, delivered to the office first thing every morning and perhaps again first thing in the afternoon if you were really popular. Dealing with and reacting to the new was a self-contained, limited activity that would take no more than an hour a day. According to the old time management principles, this left you free for the rest of the day to get on with the 'real work', which could be planned out early in the day via a simple daily to-do list and 'ABC' priority system.

Today, such systems seem archaic: it's a big challenge to create the time and attention needed to get anywhere near our real work because we're buried under 24–7 email, social media, voicemails, instant messenger, texts, intranets, conference calls, collaboration tools and the burden of staying connected. Ever got to 5pm and found you're still staring at a full to-do list, wondering where the day went? Me too.

Quite apart from the ever-increasing volume of information in our work, there are so many other reasons why time management theories of old no longer cut it. Work is more complex now than it ever has been, and yet our roles are less defined and the work itself more free-flowing: the emphasis is less on rigid management hierarchies and more on each member of the team taking personal responsibility – the pace of communication has increased dramatically and we're expected to reply or at least be 'in the loop' constantly. Not only that, but working hours are becoming longer and more flexible, catering to the needs of working parents as well as colleagues across continents.

All of this means you have to come to terms with one important thing: you will never get everything finished.

YOU WILL NEVER GET EVERYTHING FINISHED

Ask yourself this: if you've ever made a to-do list with priorities on it (for example, 'A', 'B' and 'C' priorities), did you manage to get to the 'C' listed items before more 'A'-grade opportunities or potential disasters presented themselves? Of course you didn't. And if you *did* get to those 'C' listed items, chances are you got to them because they suddenly started to rise up the ranks, becoming the more urgent 'A' and 'B' items because they were previously left unattended.

Think back to a moment in your working life when there was *nothing* more to possibly do that day. It's probably very hard to think of one in recent times; there's always a bit more business development, a bit of clearing the decks, a bit of catching up on reading or housekeeping. You're probably casting your mind back to one of your first jobs, where perhaps you worked in a bar and at the end of a long shift you could all mop down the floors, close down the bar and sit down with a beer, rejoicing in a good night's work and the satisfaction of completion. Completion is a great feeling, isn't it? The satisfaction that you've achieved something, and that it's completely done and gone, is psychologically thrilling.

The other reason completion is satisfying is that it naturally gives way to clear space. Psychologically, clear space helps provide perspective, a brief recovery from the frenetic pace of life and time to re-evaluate our priorities.

The trouble is, the modern work paradigm gives us so little sense of completion or clear space that it feels like we're constantly straining to see the light at the end of a long, long tunnel. And when the light at the end of the tunnel finally approaches, you realize it's just some nasty bloke with a torch bringing you more work to do.

LONG LIVE ATTENTION MANAGEMENT

Don't worry, though – there's a new game now, with completely new rules. Put simply, skilful *attention* management is the new key to productivity, and how well you protect and use your attention determines your success. There are some mortal enemies standing in your way, though: stress, procrastination, interruptions, distractions, low-value commitments, annoying work practices – and you need to learn to overcome these obstacles to focus on what really matters. It's time to think like a Ninja.

THE WAY OF THE PRODUCTIVITY NINJA

'We must be willing to get rid of the life we've planned so as to have the life that is waiting for us.'
– Joseph Campbell

This book is about developing a Ninja mindset and then applying it to every area of your working life – and even beyond. It is about how we turn information from new inputs or vague distractions into completed and celebrated outcomes. It is about our relationship with information at work, and how we *are* ultimately in control and how we do ultimately have enough hours in the day to get the important stuff done. (You'll notice I didn't just say get 'everything' done.)

In this chapter, I'll introduce you to the main behaviours – the way of the Ninja – that will boost your productivity, reduce your stress levels and change the way you think about your work. Necessarily, the way of the Productivity Ninja is about how we think about our work, not how we 'do' our work. Rather than being focused on specific skills, talents or tools, it is an approach to work, from which systems and frameworks can then be easily developed. I will show you how to develop those in the coming chapters, but first let's talk about the underlying principles and mindset. In the later chapters, we will apply this mindset to your everyday situations at work: your email, to-do list, projects and meetings.

DECISION-MAKING IS OUR WORK

By 9.15am on an average day in the information age, we've received more information inputs than most old-school time management theorists would have received in a week! Our work has changed so much that, for most of us, how we deal with new opportunities and new threats is what makes the difference. We no longer think about our work: thinking *is* our work. Successful careers happen for those who make the best decisions. If you want to climb the ladder in your organization, realize that your ability to react and be responsible are what you'll be judged on. The higher you go within an organization or career, the truer this is. The art of decision-making, our ability to make space for the 'quality thinking time' we need, and how we react on our gut instincts (especially when such time for thinking isn't available) defines us at work.

RESPONSIBLE VS. RESPONSE-ABLE

How quickly do you react to change? And I don't mean just realizing that things are changing, but actually digesting, understanding and responding with an appropriate action? It's long been thought that the more people get paid or achieve, the more responsible they are. If you're climbing a corporate ladder, it stands to reason that you take on more responsibility the higher you go.

But simply being 'responsible' these days isn't enough. It's become popular for footballers or managers to come out with statements like, 'I hold my hands up and say I'm responsible for my part in our embarrassing defeat'. While admitting responsibility is better than not doing so, honour in defeat still ultimately equals defeat. And in the information age, things move quickly. As a society we value those who are comfortable with positions of responsibility, but we rarely explore responsibility as something proactive and dynamic. 'I don't want the responsibility', we say, as if it's a term full only of burdens and without corresponding joys. Yet being in a position of responsibility usually also means influence. The nature of responsibility is that it should also bring reward – the ability to make an impact, create wealth and success for your organization, for society, for your family or for you. By viewing responsibility as inherently troublesome, we view it as the price to be paid for this success. We see it as a trade-off. It shouldn't be this way.

To be response-able, therefore, means you have the ability to define in the moment the actions you need to take to overcome and enjoy any new challenge. This book will give you the tools to work on your response-ability and be more response-able in three important ways:

▶ **Response-able now**

We often choose not to respond with definite actions. We procrastinate and we seek to delay things if we're feeling lazy, tired, unsure or worried about the results. The way of the Ninja will help to challenge your thinking and develop new habits so that you're proactively looking for ways to respond, rather than for ways to avoid and defer.

▶ **Response-able later**

You don't want to worry about what could go wrong on all the other projects that you're not working on right now. We'll set up systems so that you always know what your next move will be on any given project and so that you know that these systems will keep things under control for you.

▶ **Response-able if the crap hits the fan**

When you have to drop everything to deal with a crisis, it's much easier if you have a sure-fire way of knowing or remembering what you've dropped. The systems and techniques in this book will make it easier to respond when such moments come along, ensuring full focus on the job at hand.

THE CHARACTERISTICS OF THE PRODUCTIVITY NINJA

'Simplicity is the ultimate sophistication.'
– Leonardo da Vinci

What follows are the key characteristics that make up 'the way of the Productivity Ninja'. As we look at each of these in turn, you may begin to picture some of the ways these approaches can influence how you currently operate. As we go through the later chapters, I'll show you the specific tools and techniques to achieve Ninja-level productivity.

Are you a Ninja?

Zen-like Calm

Unorthodoxy

Ruthlessness

Agility

Weapon-savvy

Mindfulness

Stealth & Camouflage

Preparedness

A Ninja is not Superhuman

ZEN-LIKE CALM

ZEN-LIKE CALM

Great decision-making comes from the ability to create the time and space to think rationally and intelligently about the issue at hand. Decisions made during periods of panic are likely to be the ones we want to forget about. The Ninja realizes this, remains calm in the face of adversity, and equally calm under the pressure of information overload. You might not believe this, but it is entirely possible to have a hundred and one things to do and yet still remain absolutely calm. How do we beat stress and remain calm? I'll answer this question more fully as we look at the practical skills needed for Ninja-mastery of email, tasks, projects and meetings, but here are a few basic principles:

USE YOUR HEAD, DON'T USE YOUR HEAD!

'The mind is for having ideas, not for holding them.'
– David Allen

Be sure that you're not forgetting important items by keeping all of your support information in a system, not in your head. Be sure that you're not distracted and stressed by what you *could* be forgetting – by using a 'second brain' instead of your own head as the place where information and reminders live. This is certainly easier said than done, but once mastered, really works. I will introduce you to your very own 'second brain' and Ninja productivity habits later in this book.

TRUST YOUR SYSTEMS

You need to have trust that whatever systems you use will work. There is a danger that additional stress will be created by the uncertainty of not knowing whether your systems will help you deliver. Moving to a new computer or new software brings with it a few days of uncertainty, but many people live for years without ever really asking themselves if their systems work to the point that they really trust them to. Sticking to what you trust and trusting what you stick to are crucial. The way to foster this trust and promote the Zen-like calm you need is to regularly consider not just your work, but the *process* of your work too. Briefly but regularly reviewing *how* you work will help you to promote clearer thinking in the work itself.

LOWER YOUR EXPECTATIONS. SERIOUSLY.

Realize that you'll never get everything done. That's not the game any more. Be safe in the knowledge that you're in control, selecting the right things to do, and that you're doing as much as one human being possibly can, and you will find a way through it.

KEEP YOUR BODY IN GOOD PHYSICAL CONDITION

> *'A healthy body means*
> *a healthy mind.'*
> *– Anonymous*

Keeping fit and healthy will not only reduce stress in its own right, but will also give your brain the focus and energy it needs to produce clearer thinking and decision-making that will enable you to stay on top of your work, too. And it means you'll look hot. It's a win-win-win!

BE PREPARED & ORGANIZED, READY FOR WHEN TIMES GET ROUGH

> *'A tidy desk is a tidy mind.'*
> *– Anonymous*

Some of us look at being organized as being a bit too anal or obsessive. 'I don't have the time to be organized' is a common objection I hear when coaching clients towards Productivity Ninja status. But the truth is that when we experience periods of 'flow' – the times in our day or week when we're most productive – the last thing we want is to be thrown off track by being unable to find some crucial piece of information or by not having the tools we need readily available. We're not aiming for perfection here, but training yourself to operate from a default position of organization means you're more likely to experience regular periods of super-productive flow.

RUTHLESSNESS

RUTHLESSNESS

It's not a paradox to follow Zen-like calm with ruthlessness. We have already talked about the need to make clear-headed decisions, objectively and calmly. As well as needing to make more and better decisions, we need to be choosier, too: processing information to sort the wheat from the chaff, see the timber from the trees and sort the big opportunities from the even bigger ones. Ruthlessness isn't just about how we process information, though; it's also about our ability to protect our time and attention, focusing only on the things that add the greatest impact, even at the expense of other things that are 'worth doing'.

SAYING 'NO' TO OURSELVES

With so much information flying about, being choosy is the only way. It goes against the Western, protestant work ethic that we're so familiar with to decide *not* to do things, but that's exactly what we must do. A lot. Being much choosier about what we say 'Yes' to is an important skill – and learning to say 'No' to ourselves means not biting off more than we can chew. If you do get into situations where you've taken on too much (and I do this regularly, by the way!), you need to realize that renegotiating your commitments to yourself and others is better than burning yourself out trying to meet them all.

SAYING 'NO' TO OTHERS

Picture this. you're in a meeting that you thought you were attending purely to contribute to, and the meeting discussion begins to come around to some decisions and commitments about actions people could take at the end of the meeting. There's a particular set of actions that you're renowned for being good at, and just as it's mentioned, several pairs of eyes turn and focus on you. It's easy in this situation to over-commit. It's harder to rein the conversation back from what you *could* deliver and on to what you're *able* to deliver. It's harder still, when you know how valuable your contribution could be, to say 'No' to all of it, without feeling like you're letting the side down or losing favour with someone who matters. Saying 'No' to others is tricky. It requires steely resolve, a ruthless streak and some great tactics so that you come out smelling of roses. We'll look at this in more detail later, but make it your mission to perfect the art of saying 'No' to yourself and to others. It goes a long way.

INTERRUPTIONS

Our attention – particularly that proactive attention when we're most alert, in flow and on top of our game – is arguably our most precious resource. It needs to be nurtured and valued. At the same time, there are a million interruptions out there: emails, phone calls, thoughts, stress, colleagues, social media, the next big crisis, the next big thing. All of them need to be stopped dead in their quest to distract and derail you. We deal with this in more detail in Chapter 3, but needless to say, our ruthlessness needs to put paid to a whole lot of temptation too. We often *like* to be distracted because it's the perfect excuse for procrastination and thinking less, and Facebook or Twitter win over the report we're supposed to be finishing simply because it's easier to be in those places, having conversations, than it is to get into the difficult thinking we're supposed to be engaged in. Learning to deal with such interruptions is as much about our self-discipline as it is about our ability to say 'No' to the interruptions of others.

80–20 AND *THE POWER OF IMPACT THINKING*

'Begin with the end in mind.'
– Stephen Covey

Being ruthless also means being selective about how we achieve our goals. Using the 80–20 rule, we can start to recognize that not all of what we do creates an equal amount of impact. 20% of what we do accounts for 80% of the impact. Often, there's a temptation to aim for perfection. In some areas of our work, this perfection is healthy and even necessary, but in other cases it can be avoided and the impact on the final result hardly even noticed. So we need to be ruthless in our planning. What are we trying to achieve? Has someone else solved this problem before? Could we beg, borrow or steal a solution? What's the quickest way we can get this item off our plate and move on? These questions lead us towards thinking about innovation and a contempt for the orthodox (which we'll come to very shortly!), but with a steely focus only on the end and not on the means, we'll give ourselves a better chance of saving some time, considerably reducing the energy expended and reducing the final result only by a fraction.

WEAPON-SAVVY

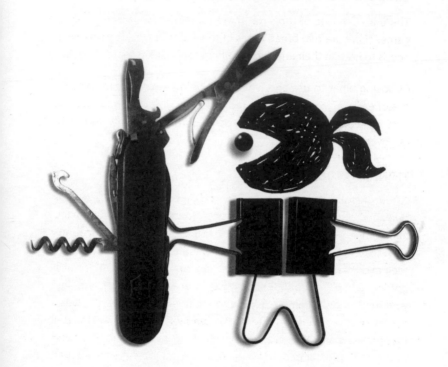

WEAPON-SAVVY

The Ninja is skilful on their own, but knows that using the right tools makes them even more effective.

CHOOSE YOUR WEAPON, KNOW YOUR TOOLS

There are a range of tools out there to help keep us on top of our game. There are two broad types of tools that the Productivity Ninja needs to have in their armoury: thinking tools and organizing tools.

Choosing what to use and when, and being aware of the capabilities of each are key to success. Tools need to give us confidence and ensure that through their productive use, we're rarely interrupted by our own ineptitude.

THINKING TOOLS

As our decisions get more complex, our need for tools to assist our thinking becomes more apparent. Strategic planning processes or line management feedback situations are often where we first encounter such tools, but their value is still underestimated. Certain tools and their explicit use can also give clients, line managers and other stakeholders additional confidence in your processes and can stimulate your thinking. For example, SWOT analysis (looking at **s**trengths, **w**eaknesses, **o**pportunities and **t**hreats) is a common business thinking tool that provides a simple structure for thinking about the present and future in a way that people can easily understand. There are a broad range of such thinking tools and frameworks that have been created to help make our lives easier and our decision-making better.

ORGANIZING TOOLS

From Microsoft Outlook and iPhone apps to the humble stapler, there are so many ways to be organized. The trick is to get to a very good level of organization rather than an excellent or mediocre level; this ensures that the time spent on getting organized receives the optimum payoff in increased productivity, rather than becoming a drain on our time and an unwelcome and unnecessary distraction.

DON'T GET SEDUCED BY 'PRODUCTIVITY PORN'

> *'Joining a Facebook group*
> *about productivity is like*
> *buying a chair about jogging.'*
> *– Merlin Mann*

Tools are there to help us get things done, but our obsession with them can occasionally become a distraction. There are some great productivity websites out there – often created or led by influential and insightful thinkers – like Merlin Mann's www.43folders.com and Leo Babauta's www.zenhabits.net, but while we do need to keep up with technology and innovation to the extent that it increases our productivity, we also need to be hyper-conscious that this is in itself 'dead time', away from the completion of our priority tasks and projects. I worry when I hear someone talk about their productivity purely and exclusively in the context of which new iPhone app they've just downloaded. These tools assist our thinking and organizing: they don't replace the need for it. Worse still, it's not uncommon for people to retype all their projects and actions from one piece of software to another under the oft-mistaken premise that they're increasing their productivity by 5% by doing this. No, that's just a day of procrastination.

MODELLING DECISION-MAKING

At the heart of the way of the Productivity Ninja is improving our ability to make decisions. By challenging ourselves to continually improve and innovate, the quality, quantity and speed of our decisions will increase. Remember that informed and clear decision-making is our aim. Thinking tools help boost our mental agility, but so does the right information.

It's often said that there are only eight stories in the world. Any challenge you're undertaking probably has a precedent, so getting out there and finding someone who is familiar with the territory of your decision making can help provide shortcuts to decisions that you thought would take you forever to master. Asking others for advice and investigating how others have tackled similar questions is a great way to come to more informed conclusions on tight timescales. Be equally free to share what you have learned with others and you'll find you are rewarded tenfold with the information and advice you get back. Learn from those willing to share, share with those willing to learn. I think we're moving towards a new age of collaboration, as our connectedness opens up new technologies that make this possible – and as I write this, I truly believe we're still hanging around on the starting blocks.

Twitter and Facebook are fantastic tools for throwing out questions or issues to a group of trusted friends and colleagues: it's so valuable getting a second, third, fourth and fifth opinion on something. It's amazing how much time and mental energy you'll save. But equally, don't be afraid to think independently and draw your own conclusions when your instinct tells you to.

STEALTH & CAMOUFLAGE

STEALTH & CAMOUFLAGE

We talked earlier about protecting your attention spans and keeping focused. It's hard to do. This is where the Ninja needs to employ a bit of old-fashioned stealth and camouflage.

IF YOU'RE IN THE LIMELIGHT, YOU MIGHT GET CAUGHT IN THE CROSSFIRE

One of the worst things you can do is always make yourself available. It's an invitation to some of your biggest enemies: distraction and interruption. Keep out of the limelight until you've got something you need others to hear. Avoid too much of the social chit chat and time-wasting that goes on in so many offices. Be a little bit elusive, a bit mysterious and even, if you have to, aloof. Protect your attention to ensure it's spent on what you decide to spend it on, not what others hijack it for. Here are a few examples:

▶ Spend as much time as you can away from your desk – work from home, in cafés, in meeting rooms, and outside. Even if you work in an open plan office where this feels impossible, you can still try to negotiate some 'thinking time' away from your desk with your line manager. And of course you can use the more ruthless and stealth-like approach of just booking vague-sounding appointments in your Outlook diary so that people just assume, 'Oh, looks like they're out of the office …'

▶ Get a gatekeeper who can help you say 'No' to appointments or meetings just not worth your while. (If you can get someone else to say 'No', it's often easier for you, and nicer for the person you're turning down!)

▶ Screen your calls and don't answer your phone unless you decide the call is likely to be more important than what you're currently working on.

▶ Book time in your calendar for creative thinking, reviewing, forward planning and other important activities. Have a personal codeword for this if you work in an office where other people can book your calendar and are unlikely to respect your autonomy if they see 'personal thinking time' or 'reading' as a calendar entry. Use 'private' or 'meeting outside of the office' instead.

▶ Set clear boundaries around things like email, Facebook chat, Skype and Instant Messenger. Get into the habit of being very conscious of when each of these is to be turned on and off. The default setting in almost every organization I've ever worked in is that Outlook (or another email client) is turned on 100% of the time. This same intrusion is increasingly true for Skype, IM and other services. It's time to wriggle away from the pressures of connectivity and 'go dark'.

GOING DARK

As well as protecting our attention from others, we must recognize the need to protect our attention from ourselves. We can be our very own worst enemy. There's a phrase in software development called 'Going Dark' which refers to the time when a developer is 'in the zone' with their programming and has subsequently stopped answering emails or responding to other communications. They can be extremely difficult to find. Those that manage software developers get frustrated by this, but also know that there's probably some amazing productivity happening … somewhere.

If your attention and focus is likely to be impeded by unlimited access to the internet and you're likely to be tempted by its millions of distraction possibilities (and who isn't?!), disconnect once in a while. Yes, a productivity book is telling you to *turn off* the internet! If I turn off my wifi connection for two hours, I know there will be no new email arriving during that time, and that it will be annoying enough having to fiddle around with turning the connection back on to keep me from doing so.

STEALTH *DELEGATION*

Finding other people to do your work for you is a great way to get more done. The problem is that the world is pretty short of people who actually want to do your work for you! Hence, a bit of stealth delegation is in order. This is unorthodox for a number of reasons, but consider first that you are unlikely to be able to claim credit for your actions and also that things may turn out differently to how you had imagined. If you're prepared to tolerate that, it's a great tactic. Better still, work out from your project list which of your projects you could afford to have others work on in different ways, or that you care least about. These are the ones to consider stealth delegating. Here are three common forms of stealth delegation. As a Ninja, you might well discover your own techniques, too.

1. Piggy backing: advertising your offer through someone else's mailout, launching your new product at someone else's event or 'borrowing' their contact list to launch something jointly. If momentum exists elsewhere in the world, jump on board.

2. Cultivating 'partners-In-crime': looking for the 'win-win' opportunities to work with equally savvy, equally useful and equally inspiring people.

3. Short-cutting: find people who've done the research, got a recommendation, learned the hard way and are eager to give their advice so that you don't make the same mistakes. A five-minute phone call to get a personal recommendation is much easier than an hour Googling the best solution. Find people whose opinions you trust – and trust them!

UNORTHODOXY

UNORTHODOXY

What's important is the end result. It doesn't matter if you use the conventional route to get there or find an easier path. Just because a seasoned professional tells you something needs to take sixteen hours, doesn't make it true. Be willing to question everything. It's important to be on constant lookout for every opportunity to take advantage of progress and innovation and do things more easily because the chances are, a lot of the people around you stopped doing that long ago. They just do things the old way and they're happy not to change it too much. We must avoid getting stuck in a rut and doing things less efficiently than we could, at all costs.

DON'T BE AFRAID TO *STAND OUT* WHEN THE TIME IS RIGHT

Doing things differently is risky, even when we've got a good hunch that we've got a better way of doing things. Managers generally prefer the status quo as it gives them an easy life, so doing the thing that challenges the status quo can often tread a fine line between glory and failure. But this isn't about chasing glory (although we'll reluctantly and graciously accept it when it comes along); it's about doing things in a better way and the satisfaction that comes from pushing boundaries to improve the process and increase productivity.

PUSHING BOUNDARIES IS EASIER *WHEN YOU'RE NOT REALLY PUSHING BOUNDARIES*

This is one of the Ninja secrets. The exact problem you face at work today is a problem that someone in another industry faced yesterday and that someone else will face tomorrow. So just as we can model decision-making, we can also model innovation from elsewhere. Injecting some fresh thinking into a situation and trying to see the problem through the lens of someone in a completely different area of work can be a useful technique. If, for example, you're looking to communicate more creatively, why not ask yourself, 'How would an advertising agency do this?' or, 'How would Nelson Mandela tackle this?', or if you need more method in among the madness, ask how a surgeon or engineer would approach the task. And, if you know people who do those kinds of jobs, call them up and ask for their perspective. You'll be surprised how effective this kind of modelling can be. Genuinely pushing boundaries is exciting, but can be a lot more time-consuming and takes a lot more effort than simple modelling. Innovation in one industry or job role can be the status quo somewhere else and vice versa.

MODELLING & PARTNERS-IN-CRIME

An obsession with unorthodoxy and innovation also means ditching some of the foolish creations of the ego: never be afraid or embarrassed or too proud to ask for advice, even if that means needing to show weakness. And never resist an opportunity to learn something new from a trusted source. Modelling the success of others is crucial. Mentoring is a great way to do this: take advice from those who have travelled the road you're setting out on, avoid making the mistakes they themselves made, and find the shortcut to success. Along with mentors, think about your 'partners-in-crime'. Who are the people travelling a similar road at the same time as you? Chances are, they all have mentors too and are learning equally important things. Never be afraid to share your learning with others as you'll be amazed at the priceless lessons you get back in return. Sometimes we resist such collaborative approaches because we believe, like some kind of superhero, that there is some added virtue in achieving things on our own or in being competitive. Remember, the only thing that matters is whether you get there; no one cares how.

BREAK RULES AND DISRESPECT BUREAUCRACY

While certain rules are worth upholding – and there are certain rules that would get you fired if you broke them – a Productivity Ninja approaches work with the mindset to focus on the end result first and work back from there. Questioning of rules, especially in relation to bureaucracy, is a great skill. Remember that if the risk of serious repercussions is limited, it's usually easier to apologize than to ask permission. There are times when we just need to show some leadership and crack on. Don't be afraid to rip up the rulebook, especially if you can trash some tired old bureaucracy along the way.

AGILITY

AGILITY

A Ninja needs to be light on their feet, able to respond with deftness to new opportunities or threats. Anything that requires a lot of shifting of thinking, quick reactions and decisions will of course need our proactive attention. And as we know, this is a finite resource. Our ability to react quickly and appropriately to new challenges really comes down to two things:

1. Our own mental 'reserves' or capacity to spend more of our days in proactive attention mode without getting tired. People do this temporarily through the use of caffeine or other stimulants, which is fine to an extent and in the short-term, but we need to think more sustainably than that.

2. Our ability to bring in other resources to aid this process – other people, more time and better technology.

KEEPING LIGHT ON OUR FEET

Just as when we talked about tools we said there was a need to focus on these in the 'fallow periods' in order that we're most agile when the going gets tough, the same process is true of developing our 'response-ability'. There are some important steps we can take on a day-to-day basis to do this:

▶ Keep organized: if we need to react, we need to be ready.

▶ Under-commit, don't over-commit your diary: it's always very tempting to bite off more than we can chew and it's even easier to find your day committed to other people's meetings. At the start of the week or month, keep space and time in your calendar, ready and able to be filled by stuff you don't know exists yet.

▶ Grow into, don't grow out of: with any organizing system you use, think one step ahead and develop systems far in advance of the capacity you need. For example, if you're going to have an upsurge in business and new clients coming on board, managing client contact information on a scruffy Excel spreadsheet that's bursting at the seams will slow you down at the crucial point. Investing the time before you need to into developing a super-hot database will seem unproductive at the time, but is actually the smarter move. In London, the Victorians built the sewers and tube lines to have ten times the required capacity. People complain about the tube system now, forgetting how ahead of its time it really was and how wise they were to think so far ahead in terms of the additional capacity requirements. All I can say is, thank goodness they did that for the sewers!

SPOTTING AN *OPPORTUNITY OR THREAT, WHEREVER IT ARRIVES FROM*

'Opportunity is missed by most people, because it is dressed in overalls and looks like work.'
– Thomas A. Edison

In order to react and respond well, we need strategic vision. We need to spot opportunity even when it knocks very softly at the door and see threats coming while they're still in the distance. Again, this takes some preparation and research and there are some useful shortcuts to use. Networking, for example, is a great way to keep your ear to the ground. Different people will have a different policy on networking, but broadly I set out to tick off these criteria, in this order:

1. Am I likely to meet interesting and useful people?

2. Is this person remarkable? Do they have something to say, or a good track record, or good enthusiasm? (If not, move on – there's nothing to see here!)

3. Can this person tell me something that informs my work and broadens my strategic sense?

4. Can we work together on something?

5. Is there an obvious win-win here that takes half the effort of the conversation itself?

Only when I get to number five do I commit. Often we get carried away with possibility, but delivery is another matter, so only pursue those that in conversation appear to be the 'no-brainers'.

MINDFULNESS

MINDFULNESS
MANAGING OUR MINDS

Our minds are our most important tool. Being emotionally intelligent and self-aware are important for so many reasons, not least because they equip you to take action. For instance, a lot of the things that make up the Ninja mindset, such as remaining calm, being ruthless and pushing the boundaries by being unorthodox, aren't easy. In fact, in many ways they go against our evolutionary design.

LISTENING TO THE 'LIZARD BRAIN' & OUR OWN RESISTANCE

Our brains have evolved a lot since we were monkeys, but one thing has hardly changed: the lizard brain. A term popularized by Seth Godin in his brilliant book *Linchpin*, this part of our brain still remembers what it was like to need to survive, to blend in, to not make a fuss. In fact, the worst thing for the lizard brain to think would be that whatever we're doing makes us stand out. Standing out from the crowd in evolutionary terms meant you'd get picked off by a predator, and this is exactly how the lizard brain still thinks!

Steven Pressfield's book *The War of Art* is a revealing and personal account of his battles as a writer against what he calls 'the resistance'. The resistance is a mindset, usually developed by the lizard brain, characterized by stress, anxiety, fear of failure, fear of success and a whole host of other emotions that whir around our brains and tell us to stand still. 'Stop. Don't do it. It's risky. Do it how others do it because that's what we know is already accepted behaviour. Innovation and unorthodoxy is a crazy idea. Creativity is just wrong.' Your job as a Ninja is to silence those thought processes as much as possible.

This sounds easy, but it's not – mainly because these thoughts are often so quiet that you don't even realize they need silencing at all. Pay close attention to yourself and your gut instincts, but also objectively observe your productivity, noticing which tasks you're drawn to and repelled by.

EMOTIONS & MEDITATION

Many people will tell you that allowing time and space to listen to your emotions, listen to your heart and just be mindful is either a waste of time or somehow 'hippy psychobabble'. The Ninja knows differently – it's all about perception. A bad day can be as much about what's going on in your head as what's going on in the office. Those that regularly practise some form of meditation will know of its benefits. In fact, meditation can help sharpen all of the other aspects of the Ninja mindset we've just discussed. I take a wide definition of meditation here that includes sitting quietly staring at a beautiful view, praying, free writing and other creativity pursuits, Yoga, walking (if the purpose is to walk, not to arrive!) and many other things. Again, the aim is to promote Zen-like calm and be focused and fully present in your work.

LISTENING TO OTHERS

As well as taking the time to listen to our own thoughts and emotions, active and effective listening is at the heart of great meetings and collaborative work. Listening to objections and hearing only feedback and connection rather than criticism and opposition is a crucial skill, too. We will come back to these themes in Chapter 10.

PREPAREDNESS

PREPAREDNESS

Last in our list of the characteristics to aspire to is one that underpins and strengthens so many of the others we've just talked about: preparedness. Zen-like calm in the heat of the battle is only possible if you're well-prepared. Agility is only possible if you're starting from a position of being prepared and ready to react immediately, producing the right response. And you're only ready to be ruthless if you've got the energy. Being prepared is about practical preparation as well as mental preparation.

PRACTICAL PREPAREDNESS

A weapon-savvy Ninja knows the added sense of control they feel when tackling a problem or project with the right tools. There used to be a time when being organized, focusing on the stationery or the geeky apps was considered nerdy or uncool. Well, the time has come to unleash your inner geek. It's time to maintain practical systems that will mean you're always prepared to tackle whatever comes your way. It may seem less cool than just 'going with the flow', but there is power in stocking up on stationery, power in investing time in the right systems and power in attacking your work from the position of being well prepared.

MENTAL PREPAREDNESS

As well as being physically well-prepared, we need to be mentally well-prepared too. This of course means mindfulness, but it also means looking after our most precious resource: our own attention and energy. As such, we need time to be off duty too. Perhaps being off duty involves a long Facebook binge or surfing rubbish on the internet. Perhaps it involves going out with friends or taking time to focus your attention on something completely different (or on nothing at all). Many people are pressured by their bosses to stay late in the office. I have talked to a lot of people who say that even though no one feels like there's anything to do, let alone feels ready to do anything, they still stay – for about five minutes after the boss has gone home. If you're in a job where you're under this kind of peer pressure, it needs to change. We'll work on that together. As for your boss, well, perhaps buying them a copy of this book would be a start!

LUNCH IS NOT FOR WIMPS

'Crunching' is a term that means buckling down, eyes on the deadline or conscious of the busy period ahead. It means not looking after yourself and not coming up for air. Crunching is a great short-term tactic when the going gets tough. But studies show that sustained periods of 'crunch' only lead to diminishing returns. In the film *Wall Street*, Gordon Gecko, played brilliantly by Michael Douglas, uttered the now legendary phrase, 'Lunch is for wimps'. It stuck in the collective consciousness and you'll still hear it used to this day. Well, lunch is not for wimps. But preparedness is for Ninjas.

PREPAREDNESS LEADS TO MAGIC

It's difficult to say why taking lunch or short breaks during the working day always brings you so quickly back to ruthless focus and your 'A' game. It just happens that way. Periods of rest are vital for preparedness. Next time you spend any meaningful length of time during the hours of nine to five *not* working and move your attention onto something completely different, just watch what happens; I'll bet that on that day, you'll get *more* done, not less. It's like a magical little secret. Different shifts in gear seem to work for different people, but it's as much in the body as in the mind. A five-minute blast of fresh air is infinitely more effective than ten minutes screwing about on the internet with your work still open in the background. The trick is to find the thing that works for you. As we look more at managing your attention and momentum later in the book, we will revisit this very unusual but startlingly effective secret.

EXERCISE: PREPAREDNESS

What you'll need: Self-awareness, space to think

How long it'll take: 20 minutes

Ninja mindset: Mindfulness

You've read through the key characteristics that make up The Way of the Productivity Ninja – Zen-like Calm, Ruthlessness, Weapon-savvy, Stealth and Camouflage, Unorthodoxy, Agility, Mindfulness, Preparedness – so take a moment to decide which ones are already quite well developed in you, and which three you think you need to focus on throughout the book.

Make a note of them here and refer back to them as you work through the book.

NEARLY A NINJA ...

....

....

....

....

....

....

A BIT OF NINJA PRACTICE NEEDED ...

....

....

....

....

....

....

NINJAS ARE NOT SUPERHUMAN ...

... BUT THEY SOMETIMES APPEAR TO BE SO

NINJAS ARE NOT SUPERHUMAN ...
... BUT THEY SOMETIMES APPEAR TO BE SO

'Life is really simple, but we insist on making it complicated.'
– Confucius

Working in this way is liberating, fun and super-productive. Sometimes as a Productivity Ninja you will seem to others like you have special powers. Sometimes it will even seem that way to you.

However, a Ninja is very different from a superhero. A Ninja is just a regular guy or girl, but with tools and skills and a very special mindset. There are no super powers and no kryptonite.

As a Ninja, you'll develop a reputation as someone who delivers, someone who is reliable, makes good decisions and takes their work seriously. Apart from when you wear your Ninja mask. Keep that private.

Ninjas are passionate, indispensable and calm under pressure. Ninjas get things done in a way that seems, well, magical.

As a Ninja, what were once routine tasks become opportunities for fun, discovery, experimentation and the unleashing of your inner geek. Thinking about the *process* of your work as well as the work itself will help you to love what you do, whatever that may be. You will gain excitement and motivation from being better at doing what you were doing before; you'll be less stressed about it; and you'll experience a momentum in your work that you never thought possible. But it's not all plain sailing either.

NINJAS ALSO OCCASIONALLY SCREW UP

'The best brewer sometimes makes bad beer.'
– German proverb

By seeking ultra-productivity, using unorthodox means and for a host of other more 'human' reasons, Ninjas are prone to screwing up once in a while. In old time management books, the time management 'gurus' would paint themselves as a picture of superhero perfection. They'd give you detailed planners to fill in, have you performing high fives in celebration of continuous massive achievement and leave you as the reader wondering how on earth they managed the impossible. Well, don't believe a word of it. We're all prone to screwing up – no matter how organized, how intelligent, or how seemingly perfect we are or are trying to be. Yes, you too.

We can aim for perfection and fail, or we can aim for Zen-like Calm, Ruthlessness, Weapon-savviness, Stealth and Camouflage, Unorthodoxy, Agility, Mindfulness and Preparedness, and succeed. Yes, we'll make mistakes. No, we won't be perfect. But what we will do is increase productivity in ways you never thought possible before.

It simply isn't possible for me to make you a superhero and if you want that, there are plenty of other books out there that will promise it but won't deliver. It's an unrealistic dream, a fantasy never fulfilled.

But it *is* possible that we can make you a Ninja.

2. WHY WE GET STRESSED

'The greatest weapon against stress is our ability to choose one thought over another.'
– William James

Chances are, if you've bought this book, you're feeling stressed. A Productivity Ninja knows that stress in some form or another is inevitable if you're ambitious and you want to get things done that really matter. Indeed, a good shot of adrenaline now and again can be a wonderful, exciting thing. However, what we also know is that stress is a barrier to the kind of relaxed concentration and Zen-like calm that we need for long-term, sustainable productivity. This chapter will open your awareness to stress and how to recognize what might be causing stress for you. We'll go on in the next chapter to look at attention management and how reducing your stress will increase your attention. Goodbye stress, hello Zen-like calm.

FIGHT OR FLIGHT: THE PHYSICAL ROOT OF STRESS

You have probably heard of the 'fight or flight' response. When our mind senses danger or risk, it produces adrenaline, increases our heart rate, with which we find a huge surge in our mental awareness and as such, in our ability to get out of said danger. When we lived in caves, such adrenaline 'rushes' gave us the edge to survive the threat of attack, or to kill for our next meal. In many ways, work is the new hunting. It's how as animals we are able to feed our families – not by killing things but by doing our bit, performing our role and getting rewarded with the money we then use to buy food and pay for shelter, thus providing our families with security. We bring home the bacon. In that sense, work is still about survival and there's still a primal instinct inside us that takes this very seriously indeed, even though we'd still actually survive if we had no work (through unemployment benefits, savings, drastic lifestyle changes or getting by with a little help from our friends).

THE PSYCHOLOGICAL CONTRACT

Sometime in the weeks before or just after starting a new job, employee and employer sign a contract. The contract puts down in writing all of the fundamentals so that both parties have a level of security, control and clarity in their relationship. But have you ever really thought about the expectations of both parties and how far they go beyond what's written down in that contract? And what about how these assumptions develop in the minds of employer and employee as things progress? Beyond the contract are things like:

Employee:

> 'There's a really nice canteen. The menu changes every day and there's always a good healthy option. This is a sign that I'm valued.'

> 'My line manager lets me be flexible if I have childcare issues that I need to work around.'

> 'The role is so varied.'

Employer:

> 'Obviously if there's additional work that needs to be done after 5pm, they'll stay and help us finish it.'

> 'We don't just expect our people to show up, we expect ingenuity, energy and passion.'

> 'Cheap hotels for work trips? They love them!'

These are all part of the psychological contract between employer and employee – things that are either unsaid, or discussed but never formally recognized as additions to the contract of employment that's been gathering dust on a shelf since you started work or since your last promotion. Changes to the psychological contract affect our happiness at work, our motivation, our self-worth and in turn the morale of the team or whole organization. They challenge our perceived sense of our value and how we're valued, and often lie at the root of stress.

Think about this scenario for a moment: your company changes none of your formal terms and conditions, but in one week does everything possible to worsen your working life. They suddenly demand you stay much later; they insist that you check your Blackberry in the evening and at weekends; your lovely boss who you have built such a good rapport with is suddenly replaced by a demanding ogre; there is trouble with the biggest client you are responsible for; and even asking for holidays or flexible working right now is met with short shrift. You're still coming home with the same pay and the same ability to run your household, but the whole office environment is now radically different to how it was a week ago. It's no longer fun, you no longer feel valued and you no longer think it fits with who you are.

If work was just about your own personal survival and as the old saying used to suggest, you 'work to live, not live to work', then you wouldn't have any thoughts of leaving that job right now. Your pay remains unchanged and what's a little extra work in the evenings?

The truth is that as well as wanting to earn a crust, we want to feel valued and feel that what we do is of some significance. We want to feel that the relationship with the organization where we spend so much of our waking time is a healthy, fair and happy one. We derive pleasure and identity from the successes of our company and even more so when we receive praise to say that we were part of that success. We're very quick to start using the word 'we' to describe our employer, our organization or our team. We all want to do great work and make our mum proud. If we love what we do, work defines us as the kind of fun person who does what they love. If we hate what we do, work *still* defines us as the kind of person who does stuff they don't enjoy in order to earn money and take responsibility for ourselves. Mum's proud either way, but only one of these will make you happy.

It's often talked about as a dream to be 'work free'. I would seriously contest that. Work gives us meaning and we need it. Why do so many millionaires continue to build their fortunes when there's really no need? Why do lottery winners say things like, 'Well, it won't change me, I'll still work part-time'? I would argue that the real quest is for financial freedom but the real reason to achieve that is to be able to choose what you work on! Bill Gates is a great example of this. I don't imagine he works any fewer hours now than he did when he was creating Microsoft. Building an exceptional company like Microsoft would make any mum proud, but it pales in comparison when his new work is striving to eradicate malaria. Tim Ferriss, author of *The 4-Hour Work Week*, talked about automating and delegating the running of a business to others in order that you could live the dream of world travel and work only four hours a week. In interviews, though, Ferriss also talks about how he's 'always busy doing stuff' and only categorizes as work those activities that he actively dislikes. I bet Tim Ferriss works about fourteen hours a day – he just doesn't see it as work because he enjoys it. Work is highly personal and central to our sense of self. No wonder, then, that even small changes to the psychological contract with our employer can leave us feeling anxious, bruised, angry, threatened or fearful. If we feel under attack or feel that we're playing a game where the stakes are high and our performance will be analysed, it's pretty natural that our adrenaline kicks in.

SYMPTOMS OF STRESS

Whatever we're working on, our adrenaline levels can drive us towards making the impossible become possible. But when we cross the line from healthy adrenaline into unhealthy, stressed out and unhappy, we move from motivation and momentum into stress and the beginnings of being stifled. There are many symptoms of stress which can be recognized – and just as many books and pieces of medical guidance listing them. This is by no means an exhaustive list, but just highlights some of the more common and frequent ones. It nevertheless makes for pretty exhausting reading!

SYMPTOMS *INCLUDE:*

Physical:

Lack of appetite, food and sugar cravings, indigestion, heartburn, constipation, insomnia, feeling tired all the time, sweating for no reason, nail biting, headaches, muscle spasms, nausea, breathlessness, fainting, crying or feeling like you want to cry, impotency, inability to sit still, high blood pressure.

Behavioural:

Difficulty concentrating, lack of motivation, difficulty in making decisions, inability to finish one task before starting the next one, fear of failure or feeling you've failed, loneliness, irritability and being rude or short with colleagues, feeling unable to cope, fear of serious illness or disease, anger, paranoia, claustrophobia, dreading the future.

'Anxiety is caused by a lack of control, organisation, preparation and action.'
– David Kekich

If you were wondering why in a book about how to be a Productivity Ninja you're reading so much about stress, hopefully that second list will give you some clues about how central our dealing with stress really is to our potential to succeed. By focusing on changing our behaviours, we can reduce the extent to which we experience physical stress, and that can only increase productivity.

RECOGNIZING STRESS TRIGGERS

'I am an old man and have known a great many troubles, but most of them never happened.'
– Mark Twain

Recognizing stress itself is important and while not easy when you're 'in the trenches', there are obvious tell-tale signs you can use to diagnose it. This is the first step to moving back towards the Zen-like calm that a Productivity Ninja needs. However, recognizing stress triggers – those elements within our work that have the *potential* to cause us stress and dealing effectively with those before we get stressed is much trickier. But it's so much better to spend ten minutes speculatively nipping stress in the bud than a couple of hours, days or even weeks recovering from the stress that was caused by us not acting early. Here we look at some common causes of stress so that in the coming chapters, as we look at adopting the Ninja mindset across your own attention, emails, to-do lists, projects and meetings, you can start to see how this mindset increases control and reduces stress.

CONTROL

Feeling out of control is one of the quickest ways to feel stress. Whether you're dealing with changes to your team, your job description, or your company culture, the beauty of developing good, mindful systems to manage your work is that it is completely in your power. It's therefore a complete no-brainer. Why wouldn't you devote a little time to developing stress-busting, clarity-enhancing, Zen-like calm-inducing ways to work? A project or set of actions feels more in control the more *clarity* you have around it, not the more you have done of it. We can actually handle a heavy workload pretty well – it's being unclear about what's within that heavy workload that induces stress.

CHANGE

Dealing with change is largely difficult because it requires a period of us losing control and having to readjust. However, change also brings with it new habits or processes to learn, time-consuming things that make the easy stuff difficult again for a period while we get to grips with doing things a different way. It also provides lots of potential for personal conflicts and a whole series of new problems to manage.

Yes, change can really bring out the worst in people. However, it's how we react to change that defines us. Time to wrestle back control, dust ourselves down and get going again.

OVERLOAD *PANIC*

Emails, phone calls, reading list, paperwork, social media … the volume of new inputs is in itself a significant stress agent. I would argue that a great deal of the stress caused by these information inputs actually comes from other forms of stress, such as those listed above and below. However, when we're already feeling stressed, the mere thought of there being *more* emails, more decisions and more distractions is just enough to add to the pain and produce utter panic. Again, with good systems in place you will win this battle, and we come on to those in detail in the next few chapters.

THE FEAR OF *LOOKING FOOLISH*

Perfectly intelligent, reasonable people get caught up in wanting to present an image of success at all times to impress their bosses, colleagues and peers. Whether we're chairing meetings, presenting at conferences or delivering on a project, a kind of performance anxiety can hit. We blag our way through meetings when we haven't done the required reading, rather than simply owning up and having a more intelligent conversation as a result. Or we try to paint a failed project in a more positive light, or put the blame elsewhere, rather than holding an honest, illuminating examination of what might have gone wrong. We want to look like the most promotable, successful, and unnervingly perfect projection of our real selves. It's a system that feeds itself: because we're so unwilling to change the rules as a culture, individuals are forced to play by these rules or else lose the wider game. Even if we know that everyone occasionally screws up.

We're often caught because we're playing two different games: we know what we'd really love to do, we know what the project most needs, but we also know we need to keep up our front and avoid looking foolish. The easy and natural thing at this point is to be as vague as possible about where a project is up to, retreat to the trenches and avoid the people who might hold us accountable or spring our little secret. Sound familiar?

FEAR OF BEING FOUND OUT

'The greatest mistake you can make in life is to be continually fearing you will make one.'
– Elbert Hubbard

It always makes me smile when you hear a really personal interview with an entertainer, politician, business leader or other person in the public eye who makes reference to the idea that they thought they were the only one using the 'fake it 'til you make it' strategy. These are the people you look to as authority figures on the top of their game, and yet they're still crippled under that confident exterior by the thought that one day they'll be found out as a fraud, that everyone will 'know' that they somehow lack the abilities to do the job that they do. People with long and successful track records in their careers still think like this. Maybe you do too. It's just another form of the fear of looking foolish. My own perspective, as a fellow sufferer of this fear, is that I think it's actually quite a useful paradigm in that it gives you the edge to be bolder, braver and more creative if harnessed in the right way, but it of course needs careful mindfulness to keep it in check.

CONFLICT

No reasonable person enjoys conflict. Those that claim to revel in it are either lying or simply not worth knowing. To do so implies some kind of inbuilt sense of joy at the misery of others. However, certain conflicts bring more productive outcomes than ignoring or denying conflict altogether. Festering conflict is a major cause of ongoing stress, whereas a courageous conversation will bring about peace, a return to calm and hopefully in time, reconciliation and respect. There are plenty of good books and training courses out there that deal with tactics and techniques for managing conflict and it's a subject worthy of further investigation.

VAGUENESS & AMBIGUITY

Underpinning so many of these causes of stress is the stress caused by dealing with vague or ambiguous information inputs. Buried somewhere deep inside that email or pep talk from your boss is the biggest potential opportunity or threat. If you don't spot it and deal with it, you'll certainly look foolish, things will be out of control and it will undoubtedly be stressful. Therefore, we're constantly panning for gold among all the rubbish that gets sent into our email inboxes and the paper chases around our offices, trying to find those nuggets of potential opportunity or the ticking time bombs we need to defuse. In many instances it's not reality but a *potential* reality that causes the stress. The potential for missed opportunities or screw-ups is always at the back of our minds. A vagueness of vision or intention can be equally as stressful. Not knowing where you're trying to steer a project, or worrying that your vision might be different from a colleague's can cause all sorts of issues.

Clarity is to calm what vagueness is to stress. We'll talk more about this in the next chapter and elsewhere in the book.

EXERCISE: STRESS AND ME

What you'll need: Self-awareness, space to think

How long it'll take: 15 minutes

Ninja mindset: Mindfulness

Let's recap on some of the specific causes of stress we've just discussed. Which of these are most likely to affect you? Score yourself between one and five to indicate which have a low effect and which have a high effect.

Stress areas

	1	2	3	4	5
Overload panic/volume of work	☐	☐	☐	☐	☐
Lack of clarity about what to do	☐	☐	☐	☐	☐
Difficult decisions	☐	☐	☐	☐	☐

Stress agents

High expectations placed on me	☐	☐	☐	☐	☐
Performance anxiety/looking foolish	☐	☐	☐	☐	☐
No one listening to me	☐	☐	☐	☐	☐
Looking foolish	☐	☐	☐	☐	☐
Conflict	☐	☐	☐	☐	☐
Changes to the way my team works	☐	☐	☐	☐	☐
Changes in the outside world	☐	☐	☐	☐	☐
Vagueness/ambiguity	☐	☐	☐	☐	☐

IT'S NOT JUST CEOs ...

Many people think the most stressful jobs are at the top of organizations. There is certainly little doubt that such jobs are stressful. Having been a CEO, I can tell you I had a number of sleepless nights and battled pretty intensely with stress and overload. I've talked to CEOs of some huge companies who tell similar stories of simply learning to live with stress, minimize it and make that an acceptable state to live in rather than having any magical powers to make it go away completely. However, there are potential stress agents at every level of every organization. Those at the lower levels of organizations and with less responsibility often have less control over their own workload, but still have the same performance. Those at the middle levels are the ones I often feel the most sympathy for: eager to please everyone around them and get on, squeezed by the pressures and agendas of their bosses and direct reports – literally caught in the middle. Stress isn't determined by rank, it's determined by the propensity of the job or situation to create stress agents and our individual ability to deal with what's thrown at us.

TIME TO REGAIN SOME PERSPECTIVE

Finally in this chapter, let's dispel two myths created in the minds of people stressed out by their work:

1. The world is ending.

    (No, it's not.)

2. Everyone else is moving quicker than me and achieving more than me.

    (You'd laugh if you knew the truth.)

Slow down. It's all going to be just fine.

THE OPPOSITE OF STRESS

Here's what we're going to aim for: 'playful, productive momentum and control'. This will give you peace of mind and increase your chances of regularly achieving the Zen-like calm you need.

Playful ... is positive, relaxed and accepts that you're allowed the freedom to succeed, even at the expense of occasionally making mistakes.

Productive ... is knowing you're making excellent choices from a place of preparedness.

Momentum ... is a flow of great work that is so exciting it leads to more great work. It does the opposite of procrastination and stress.

Control ... gives you the power and confidence to keep on going, which creates even greater momentum, greater playfulness and greater productivity.

I know this might sound like a lot to take in, but the only thing that's different here from feeling stressed out, stuck and numbed by the world around you is *what's going on in your mind*.

> 'Stress is an ignorant state. It believes that everything is an emergency. Nothing is that important. Just lie down.'
> – Natalie Goldberg

EXERCISE: ADDRESSING MY STRESS AGENTS

What you'll need:	Self-awareness, space to think
How long it'll take:	20 minutes
Ninja mindset:	Mindfulness

As we delve into how to be a Productivity Ninja throughout the book, we will address the stress agents described in this chapter, and you will be presented with lots of solutions to help you make changes that will have a far-reaching impact on your work and life.

Right now, though, we are concerned with addressing any areas that need immediate attention. It's time to start taking back control. As you look once more at the list of stress agents below, note down any obvious first steps that you can take to provide some immediate relief. Take as many or as few as you need to in order to begin to establish a feeling of Zen-like calm. Some suggestions have been made for you.

Control: *(suggestion)* – Spend five minutes clearing your desk so that you have a clear space to work in.

Write your own in here ....

....

Change: *(suggestion)* – Make a note of any areas of your life where you're experiencing change at the moment/find someone to talk to – a problem shared is a problem halved.

....

....

Overload panic: *(suggestion)* – Read Chapters 4–6 and do the exercises.

....

....

Looking foolish: *(suggestion)* – Take a risk and get clear, specific and accountable to your team about something you've been deliberately vague about.

....

....

Fear of being found out: *(suggestion)* – Use the 'fake it to make it' strategy. Make eye contact, take a deep breath, and say what you have to say with an air of confidence. It's all in the delivery.

....

....

Conflict: *(suggestion)* – Have a courageous conversation if there is any conflict with a colleague, even if the result is that you 'agree to disagree'.

....

....

Vagueness and ambiguity: *(suggestion)* – Give yourself ten minutes to *just think* about a current problem and make some notes to help structure your thinking.

....

....

Are you a Ninja?

▶ A Ninja overcomes stress at work by being prepared and practising ruthlessness in their approach to their work.

▶ A Ninja uses mindfulness to notice their main stressors and takes action to combat them.

▶ A Ninja knows how to achieve Zen-like calm: it comes from being ruthless, prepared and mindful.

3. ATTENTION MANAGEMENT

'We just want to devote ourselves to art. We're all dragged at increasing speed towards the grave. Any picture we don't make will not be made by somebody else. So we don't need to go shopping, we don't have to cook. It's a very, very simple life devoted to art.'
– Gilbert Proesch, one half of the artists, Gilbert & George

'We've trained ourselves to clear the head. It's an extraordinary thing. It feels like a desert in front of us, panning out, which we can do something with.'
– George Passmore, Gilbert and George

A lot of books have been written on the topic of 'time management' but precious little is ever written about a more subtle skill: 'attention management'. This chapter will look at some of the critical attention management habits that will propel you to Productivity Ninja status.

In this chapter, we're going to focus on helping you manage your attention in four main ways:

1. Scheduling work based on your level of attention

2. Protecting your attention from distractions

3. Improving your attention by increasing your brain's performance

4. Creating new 'pockets of attention'

But before we get onto that, let's look at why attention management is so crucial in our age of information overload.

KNOWLEDGE WORK MEANS YOU'RE NOT JUST THE WORKER, BUT THE BOSS TOO

Remember the days when you did jobs that didn't require any judgement? You worked behind the bar somewhere, or in a cake factory. These are the types of jobs where you have a big box of cherries, and down the conveyor belt comes a line of cakes with icing on them. Your job is so simple you could do it in your sleep: put one cherry on top of each cake. Not much to procrastinate about there, not many opportunities to look foolish or lose control over, and not many issues for your brain to take home at the end of the shift. In fact, these kinds of jobs use precious little of your attention at all, are easily done with a hangover and you never really need to be on top form. Sounds wonderful in some ways, doesn't it? They also have a satisfyingly simple success indicator – if you put all the cherries on all the cakes, you win. If you missed off half of them, that's not so good. It's easy with such jobs for a supervisor to check up on you and see how you're doing, and it's easy for a boss to see the bigger picture and see whether it's all working.

You might at this point be harbouring a slight pang to get back to the simplicity of these kinds of jobs. The truth is, very few of these jobs exist anymore – most of them are now automated by computers or machines, and the ones that are left are the bar jobs and coffee shop gigs that don't pay very well anyway. Many years ago, Peter Drucker predicted this future. He predicted the end of the industrial age and the dawn of the information age. People would move from the kind of functional jobs in bars and cake factories and into 'knowledge work' jobs. Knowledge work is about adding value or creating value out of information rather than performing a specific function. If you think about it, that's at the heart of what you do today, and many of the UK's more industrialized cities are now making the transition to entry level knowledge work jobs on a huge scale.

Imagine that your job involves arriving at 9am at the cake factory, getting handed a large box of cherries and as the cakes come down the conveyor belt, you put one cherry on each of the cakes. If the conveyor belt slows down, so do you. If the conveyor belt stops, you just … wait. You have scheduled breaks, scheduled relaxation time over lunch and you can predict your finish time to the minute, or even the second. Imagine it's 5pm on Friday at the cake factory and you're about to go home and start your weekend. Do you think you'll even think about cherries before 9am on Monday? Do you think you'll be sat there on Sunday evening at home, worrying about the potential things that could go wrong in your job tomorrow? Of course not. While there may well be boredom in that job, there's clarity. It's really easy to know exactly what you need to do, how you're getting on and what you might need to do to improve.

Your knowledge work job is different from putting cherries on the cakes in the factory because in your work there are so many levels of ambiguity: in the cake factory scenario, imagine all of a sudden having to be not just the person putting the cherries on the cakes but also the person checking up on the cherries, the person deciding what time the shift starts and how fast the conveyor belt goes, the person occasionally filling in for the icing person when they're on leave, the person running the shop floor and also the strategic CEO responsible for deciding whether, with all this emphasis on healthy eating in the outside world these days, the factory should just sell cherries as part of fruit salads and ditch the cakes altogether. It's exhausting isn't it? Welcome back to your world.

SIMULTANEOUSLY THE BOSS AND THE WORKER

THE BOSS AND THE WORKER

In any knowledge work job, you're really playing two different 'roles' at once: you're simultaneously the 'boss' and the 'worker'. You're responsible for:

▶ Deciding what your work is ('boss-mode')

▶ Doing the work ('worker-mode')

▶ Dealing with new information inputs (worker-mode) and reacting to them to decide whether to change your priorities as a result (boss-mode)

This creates an immediate conflict and serious potential for indecision about which role should have your attention at different times of the day: do you spend more time in boss-mode (thinking and analysing your work, ensuring its success, planning your next steps) or in worker-mode (putting cherries on cakes, in whatever form that takes in your current job)? Naturally, the grass is always greener: the time you spend in boss-mode may remind you of all the things that you need to be doing in the trenches.

Yet, while you're trying to crank through your to-do list, you'll be making mental notes about all the new projects that need some precious thinking time. Since most people do not have specific definitions or boundaries around what is boss-mode and what is worker-mode for them, they get stressed about whether they've made good decisions and often procrastinate as a result – not having good boundaries or habits here means never finishing boss-mode thinking and never being quite sure when in 'doing' (worker) mode that you're actually doing the right stuff.

STRESS IS REDUCED BY CLARITY
CLARITY IS INCREASED BY ATTENTION

This is where 'attention management' comes in – your new best friend in the battle against stress and information overload.

WHAT DOES 'ATTENTION' REALLY MEAN?

Your attention is a more limited resource than your time. Have you ever got to the end of a day when you've still got loads to do, you're still motivated to do it and you have all the tools or information that you need, yet find that you're just staring into space? Under those circumstances, you'll often tell yourself you ran out of time, but actually you just ran out of attention to give.

On other days, you might feel as if you've been in back-to-back meetings all day, and it's 4pm before you even have a chance to get any desk time in, to finally look at emails, catch up on your reading and planning, and seize control. On these days, you might really feel that you're short on time, not on attention. Wrong again. Your attention is a currency to be spent, and if you choose to give away as much as 80% of your attention to meetings, don't be surprised if that final 20% of your attention amounts to little more than dealing with a few emails, followed by time spent staring into space and feeling overwhelmed. But don't fool yourself that it was anyone else's fault – if you start to think about the time spent in meetings not just in terms of the time you lose, but also in terms of the attention and energy expended, you soon realize that complex and difficult meetings are a massive drain on your personal resources.

Attention is your currency. Time might be spent, but attention still needs to be paid. Look after this currency, as it's the most valuable currency in the world.

TIME + THE RIGHT ATTENTION AND FOCUS = DONE

ATTENTION IS FINITE

> *'Only the mediocre are
> always at their best.'*
> *– Colin Powell*

In an average day, you will have different levels of attention. For ease, a crude analysis might highlight three different types of attention:

1. **Proactive attention:**

   This is where you are fully focused, alert, in the zone and ready to make your most important decisions or tackle your most complex tasks. This level of attention is extremely important and through this book my hope is that you realize just how valuable it really is.

2. **Active attention:**

   This is where you're plugged in, ticking along, but perhaps flagging slightly. You're easily distracted, occasionally brilliant, but often sloppy too. This level of attention is useful.

3. **Inactive attention:**

   The lights are on but no one appears to be home. There's not too much brainpower left and you're likely to really struggle with complex or difficult tasks. Your attention here isn't worthless, but its value is limited.

Of course, these are crude and artificial demarcations, but useful ones to think about when trying to maximize your productivity through good attention management. I have spent the last two years watching my attention management trends and flows and talking to others about their own patterns, too.

Here's an average weekday for me:

8–9am	Active
9–11am	Proactive
11am–1pm	Active
LUNCH	Inactive
2–3pm	Inactive
3–4pm	Proactive
4–5pm	Active
5–6pm	Proactive
6–7pm	Inactive

Most of the narrative to this probably mirrors 90% of your own average work pattern, and the other 10% is unique to me. You will have your own ideas about when your attention spans are at their peak.

Let me briefly describe what's happening for me here. I don't wake up easily and I'm not much of a morning person. I take a while to get going in the mornings, so first thing, my mind is a bit foggy and I need either a coffee or at least a good idea from a plan I wrote in a previous period of proactive attention to get any momentum going. From then on, I'm pretty fresh for a good couple of hours. I'll hopefully use this time to make the big decisions that day. This then tails off before lunch, and during lunch itself. After lunch, most people are sluggish. Trust me, I run workshops and give talks that often start at this time, commonly known in the training and speaking world as 'the graveyard slot' for this reason. What's interesting for me is that then I tend to have a little spurt of very positive proactive attention, before tailing off again. And often the impending end of a workday encourages some added focus, which comes at a cost because as soon as this tails off I'm completely knackered and good for nothing more.

How much proactive attention time do I have here?

Less than you think.

Two to three hours a day, Monday to Thursday, and just one and a half to two hours on a Friday.

EXERCISE: MY ATTENTION TIMETABLE

What you'll need: Pen and paper, boss-mode proactive/active attention

How long it'll take: 20 minutes

Ninja mindset: Preparedness

▶ Take a piece of paper and map out an average day in your working life in whichever way works for you – as a flowchart, list, line chart, mind map or table.

▶ Include start and finish times, as well as any scheduled breaks and what happens immediately before and after work (e.g. the journey home, or if you check emails before you arrive).

▶ Label your attention span for each of these categories: which are your proactive times, which are active, and which are inactive?

▶ Note down what surprises you from this, and also make a note of the best and worst times to give yourself the most critical, difficult or complex tasks to do.

SEPARATING THINKING FROM DOING, BOSS FROM WORKER

'Productivity is never an accident. It is always the result of commitment to excellence, intelligent planning and focused effort.'
– Paul J. Meyer

Your goal in managing your attention is to create playful productive momentum and control, limiting stress, and being confident that you're doing the best work you can possibly do.

It's worth noting that in the course of our work, information inputs flow through four different phases of work, best remembered by the acronym, CORD. We will look at this in more detail in chapter 5, but essentially this consists of:

▶ **Capture and Collect:** Collecting information wherever it lands, but also making a note of any useful ideas as they show up (in meetings or at your desk, for example).

▶ **Organize:** Taking all of this information and making sense of it. This is where you work out what's do-able, what's important and when you might want to do it. You organize it into some form of to-do list and then hopefully, as we develop the ideas in this chapter, into a more advanced and agile system for dealing with it well.

▶ **Review:** Looking through the to-do list or your entire system with all of your projects and commitments, you choose what it is you need to be working on and when.

▶ **Do:** Completion. Putting cherries on cakes.

So, when are you in boss-mode and when are you in worker-mode? And what level of attention do you need when capturing, organizing, reviewing and doing? While of course there are exceptions, it looks something like this:

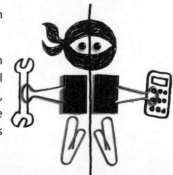

Phase of work	Inactive attention	Active attention	Proactive attention
Capture and Collect (worker-mode)	✓		
Organize (boss-mode)		✓	
Review (boss-mode)			✓
Do (worker-mode)	✓	✓	✓

What this shows us is that the boss-mode of our work, the Organize and Review phases, requires the largest part of our active and proactive attention. Thinking about our work is in many ways the hard part. If you spend a week thinking about the solution to a potentially difficult problem, the solution is easy to arrange. The arranging part is just picking up the phone, writing emails, having conversations, doing research – bread and butter stuff to a knowledge worker. It's the thinking that takes time and requires energy. Separating thinking from doing infinitely improves both.

> 'Thinking is the hardest work there is, which is the probable reason so few engage in it.'
> – Henry Ford

As we have discovered, your proactive attention is a scarce and valuable commodity in your quest to be productive and to reduce information overload and stress. Four things are required to be at your best:

1. Schedule your work according to the attention level you're operating on.

2. Protect as much of your attention as you can from the evils of distractions and interruptions.

3. Do whatever you can to increase your attention flows, 'moving up' to make periods of inactive attention active ones, and make periods of active attention proactive ones.

4. If at all possible, magic up some additional attention and time that you didn't use to have available.

1. SCHEDULE YOUR WORK BASED ON YOUR ATTENTION LEVEL

Every job will have within it a range of tasks. These will often range from making huge decisions about what to do and when to do it, through to updating contact information, filing things away or changing the printer cartridge. Once you start to focus on your attention levels, you'll start to realize that it's a criminal waste to be changing the printer cartridge during a period of proactive attention. It's like using a sledgehammer to crack a nut, although in that moment it probably feels no different to when you change the printer cartridge at any other time. Yes, attention management is certainly a subtle game.

On the page opposite you can see what I try to pigeonhole to specific attention levels if at all possible.

It's worth thinking about your natural strengths and weaknesses here. Save tasks that you find particularly difficult for when your attention level is proactive, leave the intense but easier stuff for those active attention times and try to save up the easy or dull stuff for when you're capable of little else.

YOUR PROACTIVE ATTENTION IS IN SHORT SUPPLY: USE IT WISELY

While there will be patterns to your proactive attention, it changes from day to day and sometimes from minute to minute. Therefore, to be able to schedule or select your work appropriately to your attention level, you need to have all possible options available to you so that you're always free to make informed choices from a position of confident, Zen-like calm. Since a lot of the boss-mode work of defining the best ways to achieve your tasks needs to be done when you have the proactive attention available to be able to make critical and strategic decisions, you need to ensure that you do your thinking when your attention is proactive. Finishing this thinking is what gives you the best possible range of options to choose from and the best possible information to support your decisions about what your worker-self should be doing.

Proactive attention	Active attention	Inactive attention
Key decisions	Day-to-day decisions	Filing
Project planning and reviews	Scheduling the day's work or keeping on top of action lists	Ordering stationery or other online purchases
Most phone calls (partly because I want to listen as intently as possible and partly that I generally don't enjoy them!)	Internet research	Printing stuff out
Critical emails	Most email processing	Deleting emails or throwing away paperwork I no longer need
Chairing meetings	Attending meetings	Attending meetings that I don't care about but can't otherwise avoid
Creative thinking, writing new workshop materials, etc	Preparing handouts for workshops and making sure I've got everything I need	Making coffee!

Being caught in a period of inactive or active attention and not having a clue about all the possibilities of what's out there to do next very quickly leads to a lack of clarity, stress, procrastination and bad decisions.

PROACTIVE ATTENTION & BOSS-MODE

We will talk in the upcoming chapters on managing your to-do list and actions in each of the four phases of our work: Capturing and Collecting, Organizing, Reviewing and Doing. It's likely that a prolonged period of stress will have as its root cause the fact that you have not been able to devote enough proactive attention to your boss-mode work, particularly that of reviewing your commitments and priorities. Review is the phase of your work in which you see the timber from the trees; you look objectively at the range of commitments and projects on your plate and ensure that you are as up to date as you can be about the choices you have available. This leaves much of the doing phase feeling effortless. Having done the quality thinking you need to do in boss-mode, your worker-self is truly able to feel like your job is putting cherries on cakes: no conflicts, no confusion – just playful, productive momentum and control. For this reason, prioritizing your proactive attention towards the thinking parts of your work rather than the doing should be a key goal for any Productivity Ninja.

While it sounds easy, think about your own periods of proactive attention and then think about what's going on around you during those times in the working day. I mentioned that 9–11am is good proactive time for me. That's also exactly the time that my colleagues want a piece of my time, that the majority of the day's emails and calls are flying in, exactly the time I'm having a million ideas that I want to investigate, have had appointments made for me, and so on. You need to be a pretty focused, firm and ruthless boss to make the most of this time! I regularly spend the mornings working away from the office for this very reason; I want to protect the proactive attention for my best work, and save my active and inactive attention for the parts of my job that don't need the fullest of energy or engagement.

2. PROTECTING YOUR ATTENTION FROM INTERRUPTIONS AND DISTRACTIONS

Boss-mode requires the type of thinking that only concentrated proactive attention can offer.

Our best thinking – and the kind of thinking we need to keep us feeling calm and in control – comes from having *two* things in alignment. We need to be in periods of our most proactive attention *and* we need to apply concentration to see that thinking through to its natural end. If we get distracted by something else, all that's happened is that we've done some thinking that we can't feel confident is finished; therefore, there's potential stress around the next corner because things aren't clear.

Broadly speaking, there are two types of distractions: internal distractions and external distractions.

INTERNAL DISTRACTIONS: ONE OF THE BIGGEST DISTRACTIONS WE FACE IS OUR OWN MIND

We're trying to sit down and write a report. Our worker-self is just kicking in and we've finished our boss-mode thinking as far as we can for now. So, on to the report. But, hang on – the boss is away! We're just a lowly worker in worker-mode now. No bosses around. No one would mind if we had a quick look at Facebook. Or just nipped off to make another cup of tea and have a chat with a colleague.

We face our own personal battles against distractions all the time. Everything else in the world just seems more interesting than what we're currently working on. Ever felt like you just needed to be strapped to the chair or chained to the desk in order to write, create, administrate, deal with or finish? It can sometimes feel like we're full of unique and creative ways to distract ourselves – if only we could harness such wonderful and unique creativity in work itself!

A Productivity Ninja is self-aware here and can develop better habits to combat as much of this kind of distraction as possible. Here are some of the things that you can do to help (we'll talk a lot more about this in later chapters, too):

GET NEW IDEAS OFF YOUR MIND AS QUICKLY AS POSSIBLE — SILENCE THE BOSS

As you're working on something, particularly if it's less interesting than other parts of your work, you'll hear that boss voice in your head coming up with new ideas about other projects, thinking about all the things on your mind that need to be done and generally trying to force you out of worker-mode and into boss-mode. To overcome this, you need to capture all of these thoughts so that you can come back to them later (to organize, review and, if necessary, do the actions relating to them). Have a pen and paper handy. This only works if you trust that you'll come back to these captured thoughts later on.

PROCESS EMAIL RATHER THAN CHECK EMAIL

Doing email in batches, returning your inbox to zero several times a day, severely reduces background noise and your keenness to go fiddling in your inbox looking for potential distractions. Yes, I did say zero. I will show you exactly how that's possible in the next chapter!

INTERNET FAMINES

The internet is single-handedly the biggest productivity tool and the biggest procrastination tool, all wrapped into one. Can you see an immediate problem here? The point is to be clear with yourself: decide at which times of day you want access to a fantastic wealth of information – *and* decide the times in the day that you want to avoid the temptation to get caught in a 'YouTube loop' or waste valuable attention marvelling at Facebook statuses, celebrity gossip or BBC website articles. Learn that the internet is your best friend as well as your worst enemy, and at times it needs to be as far away from your impulsive grasp as possible.

'SELECTIVE IGNORANCE'

> 'We go to the same restaurant every evening and we have the same meal, month in, month out until we decide to change it. And that will be every evening until we change our minds again. We don't like the idea of reading menus or thinking about food. It seems rather a waste of brain to us.'
> – George Passmore, Gilbert & George

'Selective ignorance' is a term Tim Ferriss uses in his book, *The 4-Hour Work Week*. He describes the idea of avoiding ever buying newspapers or consuming unnecessary media. He talks about how he 'shortcuts' this by asking his friends' trusted opinions on political issues so that he can make a good decision about who to vote for without the need for a lot of time wasted engaging in the issues, and how he deliberately avoids gadgets or internet sites that he knows can be distractions. There's also an element of personal preference to some of these: I personally love political news coverage and find the 'games' that politicians engage in pretty fascinating stuff. I would therefore hate to be taking my voting preferences from friends – as good a judge as most of my friends are! – and miss all that entertainment on the way. Likewise, many of us love nothing more than relaxing with the Sunday papers and a cup of tea. This is all about compromise though – giving up small luxuries or small wins, knowing that from less comes more. An easy one for me was that I used to spend an hour or so every week trying to keep abreast of trade press, industry news and the like. After a while I realized that the important stories were generally forwarded to me anyway, so I cancelled my subscriptions and gave myself one less distraction each week. There will be many more examples that you can begin to explore here, too.

LOOK FOR THE WORLD'S INFORMATION DJS

A great trick in reducing distractions and coping with information overload is to look for DJs rather than records. DJs are the enthusiasts who curate, edit out the crap, give you the headlines or best bits and guide your thinking. John Peel was a legendary DJ. Gilles Peterson on BBC Radio is a fine current example: he travels the world, connects with interesting people at the heart of music scenes around the world and delivers a unique mix of music for three hours every week, most of which I would never find or understand without his help. As the world produces more content, there's a good deal more worth paying attention to but infinitely more worth avoiding. TED acts as a DJ: it curates events and a website that identify a broad range of interesting ideas from diverse presenters.

I think we're moving towards the age of the 'Information DJ'. I hope Think Productive acts as a DJ too: we use our blog and LinkedIn group to find, comment on and share a whole range of perspectives on productivity. We add our own perspectives, we debate, we listen, we connect. We do this because we care. So look for the DJs, not the soulless presenters.

DON'T BE AN 'EARLY ADOPTER'

It's considered cool to be an early adopter. One glimpse at the line of people camped outside the Apple store when they introduce a new version of the iPad or iPhone is proof that people like to be the first to get their hands on new gadgets. However, it is certainly not smart to be an early adopter. Let the crowd figure stuff out, then spend time asking them for their informed opinions (which they'll be delighted to give, seeing as their aim in being an early adopter is so they get to talk about it to anyone who'll listen!) before deciding to buy. The same is true of online software. There are thousands of new sites out there purporting to be the next Facebook or LinkedIn that will revolutionize your life. Some of these things might turn out to do just that, but many of them will be consigned to history in a matter of months.

Patience is a virtue. You don't need to look cool. And even if you really want to look cool, no one really cares if you do. On your deathbed, no one will ask you what you owned or what software you used, and they certainly won't ask you whether you were among the first to have it.

BE SELF-AWARE

Your amazingly creative mind will come up with hundreds of ways to avoid stuff that's either too boring, too challenging or just unfulfilling. Keep a constant lookout for what some of these avoidance tactics might be and start to battle against them. Yours will be different, but mine have included the following over the years:

▶ Tidying my house

▶ 'Desk faffing' – symptoms include over-labelling things, refilling staplers and stationery drawers and so on

▶ Eating – sometimes this is, of course, necessary, but often spending two minutes eating a Wispa bar is just easier than thinking about or doing your work

▶ Internet research or shopping

▶ Starting conversations in the office

▶ Twitter

▶ Listening to podcasts under the false impression that spending half of your attention on something inspirational will move you forward – save those for later

▶ Fiddling around with some new internet tool or iPad app that needs lots of 'setting up' (RSS readers are a good example of this) under the mistaken impression of later time savings and payoff

▶ Talking to people on internet message boards and Facebook groups about my extremely enlightened and important opinions about who Aston Villa should sign in the upcoming transfer window

▶ Doing easier or more interesting work than the stuff that really needs doing right now.

These are all delay tactics. Some of them might be vaguely useful to you, others less so. Importantly though, they can also all be done with the most minimal attention so if you're full of proactive attention now, these things can wait.

EXTERNAL DISTRACTIONS: DEALING WITH INTERRUPTIONS

No amount of self-awareness alone will protect our attention, for one very good reason: the world is filled with other people, all with a propensity to interrupt us and steer us down a different path. As a result, we have to guard our precious attention ruthlessly against these numerous enemies. Whereas dealing with our own distractions is more like a science (observe behaviour, diagnose what's going on in our own heads, develop new behaviour, test out effectiveness, repeat), dealing with the interruptions and agendas of other people is an art form. Your deftness, skill and oft-underhanded ruthlessness is what comes to the fore here.

There are several really obvious forms of interruption that we can deal with straight away and many more subtle forms of interruption that we'll move on to later.

AVOID MOST MEETINGS YOU'RE INVITED TO

Meetings are a wonderful way to spend time indulging in other people's priorities rather than your own. Avoiding meetings that are not directly concerned with your major projects or areas of responsibility, or for which it would be possible to have an involvement in a much easier way, is critical. We all know that at times this takes some creativity and even sometimes some deception, but spending all morning in a meeting being a luxury 'extra brain' in someone else's project is a ridiculous and churlish waste of your valuable proactive attention. I'll discuss this in more detail later, but where possible, just say 'No'.

DON'T ANSWER YOUR PHONE

Phone calls are among the worst interruptions. They cost you time and energy, both in dealing with them and in 'recovering' from them (those, 'Oh, where was I again?' conversations that you have to have with yourself once you're off the call). Try this: for the periods of time that you have decided you will use to tackle proactive attention work, turn off your mobile phone and if you have a phone on your desk, set it to automatic answer machine. Over time, let the decision to leave your phone turned on be a conscious one, so that it feels like you now choose to receive calls for a period of time rather than choosing not to.

There's another great reason for doing this. Voicemail is seriously underrated as a communication medium. It's one-way communication instead of two-way. As such, the caller leaving the message gets to the root of the issue in seconds rather than in minutes and by the time you call them back, you're both halfway through the conversation that needs to happen.

CLOSE DOWN YOUR EMAIL AS OFTEN AS POSSIBLE

Amazing things happen outside of your inbox. In fact, most of the work that you produce happens outside of your inbox. We are social creatures, and the 'ping' of a new email arriving is enough to give us sufficient curiosity to drop our most important piece of work and 'check' who is reaching out to us to say hi. As we do so, we lose our place, interrupting the most important work of the day, and for what? Usually a circular 'all staff' email telling us that Julie from accounts has brought back some sweets from her holiday to Greece, or a reminder about next week's all staff meeting that you already had in your calendar anyway. Yet most people turn on their email as soon as they arrive in the morning, and turning it off is the last thing they do each evening before heading home. This means that you're constantly prone to interruptions that are easily avoided. Turning off your emails, even for just a couple of hours a day or half an hour in each hour, will give you a clearer head, reduce the noise threatening to distract you, and will help you pay attention more easily to the things that really matter.

WEAR HEADPHONES OR HAVE A VISUAL SYMBOL TO **KEEP COLLEAGUES' QUESTIONS AT BAY**

Elena is one of the stars of the Think Productive office, and is on many projects our main linchpin between our client, our Productivity Ninja delivering the workshop and our administrative support. As such, she gets a lot of questions from the rest of us in the office, all of which interrupt her flow. If she's in need of some proactive attention time she has a small china kitten that she places on the desk. Everyone else in the office, including me as her boss, knows that when we see the kitten it's a sign that she needs proactive attention time. We save up our questions or ideas for later and she stays focused. I've seen variations on this: homemade plastic signs, whiteboards, hats, police-style tape on the back of a chair – 'Stay back, there's nothing here to see' – etc. Perhaps the simplest and most effective is a big pair of headphones. As well as having the extra practical function that you can drown out the office hubbub with music (which some people love to work to, while others find difficult to concentrate with), it's also a real barrier to you hearing the bits of the conversation or questions aimed at you. If you *are* interrupted while wearing headphones, it's kind of obvious to the person interrupting you that they're breaking your flow.

WORK FROM HOME, OR **FROM SOMEWHERE ELSE**

Of course, the best way to be sure that you won't be interrupted and distracted by all the noises and annoyances of the office is to be somewhere other than the office. Working from home *can* be a good solution to this. It can also provide its own new set of distractions: 'I'll start my report just as soon as I've done last night's washing up and hoovered the lounge'. Working from home isn't for everyone. I find, though, that I do some of my best thinking work on trains and in coffee shops. These are places where the atmosphere and scenery is calming, but where there are few distractions: desk, pad, laptop and me. There's nothing to do but drink coffee and do my best work and as a result, that's often exactly what I do.

SAY 'NO'

Realize that you shouldn't feel guilty saying 'No' if someone is interrupting you at an important point in a key task, when you're on a roll during a period of productive, proactive attention. Try to schedule their query or involvement when you know your attention will be on the wane, thereby protecting your most precious attention and momentum. Don't drop everything straight away for another person's badly timed query.

REMEMBER THAT MOST INFORMATION IS CLOSE TO WORTHLESS

Be very choosy about what you drop everything to read, investigate or do anything with. In the age of information, opportunity often knocks pretty loudly, through the recommendations of friends, social media sharing and so on. It's no longer that important to scan the horizons. Letting the more important things come to you is much easier.

3. INCREASING YOUR ATTENTION: MAKING INACTIVE ATTENTION ACTIVE, MAKING ACTIVE ATTENTION PROACTIVE

In truth, if you're feeling like your mind is in a real period of inactive attention it's impossible to do that much about it. You're already tired, lacking in focus, perhaps lacking in motivation. There is, however, a lot that you can do to develop better habits that will leave your mind healthier, happier and more likely to produce prolonged periods of proactive and active attention. Before I get onto that, here are a couple of short-term fixes – the sticking plasters of attention management:

CHANGE THE VIEW

It's possible to temporarily 'trick' your brain into a short additional period of active attention if you're feeling sluggish and inactive. To do this, you need to jolt your brain into needing to feel its way around again. If I'm asked to facilitate a long meeting, I will ask people to move chairs in the afternoon and face a different direction. Just this small movement that changes the view is enough to awaken your consciousness and jolt it into increased attention. If you're working on a long report, move to a new part of the room every half an hour or so. If you're working on an Excel spreadsheet, change all the fonts to red and green just for half an hour and then change it all back. These tweaks in perspective can really help to keep you going that bit longer than you really have the energy for.

CHANGE THE GAME

If you're really battling to stay focused, change the game every 30–60 minutes. Don't dwell on that report, staring into space; instead do half an hour of email, half an hour of the report, half an hour of something completely different, half an hour of the report, and so on. Keep your attention on its toes and keep moving.

AIR

Get outside and go for a quick walk. The fresh air in your lungs, the movement, the changes in sights, sounds, smells and thought patterns will awaken you again for the next little while. If you can't get outside, simply open a window and take some deep breaths of fresh air, with five minutes just to admire the view and notice your surroundings. Such time to 'just be' is precious and again, it'll awaken the senses and switch your attention back into gear.

STRATEGIC CAFFEINE (BUT SEE BELOW!)

A short caffeine fix at the right time can be a handy Ninja move. If you're tired, you'll 'crash' afterwards and end up in the worst kind of inactive attention you can experience. But for now, load up the cafetière, strap in and let's go!

BRAIN *MAINTENANCE*

> 'In times of life crisis, whether wild fires or smouldering stress, the first thing I do is go back to basics ... am I eating right, am I getting enough sleep, am I getting some physical and mental exercise everyday.'
> – Edward Albert

The above are just the short-term fixes that over the course of a year will offer you precious little impact. You may find a couple of days go better as a result, but what you see below are the holy trinity of *increasing* your attention levels regularly: nutrition, physical fitness and meditation. Your brain is a muscle and like any muscle, it is linked to your overall physical health and fitness. A healthy body truly is a healthy mind. Too many of the blogs and books on productivity focus just on shortcuts, tips and ways of using the tool of your mind, without paying any attention to how you might improve the tool, increase capacity and boost your personal potential to create impact. What follows is a quick tour of several things that can work wonders in increasing your attention, focus, alertness and all-round brain performance. You may find a few of these suggestions common sense, and you may also find some of them downright weird. You don't have to try them all, but bear with me.

BRAIN *FUEL*

There are hundreds of books out there that focus wholly on nutrition. I'd recommend it as an area you spend some time thinking about, researching

and planning. Not only is it good for your productivity, but good nutrition can make you happier and help you lead a healthier, longer life too. Bonus! So while nutrition is an area to definitely spend some time on beyond this book, here are ten quick rules of the road:

▶ **Drink water – even when you're not thirsty**

Dehydration is one of the major causes of lost concentration. If you're feeling thirsty, it's too late. The body will only let you know the signs of thirst when you're already pretty dehydrated. Keep a large glass or water bottle on your desk at all times and figure out how to incorporate drinking water into your daily routine if you're not doing it habitually.

▶ **Five or six small meals are better than three big ones**

For your body, it takes energy to make energy. If you can spend the day regularly eating small meals rather than having points in the day where you're either starved or stuffed, you'll create a more balanced release of energy, keeping your brain more focused. Have a small breakfast at home and another when you reach the office. Eat half of your lunch a bit earlier and half a bit later. Buddhists practise eating until 80% full, not 100% – this simple but counter-intuitive habit can prevent sluggishness and makes digestion easier. When you eat, don't do anything else – one of the main reasons we get too full is because we don't notice soon enough!

▶ **Eat breakfast**

Yes, that old chestnut. It's a cliché because it's true. Fire up your metabolism early in the day and get the brain fuelled and ready for action.

▶ **Eat vitamin-heavy food and cut out the crap**

It's also not rocket science to say that natural, raw, organic ingredients are going to do your body a lot more good than another McDonald's. Think about the overall balance of your diet.

That doesn't need to mean being a martyr and certainly we shouldn't always associate good eating with diets or weight loss – and a little of what you fancy can do you good! But you should ensure you eat a good range of colours of vegetables and varied, low fat sources of protein such as lean meat, fish and beans.

▶ **Use caffeine wisely or cut it out**

As a sparsely used weapon, coffee or tea can be great; as a crutch it's so unproductive. Aim for one coffee a day and if you need to boost your energy at other times, try snacking on apples as an alternative (it works surprisingly well!).

▶ **Think about your Glycemic Index (GI)**

As well as thinking about the quality of the food that you put into your body, think about how slowly or quickly the energy gets released. Foods that have a low GI rating mean they release their energy more slowly and therefore more consistently. High GI foods can leave you constantly reaching highs and lows, rather than experiencing a steady flow of energy throughout the day. Low GI foods include beans, green vegetables, oranges, sunflower seeds, eggs, peanuts, apples, tuna, pears and peaches. Medium GI foods include bananas, granola, crisps, rice, sugar, granola, cereal, croissants and kiwi fruit. High GIs are things like potatoes, sweets, fizzy drinks, biscuits, some breads, chips and perhaps more surprisingly, things like carrots, watermelon, raisins and dried dates. Keep your focus on low GI foods for a more sustained and consistent energy release. For the same reason, a large, carb-heavy lunch will leave you sluggish straight after lunch, followed by a high, followed by a dip! For a good directory of low-GI recipes, try the BBC good food website: http://www.bbcgoodfood.com/recipes/collection/low-gi

▶ **Avoid sugary drinks and energy drinks**

Like caffeine, sugar is a great temporary solution to increasing your energy and therefore your short-term attention. It's an equally unsustainable long-term option. Drink water or fruit juices instead of lots of fizzy drinks, although be aware that fruit juices can be equally high in (natural) sugars! The proliferation of energy drinks in offices really is worrying. I have seen people twitching from withdrawal and actually becoming a distraction to the rest of the office as they're either unaware of the huge highs and lows that these drinks create, or simply unable to manage it. Avoid.

▶ **Use 'brain fuel' supplements**

There are a range of supplements on the market that are recommended to improve cognitive performance, the nervous system and physical suppleness. There are also detractors who will say you should only get such vitamins and minerals from real food, not from supplements. While I am sure getting everything you need from the perfect diet is the best option, it's simply not always feasible in today's fast-paced age. You can research particular supplements if you have specific requirements, but personally I think a fish oil tablet for the brain, zinc for immunity and a good multivitamin for overall health and well-being are all you really need.

▶ **Sleep**

Losing sleep is sometimes inevitable, but nevertheless do all you can to improve both the quality and quantity of your sleep. Want to know one of my guilty secrets? If I have a whole day working from home, I will often have a little 'power nap' just after lunch or mid-afternoon. Even twenty minutes of quiet darkness is enough to recharge and revive. I also know a couple of people who work in corporate law firms who swear by this – and luckily there they provide 'pods' for the people who sleep there overnight, so they can nap whenever they need to! I'll also admit I've napped under my desk in a busy office before now (using stealth and camouflage so that no one noticed!), under the table in a meeting room and even in a small storage cupboard.

PHYSICAL FITNESS

To reiterate: a healthy body really does mean a healthy mind. As well as nutrition, it's important to take care of your body with regular exercise. You've probably heard the doctor mention this, that woman on TV has mentioned this, and probably the annoyingly fit and active cousin in your family has, too. Again, it's a cliché because it's such valuable advice.

It doesn't need to be strenuous. A few short periods of, say, half an hour exercising each week is enough. If you live two or three miles from your office, you could probably get everything you need by simply walking to and from work more often than not.

Establishing a regular gym routine can also be a great way to keep fit as well as improve your strength and physical resilience. I tend to aim for three gym sessions each week (usually two mornings before I start work and then one session at the weekend). The important thing is to find something that you can fall into an easy routine with and that works for you. Celebrate it when momentum is good, but please don't beat yourself up if there's a week when it doesn't quite happen. It won't make a huge difference in the short-term. Ninjas are human beings, after all.

MEDITATION & SWITCHING OFF

In his book, *The Happiness Hypothesis*, Jonathan Haidt presents a compelling thesis that one of the only things proven to make you happier is regular practice of meditation. Meditation comes in many forms and is also often wrapped up with mysticism, religions and cults, which many of us can find unsettling or unpalatable. It's the practice of being present, focused only on yourself and your connection to the world around you. *The Happiness Hypothesis* also presents a brilliant analogy that allowed me to understand meditation in a much deeper way.

THE ELEPHANT AND THE MONKEY

Your mind is like a monkey riding an elephant. The monkey represents your conscious mind. It chatters away, has a million ideas a second and is constantly in a state of agitation. The elephant, meanwhile, represents your subconscious mind. It carries all the things going on beneath the surface. The monkey is of course too small to control the direction of the elephant, whereas the elephant isn't often able communicate the journey it wants to take. During meditation, you're trying to silence the monkey or at least ignore it and let its chatter pass you by. You're trying to find out what that elephant is saying and then have the elephant and monkey work in harmony.

MEDITATION DOESN'T NEED TO BE HARD

In our constantly wired world, we can sometimes forget to listen to ourselves. The monkey in our head is fed by work, stress, news, content, Facebook posts, tweets, blogs, newspapers, TV, radio chit chat and the relentless pace of 21st century life. Taking time to listen to our emotional responses, calming ourselves down, making space to be grateful for the world around us ... all of these things are shunned and excluded from our culture of constant connection. I spent about four years being interested in meditation, dabbling in it and yet never really finding the time for it (or to put it another way, the energy to prioritize it). Then, in conversation with a meditation teacher one day, where I was doing my usual monkey brained thing of asking for the 'best book recommendation' or 'best podcast', this meditation teacher looked me in the eye and said, 'Dude, just sit'. And really that was all I needed to hear. There are a million versions of the perfect way to meditate, a million people trying to attach their own meaning or pseudo-religious explanation for it, but at its heart, to meditate is just to sit and do nothing. Listen to the silence. It's unnerving at first but you'll learn to enjoy it.

NOT HAVING TIME TO MEDITATE IS NEVER THE REASON WE DON'T MEDITATE

Meditation can be hard. It requires practice. But get into the swing of it and you can meditate pretty much anywhere: from crowded tubes to driving along the motorway, from walking home to queuing in the supermarket. And if you're new to it – or you just want to make it as easy as possible for yourself – a great tip would be to get an app for your phone or some kind of guided audio meditation series. My favourites are a couple of simple and rather delightful iPhone and Android apps called 'buddhify' and 'Headspace'. Both of these bring a modern, practical and very 21st-century feel to meditation. For just a couple of pounds you have a wealth of short, guided meditations at your fingertips, each designed to help you experience clarity, connection, stability and embodiment. The audios even come purpose-built to suit wherever you happen to be, with options for travelling, walking, the gym and home. Just search 'buddhify' or 'Headspace' in the iPhone or Android app stores. (Oh, and just so you're clear, they don't pay me to mention them; I just enjoy using the apps and I think you will too. The same goes for all the other things I mention later in the book!)

SWITCHING OFF PRODUCES RENEWAL

Much like turning off our computers in the evening, switching off our brains and allowing silence, space and rest to permeate them is so important not only to our mental health but to our ability to produce proactive attention and stay on top form. Give yourself permission to switch off at night and at weekends – don't give in to the pressure to constantly work late and burn yourself out. Remember that you're switching off to *boost* your productivity.

SMARTPHONES ARE TOO SMART TO BE IGNORED

The makers of Blackberry and other similar mobile email devices know exactly how to make them 'sticky', easy to use and addictive. It's rare that I meet anyone who feels able to have the Blackberry turned on during the evening and yet resist the temptation to check or react to that little red light, flashing away on the table. To truly switch off, designate a time in the evening when your smartphone goes off and stays off. Proper renewal comes from rest and silence: silence half-interrupted is just more low-level noise.

TAKE A *DEEP BREATH*

Regularly take a deep breath. Remember as you do so that what you are doing is enough. Take a moment to feel grateful for everything around you. Taking stock is important and helps prepare a Ninja for tomorrow's battles.

4. THE MAGIC OF CREATING ADDITIONAL POCKETS OF ATTENTION

Finally, what if you could find additional pockets of attention where there were previously none? I'm not talking about extending your working hours here, but perhaps using some of the points in your day that you might currently not have considered. Opportunity is everywhere – as long as we're prepared.

CALLS & WALKING

Every day I have at least two periods where I'm walking somewhere for five or ten minutes. This is where I make most of my phone calls. Why make calls when I'm at my desk and have so many other things available to me, when I can do this when I'd otherwise be, well, just walking? I can't do these calls unless I'm prepared, though. I need a regular discipline of adding phone numbers to my Blackberry and a regularly updated list of what calls I can make on the move.

READING & WAITING

Similarly, I keep both a physical and a digital file of reading materials, primarily as a way of avoiding having to read things at my desk when again, there are other things I could be doing there that require more resources to be available. My physical 'Reading' file is simply an A4 document wallet. It lives in my bag and is constantly being filled up and emptied. My digital file is one I keep on the iPad using the app, Instapaper. Instapaper allows me to save interesting pages from the web, documents, and emails, and then access them wherever I am (and without the need for a 3G connection either). I read on trains, on the tube (my particular favourite, as I get a geeky little thrill from leaving interesting articles behind for other passengers to discover!), in the dentist's waiting room, in receptions if I arrive early for a meeting and so on. It's also sometimes nice to catch up your reading at home for an hour, while relaxing with a cup of tea.

THINKING & TRAVELLING

One of my Think Productive colleagues lives just outside London and travels into the city on a motorbike. By keeping a list of all the big decisions and thinking he has coming up, he can refer to this just before he turns the key and starts the engine running; it sets him up to use that time really productively. For several years I lived in London and rode a motorbike (by far the best way of getting around the city) but all I could think about when I rode my bike was, 'Don't die, don't die, don't die', so I'm in awe of the confidence needed to also use this time for useful thinking! There are many, many other examples of times a 'Thinking List' comes in handy: at airports, in queues, when driving, while attending functions you don't really care about, or watching films your partner wanted to see but you hate (do it subtly though!), and many more. A great tip is to keep this list synchronized to your phone. Since you always have your phone with you, the list is always there when you find an opportunity arises. Again, you need to be prepared for this to work!

COFFEE & *CONVERSATIONS*

We're about to move on and look at the dreaded medium of email, so think about all those internal emails that fly around the office from people who sit just a few desks away. While the kettle is being boiled or the coffee made, use this time to have quick conversations in reply to some of those emails. Before you get up to make a drink, do a quick scan of your email inbox, picking out two or three potential targets. Then, your goal is to hunt them down between now and when you sit back down with your hot beverage. Make it a game! Particularly focus on the conversations that are so much more easily done in person than on email, which will save you a bucketful of time later on. Sometimes a useful way to decide this is to think about which emails might lead you to reply with a series of questions – usually in a two-way conversation, the number of questions you need to answer is seriously reduced.

EXERCISE: CREATING AN ATTENTION AND FOCUS MANAGEMENT PLAN

What you'll need: Pen and paper, boss-mode proactive attention

How long it'll take: 30 minutes

Ninja mindset: Mindfulness, Agility, Preparedness, Ruthlessness

Let's create an attention and focus management action plan specifically for you! Review and rate the attention management techniques and ideas on the next pages and note which ones you do already, which you'll try (and when), which you might try, and which you're sure you'll never try. Then, pick three that you think you would find useful, and give them a try!

Do consistently already	1
Could do more	2
Will try	3
Might try	4
Will never try	5

1. **Schedule your work based on your attention level**

	1	2	3	4	5
Identify periods of proactive, active and inactive attention	☐	☐	☐	☐	☐
Identify the parts of your work that require boss-mode	☐	☐	☐	☐	☐
Schedule in times for boss-mode work	☐	☐	☐	☐	☐

2. **Protecting your attention from interruptions and distractions**

   Distracting yourself

	1	2	3	4	5
Get new ideas off your mind as quickly as possible	☐	☐	☐	☐	☐
Process email rather than check email	☐	☐	☐	☐	☐
Internet famines	☐	☐	☐	☐	☐
Practise 'selective ignorance'	☐	☐	☐	☐	☐
Look for the world's Information DJs	☐	☐	☐	☐	☐
Don't be an 'early adopter'	☐	☐	☐	☐	☐
Be self-aware	☐	☐	☐	☐	☐

   Interruptions by others

Avoid most meetings you're invited to	☐	☐	☐	☐	☐
Don't answer your phone	☐	☐	☐	☐	☐
Close down your email as often as possible	☐	☐	☐	☐	☐
Use headphones or a visual symbol to stop interruptions	☐	☐	☐	☐	☐
Work from home, or from somewhere else	☐	☐	☐	☐	☐
Say 'No'	☐	☐	☐	☐	☐
Remember that most information is close to worthless	☐	☐	☐	☐	☐

3. **Increasing your attention: making inactive attention active, making active attention proactive**

	1	2	3	4	5
Change the view	☐	☐	☐	☐	☐
Change the game	☐	☐	☐	☐	☐
Air	☐	☐	☐	☐	☐
Strategic caffeine	☐	☐	☐	☐	☐
Brain maintenance	☐	☐	☐	☐	☐
Drink water – even when you're not thirsty	☐	☐	☐	☐	☐
Five or six small meals a day	☐	☐	☐	☐	☐
Avoid sugary drinks and energy drinks	☐	☐	☐	☐	☐
Use brain fuel supplements	☐	☐	☐	☐	☐
Get better sleep	☐	☐	☐	☐	☐
Physical fitness	☐	☐	☐	☐	☐
Meditation	☐	☐	☐	☐	☐
Switch off your smartphone	☐	☐	☐	☐	☐
Take a deep breath	☐	☐	☐	☐	☐

4. **The magic of creating additional pockets of attention**

	1	2	3	4	5
Make calls while walking	☐	☐	☐	☐	☐
Prepare reading material for times when you're waiting	☐	☐	☐	☐	☐
Do your thinking while travelling	☐	☐	☐	☐	☐
Use coffee breaks to have quick conversations	☐	☐	☐	☐	☐

Are you a Ninja?

▶ A Ninja is ruthless in choosing where to put their attention.

▶ A Ninja is prepared, able to match the right levels of their attention to the right tasks.

▶ A Ninja is agile and moves fluidly through their day, maximizing their attention levels to make magic happen.

4. NINJA EMAIL

In the last chapter we looked at how managing our attention is the new key to Ninja-level productivity. The reason this is so crucial these days is simple: information overload.

Information overload – not just from email, but from the internet, social networking sites, 24-hour news, work intranets and the sheer speed and volume of modern knowledge work – is a much bigger challenge than it was even two years ago, let alone ten years ago, and this carries a major threat to our productivity. The more information we subject ourselves to, the more likely our attention moves away from the things we really need to focus on.

> 'One of the most important soft skills you can have is figuring out how to deal with a high volume of email. And the only way to do that is to put some kind of a system in place that's simple and repeatable and is going to allow you to have an actual life outside of email.'
> – Merlin Mann, 43folders.com and creator of Inbox Zero

Email in particular is a prime offender here. Research carried out by the Universities of Glasgow and Paisley has discovered that one third of email users get stressed by the heavy volume of emails they receive.

When I was a busy Chief Executive, and before I had any need to invest time in thinking about my own productivity (since, as a Chief Executive, I had plenty of people in the organization to be productive on my behalf!), my email management was completely out of control and it stressed me out. I had an inbox with 3,000 emails not yet dealt with – and rising! – and I would all too often need prompting to meet necessary commitments and deadlines. This approach would frequently mean I would miss opportunities to be proactive as well as obviously miss the deadlines concealed way down somewhere in the depths of my inbox.

Of course, even more stressful than knowing you've missed something vital that you needed to act on is *not* knowing that you're missing something vital that you need to act on! The fact that you don't even know what other opportunities or threats lie buried in that stack of emails, and how important that information and those opportunities could potentially be, is at the root of the stress most people feel about their email, and the obligation people feel to be constantly connected to it.

People become a slave to their email account as it piles up even further and it quickly becomes a constant drain on attention. When I was a Chief Executive I was never off my emails: I was constantly distracted by new emails coming in, and spent half my time scrolling up, scrolling down, scrolling up, scrolling down – never actually fixing the mountainous problem in front of me, just regularly reminding myself that the mountain was still there to be climbed. Sound familiar at all?

THE PARADIGM SHIFT: *CONNECTIVITY VS. PRODUCTIVITY*

Today, my email practice is very different. I have a system in place that gets my inbox to zero several times a day, leaving me clear about what opportunities or threats are lurking, and miraculously, I'm also able to track and follow up on particular emails at the right times so that things don't fall through the cracks and get lost in the back and forth of email. In this chapter I'll show you how this works and by following the exercises in this book, we'll get your email inbox to zero in the next couple of hours if you're up for it.

BEING 'CONNECTED' *REQUIRES VERY LITTLE THINKING.* DEFINING THE MEANING OF INPUTS *REQUIRES A LOT OF THINKING*

It's time for you to rethink email. Let's start with the uncomfortable truth about the way that we work. As soon as more than one thing has our attention and we experience information overload, our instinctive reaction is that we want to feel busy in order to feel like we're making progress. Because as a species we're inherently lazy, we gravitate to the easiest way to achieve this illusion of progress.

We check for what's new, we scroll up and down, we check for what's new, we scroll up and down, we fiddle around creating archive folders, we check for other new information (for example on our social media profiles or the news or our phone) and generally begin to develop an addiction to being connected. What we're addicted to here is the illusion of productivity for a minimal payoff of thinking.

Getting your inbox to zero breaks out of this bad habit and changes the way you see email; you instead become addicted to being safe in the knowledge that all of the decision-making and thinking work has been done. The system itself forces Ninja-like decisiveness and discipline that's needed for you to make the difficult decisions about emails as soon as you read them, reducing procrastination time, increasing clarity about your work and vastly reducing the stress that email overload causes.

'What gets measured gets managed.'
– Peter Drucker

The surprising thing – and one that most people never discover – is that once your email inbox is at zero, keeping it there is pretty easy. After all, there's no mountain left to climb, just today's molehill. In fact, one of the nicest things about using such a system is how easy it is to take couple of days out of the office, knowing that when you return you only have that many days' processing to do, because you're starting from a zero position before you leave. Also, your ability to make decisions about each email will be so enhanced that you can go away for a week's annual leave and come back and clear all your emails in a matter of an hour or so. And if you happen to experience a heavy volume of emails for a few days, and start to see your inbox building up again, you can easily measure this and estimate how long it will take to get you back to zero. Email changes from being a task that seems like an amorphous mass of work that will never be finished, into a quantifiable conveyor belt where every single email has a possible decision that can be made about it straight away. Sounds simple doesn't it? Well, the good news is that is really is!

THE MINDSET YOU NEED TO KEEP YOUR INBOX AT ZERO

There are three mindset changes required to implement this system that will wean you off your addiction to being connected to email and encourage you to develop an addiction to decisiveness and productivity instead.

YOUR INBOX IS JUST *A PLACE WHERE EMAILS LAND*

Your inbox is not your to-do list. I cannot emphasize this enough. Your inbox is not your to-do list. It is nothing more than a holding pen for where new inputs land. We often try to keep emails in our inbox because we don't want to lose them or we want to come back to them. But the really meaningful work goes on outside of the email inbox and using it as your primary to-do list reminder will mean either that things from elsewhere are missed or you end up having to email yourself. A lot. In addition, using your inbox as a to-do list mixes your to-do reminders with all the other noise that your inbox throws at you, so it can be difficult to know what's 'to do' versus 'what's happening' versus what can be ignored.

We need to create new holding pens for these very differently categorized items otherwise we'll keep having to make the decisions about what's actionable and what's not over and over again. Your inbox is to your work what an airport runway is to your holiday. The impact of an email isn't felt in the inbox it lands in; it ends with an action, a reply, something read and filed, or something deleted.

DON'T LET YOUR INBOX *NAG YOU ALL DAY*

Your inbox is full of potentially exciting information to get distracted with and this information is piling up all the time! 'What if there's something vital in there? Better quickly go and see what it is!' Checking too often can become a deadly disease. Turn off every sound and graphic. That way, you can revisit the inbox when you're ready to, not when the inbox is nagging you to return.

DON'T *'CHECK'* YOUR EMAILS, *'PROCESS'* YOUR EMAILS

This might sound really simple, but it's one of those subtle changes that's actually profound. Every time you open your inbox, your mind-set is not to check what's new, but to make the decisions and create the momentum needed to move those emails to where they need to get to. You can only get it out of your inbox if every option you need has an obvious next step – otherwise your mind will do what it probably does now and say, 'Err, not sure where that goes. I'll come back to that one later'. The system I'm about to show you will mean it's no longer easier to procrastinate than it is to take action – ever again.

REGULAR REVIEW

Making time to follow up, double check, print, clean up and generally do some housekeeping on your email system provides a regular chance to do some routine maintenance and a little bit of strategic-level review. After all, it's important that we measure the effectiveness of any system; one of the key problems with how most people use Outlook or Gmail is that they don't feel there's any way that they can gain control, so they don't think there's anything to measure.

D IS FOR DECISION ...

Here's a liberating thought for you. With every single email that arrives, there are only seven possible things you can do:

- ▶ **Delete it**, or file it away

- ▶ **Do it now** (if less than a two minute action, automatically do it then and there)

- ▶ **Do it later**

- ▶ **Decide** it doesn't need an action, but file it for reference or future use

▶ **Delegate** it for someone else to do

▶ **Defer the decision** about whether the action needs doing to a later stage (usually by adding to your calendar)

▶ **Decide** there is no action from you, but that you want to track whether someone else follows through.

Those are the *only* decisions we can make about each and every email. The point is that most people delay making those decisions, to the point that valuable information is lost in and amongst a lot of stuff that should have been deleted long ago.

THE *800–20 RULE!*

For a lot of people that I coach to get their inboxes to zero, one of the common themes and questions is about the ratio of actionable versus non-actionable items. Now this will probably shock you: no more than 20% will be actionable. I like to think of this as a version of Pareto's 80–20 rule: about 20% of your emails will add 80% of the possible impact you can have through your use of email. This leaves at least 80% of the emails you receive in the category of low priority, noisy, nice to have or plain useless. I would actually go further than this and say that often when I'm coaching people, the numbers are even more extreme. Email has taken over our working lives, over-communication is valued above silence and thinking things through, and sending an email is often used as a substitution for taking responsibility for prac-tising clear thinking. As a result, so many organizations are crippled by the CC button, the reply all button and some seriously bad habits.

I will regularly have someone with 800 unread or un-dealt with emails in their inbox at the start of a session and a couple of hours later there are only around 20 emails left that require any significant action. So don't think 80–20, think 800–20.

For every 800 emails you have, there will be around 20 there that will matter and 780 that can either be deleted, filed or at worst, very quickly replied to in just a few seconds. Instead of feeling burdened by a thousand emails, think of it instead as two-dozen conversations. The stuff that really matters is inherently manageable, but it *does* require some ruthless focus to find it in among the deluge of 'cakes in the kitchen' emails, software notifications, 'reply all's and FYIs.

WHAT'S THE **WORST THING** THAT COULD HAPPEN?

Think of it this way: if your entire email inbox crashed tomorrow, what would you lose? I'm not asking how many emails would you lose, but how many opportunities to get a leg up or prevent a screw up would be missed? How would the world be different? We place such an importance on each and every email but it's the actions and information outside of our inboxes that really matter.

There's a definite nervousness around the way we think about email. In fact, when I coach people, often the word is fear. It's a fear of screwing up, a fear of acting without permission and a fear of being reckless in deleting emails that might later be needed. All of these fears are understandable but they are getting in the way of our ability to be productive, focused, measured and relaxed.

Firstly, emails are almost always retrievable. It might cost your IT department a few quid to go searching through old back-ups, but in effect once an email is written, there's always a way to get it back somehow. It really depends on the relative value of what's in the email versus the actual cost of retrieving it. And therein lies my point. It's not the *email* that is creating value, it's the information, commitments or actions held inside the email. Could the sender resend it? Does anyone else have a copy? Could you get that same information or commitment some other way? Usually, yes.

I hate to demean your sense of status and importance, but those emails probably aren't going to bring down your company, nor are they going to bring about world peace. They're just little bunches of electronic information that we love to get obsessed about and addicted to. They're not pets. You don't win by having the largest and biggest tower of un-dealt with stuff. It's time to get ruthless.

If you're really worried about deleting things, here are two simple things you can do. First of all, change your deleted items folder settings so that it empties not every time you close your mailbox, but maybe once every two weeks or once a month. That way, you've got an automatic safety net. If something didn't seem important to you when you deleted the email and your boss now tells you it is, chances are that two weeks is a decent window to realize and retrieve. Secondly, use filing into reference folders as a substitute for deleting. Don't worry about overloading your reference folders: most people use their folders much less than they think anyway, but with programs like Outlook you can so easily sort by date, subject and sender, or of course perform a search function, that the chances of actually losing stuff in there – even if those folders had a lot more items in – are slim to none.

RETHINKING YOUR EMAIL INBOX

Over the next few pages, I will illustrate some ways to rethink your email inbox, from being potential cause of stress and distraction to a powerful centre for keeping on top of every single information input you encounter. These ideas will vary slightly depending on which email server you use, but the basic theory is always the same.

THE THREE SPACES IN YOUR EMAIL INBOX

One of the main reasons that an email inbox becomes stressful is that your brain is trying to use the inbox itself to perform too many different functions. Typically, your inbox will be:

▶ Where new emails land

▶ Where the backlog of old, unread or unprocessed emails is piling up

▶ Where you're keeping emails you haven't dealt with yet but you know you need to

▶ Where you're keeping emails you *have* dealt with, as a reminder that someone else needs to do something

▶ Where you're keeping old emails that contain useful information you might want to come back to

▶ Where you're keeping emails you've 'flagged' as in need of further work sometime in the future, just as soon as 'work calms down again' (ever noticed it never does, by the way?), or until you've worked out what exactly needs to be done.

So if you're scrolling up and down your inbox looking for some clarity, is it surprising that it's pretty hard to find? Behind any of those emails could be some important piece of information, and even the sight of those emails will leave you wondering what it might be. Working this way, it's natural that your inbox serves more as a trigger of the things you know you don't have time to deal with right now (causing stress) than it does as a productive tool to aid decision-making and positive workflow.

So it's time to separate out what we're using the email inbox for. We're going to separate the inbox into three main spaces:

▶ **The processing folders** – where 'live' work is kept

▶ **The reference library** – where old emails we've dealt with are kept in case we need them in future

▶ **The main inbox space** – where new emails land.

Let's talk about those three spaces in more detail, starting with the processing folders.

INBOX SPACE 1: THE PROCESSING FOLDERS

We need to separate the unnecessary noise landing in our email inbox from the small number of items that have value. To do this, the useful items are instead kept in three processing folders – @Action, @Read and @Waiting – which become our main focus points. (The '@' sign is there because the email provider I use categorizes folders alphabetically, so this keeps them at the top.) These processing folders are where anything you're currently working on will be kept and where the most time and attention is spent. And because they contain nothing other than what we're actually working on, the processing folders actually become your record and measure of your current activity. Ever wanted to know for sure how many email replies you still have left to do, how much there is to read in a week or how many items you're waiting on your colleagues to complete for you? Well, now you can!

@ACTION

You may be used to using your main inbox space as the main place you look at to focus on your work, pick up next tasks to do and so on. Very quickly, using this system you will shift your attention, making the @Action folder your main hangout. In this one neat little folder is everything you're actually working on – nothing more, nothing less.

What goes in the @Action folder?

▶   Any email that you've received where you know a reply or other email action is needed and where the action will take longer than two minutes.

What doesn't belong in the @Action folder?

▶   Any emails where the response is a *non-email* related action (for example, where the email you've received prompts your decision to call someone, look into something, bring up something at a meeting, or generally deal with it in a way where the reminder is better stored on some kind of to-do list rather than in your inbox). We'll talk about the idea of keeping such items on a Master Actions List, part of your new 'second brain', in the next few chapters!

▶ Any emails that can be replied to or dealt with in less than two minutes – just do those straight away, rather than clogging up your action folder with them!

▶ Any emails where you 'think there's probably something to do' but haven't decided what the action is – don't be lazy in your thinking. Put it back in the inbox and work out the next step before you continue!

@READ

One of the problems we face with high volumes of email is that so many of the emails that we need to avoid are disguised as useful, exciting and important things to read! If you work in any organization with more than about twenty staff, you'll know that at least one person in your organization is responsible for 'keeping everyone in the loop'. As well as all of that internal communications stuff you receive, you'll be getting a lot of emails from people wanting to grab just a few seconds of your attention to inform you about some kind of new initiative or general update. While much of this is necessary, it comes in the form of interruptions. Furthermore, these are among the most toxic of attention-sapping interruptions because they just *feel* so useful! I regularly come across intelligent, reasonable, senior people in organizations who are gripped with fear and guilt about keeping on top of the barrage of internal memos, briefings and updates that they receive, often left wondering if their bosses are about to test their knowledge and memory of these things at a later date, or worrying about the prospect of looking foolish in a meeting because they've 'missed' something.

The @Read folder therefore provides a vital function. It forces us, during our email processing, to ask the question about whether this is really something we should commit our time to. Yes, it would undoubtedly be useful to read each and every one of these things.

But how useful on a scale of one to a hundred? Useful in a 'change the world, light bulb moment' kind of way? Or useful in a, 'Well I feel abreast with corporate issues, well done me' kind of way?

What goes in the @Read folder?

▶ Anything that you want to scan your eyeballs over at a later stage *rather than read as soon as it lands in your inbox.*

What doesn't belong in the @Read folder?

▶ Anything where you know there's an action to perform. Make the distinction that the @Action folder is where you keep anything that needs an action, no matter how long those emails are!

▶ Anything that can be read and then either deleted or filed in less than two minutes (just do those as you go!).

▶ Any emails you don't know whether you need to read or not – don't move things there until you have made a definite decision of commitment. And be ruthless. Time spent reading someone else's report is time not spent on creating impact and value. So be careful where you plan to put your attention.

The @Read folder gives you the opportunity to save up big piles of reading for quieter periods and periods of inactive attention. Returning once a week to the @Read folder will have you speed reading ruthlessly through things that could easily have proved major distractions when you really needed to focus on other things. So using the @Read folder as a reminder to stay ruthless and focused is a huge Ninja advantage.

@WAITING

Ever been working on something, done your bit, delivered things on time and then been let down by the ineptitude of other people? Yep, me too. The last of our processing folders is designed to ensure this doesn't happen. The @Waiting folder is where you hold emails that serve as a reminder that you're waiting on someone else to do something. It's like your portfolio of people to nag, prod and annoy. I tend to store up 'waiting' items and then about once a week, I'll spend a few minutes systematically running through each of these in the @Waiting folder, deleting those that I know have been completed in the last few days, and perhaps sending out gentle reminders to those people I'm still waiting on. It's a great way to ensure things don't slip between the cracks.

What goes in the @Waiting folder?

▶ Any emails where you're waiting on someone else to do something *and* where you are committed to seeing a successful conclusion (if you don't care, why track it anyway?).

▶ Emails you have sent that you would like to track in this same way.

What doesn't belong in the @Waiting folder?

▶ Anything where you're not clear on who or what you're waiting on (these need to be thought through properly before you move them in here – @Waiting is *not* a catch-all for the stuff you don't want to think about right now!

INBOX SPACE 2: THE REFERENCE FOLDERS

Below the processing folders, where the magic happens at a frenetic pace, is an altogether more serene world. Your reference folders are like walking into a large public library – quiet, reassuring and full of useful information you might need. It's important to make the distinction here that nothing that sits in any of the folders in your reference library is actually actionable. These are purely folders that you're using to store reference material or useful information that you might need at some point in the future.

Contrary to how most people habitually and naturally manage their folders, it's worth pointing out that the most important consideration with regards to organizing your reference folders is not the issue of making it easy to find stuff again in the future. Thinking in this way leads to one very bad habit that will ruin your productivity.

THE CURSE OF THE SUB FOLDERS AND SUB-SUB FOLDERS

Take a quick glance at the reference folders you have already. At least half of the people I coach have far too many of these. Having too many folders is bad for productivity because it creates unnecessary thinking work just at the point where you're trying to get your inbox back down to zero. It is important to remove any friction to transferring non-actionable items from the inbox, so getting them into trusted folders as quickly and effortlessly as possible is key. Notice I said 'trusted' there, not intricate.

Most people do not trust their Outlook or other program to help them retrieve things and therefore set up lots of folders, each with very specific themes, to try to ensure they trust their folders. However, from within each folder in Outlook, you can arrange the emails there by name, by subject, by date and actually in a whole host of other ways too. Alongside this, there is obviously the separate ability to run a search. Your search can cover your whole inbox. Many people's previous experience with using the search function is that it wasn't very good. True, the 2003 Outlook and versions prior to it didn't have the most powerful search function, but the more recent versions seem to have made this much more effective. And of course, if you're a Gmail user, you have the power of Google search behind this, too!

A LARGE BUCKET OR A DOZEN TINY CUPS?

Not convinced? Think about it this way: imagine you are holding a screwed up piece of paper in your hand and you want to throw it away into the bin, making sure it lands in the bin and doesn't bounce out onto the floor. I am now going to offer you the choice of two different things to aim at. Do you want to be aiming at a huge bucket with a large open mouth, or at a dozen tiny cups on the floor? And while I'm at it, I can't tell you for sure which of those trinkets will be the correct one to aim at. If you're clinging on to the need to keep hundreds of folders and sub-folders, think about how this relates to your email usage. A smaller number of bigger and braver buckets removes friction and helps you make quicker and better decisions. And here's the really counter-intuitive bit: since there are fewer places to look when you do want to retrieve an email, emails are actually *easier* to find, not harder, when you have fewer folders!

SOME USEFUL FOLDERS *TO KEEP*

The exact folders you need will depend on your role and responsibilities and specifically, on how important the themed or categorized storage of emails is to your role. However, there are a number of folders that over the years I have found very useful. Since I spend a lot of time talking to people about their email folders and categorizations (and can honestly say the topic never bores me despite how geeky that last sentence must sound!) then along the way I have picked up a few good tips from people and also noticed what tends to work well – or not.

CONFIRMATIONS/'THE SAFE PLACE'

In this folder I keep all kinds of email confirmations: ticket bookings for theatre events, boarding passes for flights, licence keys for software I've bought, emails confirming passwords or things I might forget and so on.

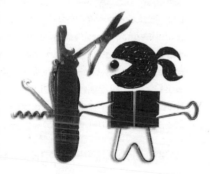

FINANCE

I store all financial information separately. I decided to do this after spending a day piecing together all my financial transactions for my accountant one year after a financial year end, but it's equally as useful if you're working in a company where you're dealing with purchase orders, invoices and the like.

F&F/PERSONAL

Friends and family. Many people also call this one 'Personal' or 'Home'. There isn't much logic to needing to keep these separate to be honest – it just makes sense to a lot of people. Could I still find the round robin email suggesting travel plans for next month's get together if it was in a big bucket folder called 'Archive' that also contained lots of work emails? Yes of course, but it seems to make psychological sense to put some distance between work and life.

CIRCULARS/NOTIFICATIONS/NEWSLETTERS/BACON EMAIL

Gripped by the deluge of hundreds of internal communication emails, updates from social network sites like Linkedin, Facebook and Twitter and automatic notifications? This folder is a great place to keep all of that low-value noise. Once you have this folder set up, it's time to get Ninja ruthless. Set up rules in your Outlook so that emails that you receive regularly and where you know there won't be any immediate actions needed can be filed straight into the folder rather than even appearing in your inbox at all. You may be asking why you shouldn't unsubscribe from those notifications in the first place? Well, at Think Productive we call these kinds of emails 'Bacon'. It's not quite spam as it's kind of worth having; you don't want it around you every day, but occasionally it provides some real value. Now and then I change my mind over what's bacon and what's spam depending on what I'm working on. At that point I'll unsubscribe from a few things, but given that it's never a huge drain on my attention, it's not an issue that needs too much consideration. There's work to be done, remember!

'THINK PRODUCTIVE' (MINE)/'JOB' OR 'ORGANIZATION' (YOURS)

Yes, I have one folder where I keep *everything* related to Think Productive. One. No subfolders below this. No intricate client-by-client archive, no dated workshop archive. One folder. Do I lose stuff? Rarely. Do I lose stuff less often now with this system than I did when I had hundreds of sub-folders as well? Yes, of course! Hopefully by now, you're convinced of the reason for this. And I challenge you to experiment with your own folders and do the same.

Z_GENERAL REFERENCE/ MISCELLANEOUS/ ANY OTHER STUFF

Anything that doesn't fit any of the above categories goes into a big catch-all bucket called 'General Reference'. I use 'Z_' to make sure this folder appears at the bottom of my list so that it's out of the way. It's usually important to have clear definitions of your folders, but this might be the one exception. However, this folder plays an important role: it prevents you from feeling the need to create lots of folders for new situations. Got that urge to create a new folder for one email? Throw it into 'General Reference' instead!

BIG BUCKETS INSTEAD OF SMALLER CUPS — THE OCCASIONAL CASE AGAINST

Occasionally in a workshop I encounter some serious resistance to the idea of structuring folders as big buckets. Such concerns are of course worth listening to and I've come to the conclusion that there are a small number of exceptions to the 'big bucket folders' rule. One group of people who do like to keep a separate storage of emails in small cups rather than bigger buckets are Human Resources (HR) managers, managing specific cases of performance appraisal, grievance and so on. It is very common for HR managers to keep a separate folder for each ongoing case. The case might include emails from the person under investigation, as well as their line manager, witnesses, lawyers and so on. Subject lines might be quite deliberately nuanced or confidential and it may be necessary in future to present all of the emails relating to that one case to someone making the final decision. But before you get carried away thinking you have hundreds of examples like this that might also be exceptions, ask yourself whether you really need to present the folder to anyone in future, or store it as a specific-issue archive for any kind of official purpose. If the answer is no, the chances are big buckets are still the way to go, much as you might be resisting the idea initially. Don't worry, you'll begin to trust this new structure over the next few days!

INBOX SPACE 3: THE MAIN INBOX SPACE

Remember your inbox? It's that space that you used to spend all your time in! Well, now it performs only one function: it's just the place where new emails land and wait to be organized.

With these processing folders in place, and a good reference library system below this, there is now always something you can do with any single email that comes in. There's never any excuse to leave something in your inbox because you can apply the 'one touch' rule to make sure that once opened, an email is never closed and put back in your inbox pending further procrastination. Ever.

In the first few days of adopting this new, Ninja approach to email, you may be tempted to spend too much of your time back in the inbox itself. And you might also be worried that squirrelling your most vital emails into those top three folders will mean they're out of sight and out of mind. Old habits die hard.

The truth is we resist change and we need to be conscious of our habits in order to change them for the better. So as you adopt these new processes, be very clear in your own mind as to why you are spending time on your email and plan your email time into two very different modes:

1. Organize mode – time spent in your inbox ruthlessly deleting, filing and deciding

2. Do mode – time spent in the processing folders, taking actions, replying to emails, managing your reading and tracking what you're waiting on others to do.

Let's focus here on the time you spend in the inbox itself – in Organize mode – which will see your inbox hurtling from its current position all the way down to zero with amazing speed!

GETTING YOUR INBOX **BACK TO ZERO**

After any period away from your inbox, you can expect a build-up of unread, un-organized emails. To get this back to zero, you'll need to:

▶ Hack most of them

▶ Process the rest, one by one

HACKING: BULK FILING AND BULK DELETING

To keep your inbox at zero, you'll need to be comfortable with using the delete button more regularly, cheating where possible and being ruthless. Remember that at least 80% of your emails do not require any significant action, so you can afford to be pretty cutthroat, but at the same time, you definitely can't afford to be reckless. What we're looking for here is clarity and the Zen-like calm which comes from feeling prepared, up-to-date and in control.

'Hacking' involves looking for opportunities to say no and hit delete, weeding out all that unnecessary noise and quickly identifying the relatively small number of items that do require further attention. Hacking is about finding the cheats, shortcuts and Ninja moves that produce quick wins, speed and momentum. While hacking, the mindset should be ruthless and big-picture focused (resist the temptation while hacking to *ever* read any email all the way through!). Use the inbox views to look for the biggest, quickest and most potent hacks. On Outlook, the three most obvious views are to sort emails by:

Who they're **FROM**

The email's **SUBJECT**

The email's **DATE**

If you find your momentum is starting to fade, change the view. Other opportunities *will* exist somewhere in that stack of emails, but changing the view makes them easier to spot.

The other view you may find useful is flags. Not everyone uses flags and personally I have to say I'm not a fan (and with this system you can either choose to use flags to add an extra (red) layer of urgency to your processing folders, or simply let the processing folders provide you with all the distinctions and boundaries you need). If you are a flag fan, this view should quickly give you a sense not necessarily of what's actionable, but certainly of what you and others have marked as urgent or important.

WHAT TO **HACK AWAY**

Here are a few things to look for on each view as you hack:

DATE view

The most obvious quick win. Start at the bottom, and scan upwards. What you'll usually find is that there are one or two emails from a *long* time ago which you might still feel are important, but the chances are, they're reference rather than actionable. File them.

▶ Email death row. Decide on a date – let's say anything older than six months. Move every email older than this into a folder called 'Email death row'. These emails are waiting to die. They are guilty of distracting you, using up your precious attention, and adding no value. Add a time in your calendar, perhaps six weeks ahead, and if by that date you haven't needed anything in that folder, delete it.

SUBJECT view

▶ Strings of conversations. Where there's been a frenzied conversation of 20 emails, you can usually delete the first 19, as the final email should contain a string of all the others.

▶ Subject lines that relate to dates or events that have already passed or been finished.

▶ Circulars – daily, weekly or monthly round-up emails. Coming across these now might be a good time to set up some rules so that in future these file straight into a reference folder such as the 'Circulars' folder mentioned earlier.

FROM view

▶ Emails from people who have left your organization.

▶ Emails from the reception desk exclaiming, 'Cakes in the kitchen' or 'Taxi for someone you've never heard of'.

▶ Emails from colleagues and friends who send you 'funny' attachments. Just delete them all, they're really not that funny. Oh, OK, save that great one you got from your friend the other week with the kittens. But the rest of them need to go.

▶ Emails from people whose main interactions with you were on projects that have been finished.

As you hack, you might come across a few emails that you want to add to your processing folders, or quick actionable ones that you can do in less than two minutes. This is fine, but try to resist getting into too much detailed thinking. Hacking should always be focused on quick wins, easy targets, cheats and anything else that can keep momentum going.

Wherever possible, stick to batch filing and batch deleting. You might find it helpful to ruthlessly ignore anyone whose emails might require more complex decision-making and deliberately *not* try hacking emails from your boss, biggest client or other significant stakeholder in your working world. While hacking, your momentum and ruthlessness is key, whereas you'll have an opportunity to move on to a more mindful and slower pace in a few minutes when we look at processing the remaining emails one by one. It's not cheating to leave some of these people well alone until you've finished hacking and are moving into processing.

Once your hacking is done, you're well on the way to a zero inbox. It's different for everyone, but you should find you're left with a significantly lower number of emails ready for processing. As a rough guide, if you started with anywhere near 1,000 or more emails in your inbox, hacking should get you down to somewhere around or below 100. If you started with around 200 emails, hacking should leave you with 50 to process. Those are rough numbers of course, but they are a couple of the common patterns I see when coaching people.

If you're a little bit tired from hacking and finding your active attention on the wane (don't worry, making quick decisions for a long period of time is about the most tiring thing you can do in a knowledge work job!) then take a short break so that you begin processing when you have a good level of attention left for the all-important decision-making.

PROCESSING EMAILS, ONE BY ONE

Now you're left with those emails in the inbox that need a bit more thought and organization. This is where a more considered and careful approach is needed – and where your processing folders really start to prove very useful indeed.

Again, we're looking for momentum here, except this time you're going to focus on each email one by one. Avoid the temptation to cherry pick. It *is* tempting to look for the ones where you know easily what's needed, the ones you feel most strongly about getting done, or the ones from the people you're most keen to connect with.

It's equally tempting to procrastinate and leave emails that might require some extra thinking before you can decide on their destination, or where your reply might make you the bad guy ('We've decided not to go ahead with the project', 'I'm afraid I haven't had time to find what you needed', 'I'm running late on this and am sorry for not keeping you more in the loop').

If you cherry pick the best ones and procrastinate over the worst ones, I guarantee that the following scenario will happen. You will use up all your most proactive attention on hacking and the first part of processing, and just as your attention starts to wane, you'll find yourself staring at thirty or forty of the hardest emails: the ones you were avoiding. And you'll feel worse for it. Getting to zero from here is of course possible, but you'll be wading through treacle to do it.

Processing one by one means exactly that. As you do so, apply the two-minute rule: anything that can be fired off in less than two minutes should be dealt with as you see it, rather than trying to store these in the @Action folder. As you process, some of what you read you'll still want to file as reference or delete, but you should find that as you hit the 'home straight', you'll be more engaged with your three processing folders and a bit less focused on the delete button than you were when you were blissfully hacking a few minutes ago.

THE *30-SECOND* EYEBALL

Since processing is about separating the wheat from the chaff, the first question to ask with any email you process is 'Is this information important to me, at all?'. Usually, when faced with that question, a 'yes' or 'no' answer can be established very quickly (remember at this stage, you're only establishing importance, not the need for action!). For all other emails, the answer is 'maybe'. If you answer 'maybe', you need to use the '30-second eyeball'.

You have 30 seconds to establish whether the email is important to you at all. You don't have to complete the reading or replying in that 30 seconds, but in that 30 seconds you do need to change your 'maybe' to a 'yes' or a 'no'. So at the end of the 30-second eyeball, you've either scanned and deleted it, moved it somewhere for further reading or decided that an action is needed.

The 4 Stages of getting your inbox to zero:

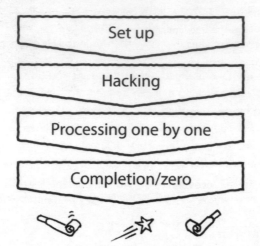

Set up

Hacking

Processing one by one

Completion/zero

EXERCISE: GETTING YOUR INBOX TO ZERO

What you'll need: Your email inbox,
this book,
proactive attention –
no interruptions!

How long it'll take: 2 hours

Ninja mindset: Ruthlessness

STAGE ONE: *SET UP*

Set up your three processing folders in your inbox:

> **@Action**
>
> **@Read**
>
> **@Waiting**

(Optional) Depending on what you already have set up as your reference folder structure, you might want to make some changes:

▶ Get rid of *any* subfolders.

▶ Reduce the number of reference folders you have so that they fit onto one screen, meaning you won't have to scroll up and down Outlook once you're trying to rapidly process emails into these reference folders.

▶ If you are overwhelmed by your multitude of 'tiny cup' reference folders and want to think about this some more before you make permanent changes, consider using a small number of new, 'big bucket' folders which start with a number (e.g., '1.Circulars', '2.Confirmations', '3.F&F', '4.Job' and whatever else you need). Folders with numbers will sit above the rest of your reference folders, but below the '@' folders you've just set up as your processing folders. This is handy as you can focus your mind solely on these new folders, all in one place and you can use this as a temporary solution while you spend some more time thinking about the best structure for your reference folders going forward. If you're untangling years of complexity here, it's easier to make good decisions about your folders during the hacking stage that's coming up right now, because you'll see when you're hacking which folders are used more regularly and which are likely to be less relevant in the future.

STAGE TWO: *HACKING*

Remember, hacking is about looking for the quick wins, and most quick wins involve either reference filing or the delete button. Most hacking won't even require you to read the email itself: the subject lines alone in most cases should tell you all you need to know (i.e. that an email is not actionable). Failing this, I recommend opening the reading pane so that you can see with a deft glance what your decision will be, rather than having to click the email open and closed.

Where to start?

If you have a lot of old emails, start with 'Email death row', a single folder where you can safely chuck all of the stuff that's so old that there won't be actions required. This will feel unorthodox and perhaps overly ruthless but don't worry. It's all still there in the 'death row' folder for you to come back and read later, but as time goes on you'll become more comfortable with the idea that you have better things to spend your attention on than old emails that didn't change the world six months ago.

Next, we're going to be using the 'Arrange By' button at the top of your inbox. Click to arrange by 'From'. This will bunch all of your emails together based on who the sender is. Now look for opportunities to 'cull' people!

▶   Hack based on 'From' (sender)

▶ Move from A–Z, focusing only on 'quick wins' or until you feel your momentum slipping

▶ Then hack based on 'Subject' and do the same

▶ Then move back to 'Date', back to 'Subject', back to 'From'.

Keep things fresh. Keep it moving. Get ruthless.

When you start to find yourself struggling to find *any* opportunities to deal with groups of two or more emails in a single move, your hacking job is done. It's time to move on to processing, one by one.

STAGE THREE: *PROCESSING ONE BY ONE*

Processing one by one is a more mindful and considered stage than hacking. Make sure you follow the questions and use them as an opportunity to be ruthless, decisive and focused on the potential impact – or not – of each email.

So as you process, you'll start to find that you have:

▶ A folder with a few emails that you know you need to action

▶ A folder with a couple of reports to print and read

▶ A folder containing emails that you're tracking other people's actions on, and can chase them with later.

Don't blur the boundaries

The questions on the email processing diagram here are designed to avoid a blurring of boundaries. It's important that the @Action folder in particular is considered a sacred space and is not clogged up with lots of stuff that should not or need not be there. Some common blurring of the boundaries to avoid are:

▶ Putting things in the @Read folder because you haven't made an action decision on them – decide if it's actionable first. Only move it to the @Read folder if there's definitely no action.

▶ Putting the things that can be done in less than two minutes into the @Action folder. It's the easiest way to clog up your @Action folder and procrastinate over those fiddly small jobs. Do the quick stuff straight away!

▶ Filling the @Waiting folder with things you want to delay a decision about. It should only be in this folder if you've taken an action and you're waiting to 'receive' an action from someone else.

STAGE FOUR: *COMPLETION*

So that's it! You're staring at some white space on the screen where previously you had a pile of stuff looking distinctly like it was out of control.

There are two types of completion: inbox zero and email at *complete* zero. I try to get to inbox zero every time I shut down Outlook. That for me is at least once a day and can be several times a day, depending on what else I'm doing. As I shut down Outlook, I'm left with a state of clarity: I know the decisions I've made about the meaning and potential impact of every single email in my world. It doesn't mean it's all finished at that point, but I'm totally confident there are no landmines or goldmines lurking undiscovered in there. Nothing is going to blow up or bite me on the backside. It's all in hand.

In the middle of a workday, or the middle of a busy week, processing your inbox to zero gives you a satisfying moment of mental completion, and it also prevents your attention from being spent on worrying, checking or stressing about feeling out of control.

Complete zero – where both your inbox and @Action folder are at zero, and where you have also paid some attention to your @Read and @Waiting folders – is something I try to get to once a week. It doesn't always happen and it's not worth becoming obsessed about (some things do naturally run on longer than the arbitrary point in the week you designate for a complete zero assault – and this is fine), but even when it doesn't quite happen I can get close to it. It takes the feeling of completion to an even greater and more profound level.

Ninja Email Processing...

Is the information important to ME at all?

- **No** → Delete!
- **Maybe** → 30-second eyeball, then...
- **Yes** → **Action?** Am I committed to an action here?

30-second eyeball, then... (No action but...)

- ...I want to think about this again sometime in the future → Add to calendar then file the email in... → Reference Folders
- ...I want to keep it → Reference Folders
- ...I want to keep track of someone else's action → @Waiting
- ...I need to read further

Am I committed to an action here?

- **No** → Is it important for me to read/know this soon?
  - **Yes** → @Read
  - **No** → Reference Folders
- **Yes** → Can I do it in 2 mins or less?
  - **No** → @Action → **Then later...** → Do!
  - **Yes** → Do!

Okay, so now to file the original email

Do I need a reminder to track someone else's action on this?
- **Yes** → @Waiting
- **No** → Reference Folders

Do!

Picture it: there's nothing more to do here. **Nothing.**

And here's the even greater news. It takes *less* energy and attention thinking about your emails when you're at complete zero or inbox zero than it does with a stack of 2,000 potential surprises. Trust me, I've been there too. And I'm not planning on going back there anytime soon.

TURNING EMAIL *OFF*

Now that your inbox is at zero, there is another, controversial productivity tool at your disposal. It's the slide on our 'Getting Your Inbox to Zero' workshop that divides opinion like no other. It suggests that every now and then, you might like to sit at your desk, engaged in your creative work, thinking, decisions, administration, conversations and other essential tasks yet at the same time, your email is turned off completely. To some, this is common sense – although even those who recognize the value in 'going dark' and boosting productivity by reducing connectivity will often say it's something they don't manage themselves as often as they would like.

To others in the room it meets with a stony silence. It's designed to feel provocative of course, but think about it for a second. You will regularly leave your email turned off or unattended when you're in a meeting or when you're on holiday, but the thought of doing this at your desk is still terrifying. This is a habit and mindset issue more than being about actual need. Don't get me wrong, if I have a day when my job is to wait to receive the email telling us we're ready to execute on a really important project, I'll be monitoring my email inbox too. But most days, I use the mornings to go dark and deliberately stack up my emails while giving myself some more concentrated proactive attention, unspoilt by interruptions.

If my team need me, I'm on the phone, but I'm grown up enough to know that I'm much less indispensable than I think. You are too, by the way. Your team will be fine without you, as long as they know the rules!

So, if you're like most people these days and you're what I would call a 'connectivity addict' then it's important to challenge yourself and spend some time going dark. It's time for your period of 'email cold turkey'.

Here are four potential schedules for going dark with email. Which could you most easily implement? Which would be fun to experiment with just for a day or perhaps for a week?

▶ **50–50:** this is my usual approach. I will do an 'emergency scan' just before 9am to check there's nothing urgent, then close email down until 1pm. I start hacking, processing and replying to things from 2pm and leave Outlook on all afternoon.

▶ **3 regular times:** hack and process to zero three times a day. Early morning, lunch and end of day are three good times here. Allow approximately 45 minutes for each session and then aim to reduce this over time. This is what I do if I am out of the office in meetings or running workshops.

▶ **The hourly dash:** for those of you in particularly reactive roles or fast-paced work cultures, it's difficult to imagine leaving a client's question pending from 9am until 2pm. But that doesn't mean you can't batch up emails like the rest of us and improve your efficiency. Schedule ten minutes every hour at a set point in each hour to hack and process.

▶ **Extreme:** Tim Ferriss in *The 4-Hour Work Week* proposes once a week, for an hour. He doesn't even look at his inbox for the rest of the week. He uses a range of interesting outsourcing and automation techniques to make this possible, but it's certainly not something that everyone could do. It's a fascinating idea though and even if you don't feel you could adopt it, it's worth spending a few minutes asking yourself why it's not possible for you. As you explore your reaction to the idea, what does it tell you about your own email habits, or your connectivity addiction? And I wonder if you'll feel differently about it once your inbox is at zero …

Are you a Ninja?

▶ A Ninja takes a ruthless approach to email.

▶ A Ninja approaches email in an unorthodox way, separating out thinking from doing and the wheat from the chaff.

▶ A Ninja is weapon-savvy enough to know how to make tools do the work so that they don't have to.

5. NINJA PRODUCTIVITY: THE CORD PRODUCTIVITY MODEL

HOW STRONG IS YOUR CORD?

As we discussed at the beginning of this book, the old time management techniques are no longer sufficient to ensure we have a good grasp of all the various tasks and projects we're managing, let alone sufficient to help us react quickly and responsibly to the myriad of information inputs we're being bombarded with all the time.

Over the next four chapters I will introduce you to four distinct habits – Capture and Collect, Organize, Review and Do – that are the cornerstone of achieving relaxed control: the CORD Productivity Model. This model has been tried and tested by Think Productive's workshop delegates from organizations large and small, across the UK and Europe. It consists of four key habits that flow from one to the next: master each step and your workload will be like a strong, unbroken cord (hence the name!).

Each of these habits together make up a stronger whole than the sum of their parts. So if you Capture & Collect well, it's easier to Organize. If you Organize well, it's easier to Review. And if you do all of those well, then Doing becomes effortless – and makes it easier to Capture and Collect, Organize and Review!

So in this chapter, we'll focus on the four key habits that make up the CORD model and think about how this relates to your habits, so that you can strengthen your CORD – and create a chain of effortless and brilliant productivity!

CAPTURE AND COLLECT

This is where you harness all of your information inputs. This might be your own ideas, actions established during conversations with colleagues, paperwork, voicemails, social media notifications and of course the email inbox. Keeping each of these at zero, in the same way we've just done with your email inbox leads to the Zen-like calm and preparedness a Ninja needs.

ORGANIZE

Once we have all of those information inputs captured and collected together, the Organize habit is where we start to ask the crucial questions to ensure ruthless focus and peace of mind. It's about applying consistent thinking and developing habits that get you to the heart of action decisions as quickly and effortlessly as possible.

REVIEW

The Review habit comprises daily and weekly checklists designed to help you direct your attention and focus for optimum efficiency, mindfulness and agility. Do you remember we talked about how in knowledge work you're both the boss and the worker all at the same time? Well, the Review habit gives our inner boss the chance to shine and gives us the chance to step out of the chaos to find some clarity.

DO

Of course, all of the above habits are of little use or value unless we're in the habit of doing things! The Do habit focuses on working with your attention and energy levels, choices, tactics and momentum for optimum efficiency. It's also about developing the mindfulness and unorthodoxy needed to avoid procrastination, keep things moving and feel positive about your work.

FROM UNCONSCIOUS *INCOMPETENCE* TO UNCONSCIOUS *COMPETENCE*

In thinking about the question 'how strong is your CORD', what you're really being asked to do is think about your habits. The 'Four Stages of Competence' model is widely used in management schools and in learning and development to look at how people develop skills and put theory into practice. So let's spend a few moments here looking at how you learn and looking at what you're going to need to do to change your habits.

I would encourage you to constantly think about these four stages during the next four chapters. Be self-critical enough to diagnose where your biggest productivity improvements may come from.

The journey from unconscious incompetence to unconscious competence is the journey from complete novice to seasoned – and habitual – 'pro'. If you think about how you learn anything at all, it will follow this same path. For now, I'm going to use the example of driving a car, but even if you don't drive, I'm sure you can imagine the stages and examples I'm describing.

UNCONSCIOUS INCOMPETENCE

Before you could drive a car, what did that driving look like to you? It looked almost magical! All of those knobs and levers and buttons and turning of keys and looking in mirrors. So complicated. If I asked you to turn the car on and drive to the shops, you wouldn't know how to do it, and you wouldn't know what you needed to learn to change this.

CONSCIOUS INCOMPETENCE

Fast-forward a few years to one of your first driving lessons. You're sat in the driving seat and your teacher asks you to pull out onto the road. To your horror, you stall the car. Oh dear. Flustered and panicked, you do your best to get going again, and within a few moments you find yourself calmly reflecting on what just happened. Perhaps it was the clutch, or perhaps you weren't in the correct gear, or you didn't give the accelerator enough revs. Whatever happened, you can start to recognize what that problem was and make sure that next time, you'll be more careful. Because next time, you'll be conscious of what you're doing so that you make sure it doesn't happen again.

CONSCIOUS COMPETENCE

Do you remember the day of your driving test? Chances are the adrenaline was flowing and you were doing everything you could to keep focused on every single movement. You're conscious of making sure you practise your 'mirror-signal-manoeuvre' technique, you're feeding the wheel without crossing your hands over each other in a way that you *only* ever do before you've got your driving licence and during the test, the only thing on your mind is the driving test. Do it right. Do it right. Stay focused.

And it works – you pass! But it required fierce concentration and strong, proactive attention to get there.

UNCONSCIOUS COMPETENCE

But think about how you drive now! You're no longer thinking about mirror-signal-manoeuvre; you're talking to the person next to you about what you're going to eat for your dinner. Or you might even be sat there eating your dinner while you drive! You're thinking about other things, listening to podcasts, the radio or an audio book and generally the driving part of what you're doing is pretty effortless. It's a habit. You don't need to think about your driving; you just drive.

EFFORTLESS PRODUCTIVITY

Welcome, my friends, to unconscious competence. Whatever you're doing is just a habit. You don't need to think about it at all, you just do it. We're going to work on your productivity habits in the next few chapters. In fact, it could be said that the entire aim of this book is to encourage you to think more  about your own productivity behaviours in terms of your current habits (conscious competence), but only so that you can improve these habits so that you rarely have to think about your productivity ever again (unconscious competence) – because once you've developed strong, productive habits, well, the magic just happens. No effort, no consciousness of your competence, just habitual brilliance.

BUT THEN HOW DO WE IMPROVE ON EFFORTLESS BRILLIANCE?

Think back to conscious competence and your driving skills for one moment. Can you honestly, hand on heart, say that you are the safest and best driver that you know? Or the best driver you could possibly be? If you took that test again tomorrow, would you pass? Because that's the other thing about our habits – we develop unconscious competence that makes our productivity effortless, but we can also develop bad habits at the very same time. We can get lazy over time, too, and mistakes and errors can get made that wouldn't have been made if we were slightly more focused or consciously aware of what we were doing. In short, there is always room for improvement. There is never a final point to reach where it doesn't get any better and unfortunately, there is no secret formula for perfection.

Changing your habits is one of the most difficult things you will ever do. What's needed to achieve the habit shifts that lead to improved productivity is to be mindful enough of your existing habits so as to know where the improvements can come from. While this sounds like the easiest thing in the world, I'm sure we all know that it can be anything but.

This is where it gets really tricky. Learning how to improve your good habits still further is actually harder if you're contented with what you *perceive* as the pinnacle of unconscious competence. A Ninja needs the mindfulness to regularly question what's going well as well as what's going badly. It's all about trying to regularly revisit conscious competence, which in turn provides us with the insights we need for regular self-improvement. Thinking about the process of your work as well as the work itself – and hence seeing where those processes could possibly be further improved – is difficult unless we build into our work some mechanisms to keep us questioning and learning.

This is where the CORD Productivity Model comes in. It helps us to think about the process of work: are you Collecting and Capturing everything effectively? Are you Organizing the data and action reminders? Are you Reviewing what's on your list and keeping a good overview of this? Are you getting good momentum when the 'Do' time comes? These four habits, which will be the focus of the next four chapters, are the core mental processes of any modern day knowledge worker.

HOW TO USE THE CORD PRODUCTIVITY MODEL

There are two distinct ways to use the CORD model. You can use it to manage your personal workflow, and also to structure your days and weeks in order to remain as agile and adaptable as possible to whatever comes your way. It also gives you the confidence to know that whatever you're working on is the best possible thing you can be doing at any given moment.

Workflow

We all need to think about our personal workflow, and in particular the flow from information inputs to completion of tasks. Using the CORD model, any piece of information will be captured or collected. You will then organize the information, deciding whether action is necessary. If it is necessary to do something, you'll need to review this in the context of all the other things you *could* be doing at that time and at some stage you'll need to get that task completed. While it might feel like a logical thing to follow that first item all the way through to completion in one go, it might not be the best choice you could make if you also have lots of other things you could be doing at that time. But nevertheless, using the CORD model with your workflow will help you constantly push even the most troublesome of items through towards completion, productivity and impact.

Spinning plates

You can also view CORD as a diagnostic tool and as a constant reminder that our work is no longer just about doing, but about thinking too. So for example, as I write this sentence, I know that I am up against a deadline from my editor. As a consequence, I know that I have neglected my capturing and collecting, organizing and reviewing. But because I *know* this, I know exactly how to get every-thing back under control when I reach the editor's deadline tomorrow and I'm not stressed about leaving those things in the meantime. Our work is like spinning four different plates every day or every week – if we are not paying enough attention to one of the four elements of CORD, we'll quickly start to feel stressed. Here's why spinning each of these four different plates really matters, and what happens to our stress levels if we neglect one or more of them:

Not enough ...	Leads to ...
Capture and Collect	... feeling overwhelmed as new information inputs arrive and are not dealt with, feeling uncertain about what we should be doing and feeling stressed that we might be missing things.
Organize	... a lack of clarity about how long things might take, which tasks are the highest priority and an unrealistic impression of what's really on our plate.
Review	... feeling unsure that we're on top of our work, an inability to put things in perspective, a level of constant stress that leads us to inefficiency, a constant sense of panic and a reactive rather than proactive style of working.
Do	... work piling up not done! There are times when we're resisting the actual doing in favour of more organizing or tinkering. This might otherwise be labelled 'procrastination' and it's crippling if it sets in – as we all know!

HOW STRONG IS YOUR CORD?

You can also look at your overall productivity as being as strong as the weakest link in your CORD. Visualize CORD as a piece of cord – how much can you stretch yours? Where would it break? Consistent neglect of one of the four habits will undermine the other three. So your overall performance depends on getting each of these four things right.

The confidence to answer the most important question in knowledge work

Here's the question that the CORD Productivity Model will allow you to answer:

> 'Am I confident that whatever I'm doing at this moment is the most appropriate thing I can be doing?'

While this might sound like a simple question, how often do you really know the answer? Not knowing the answer to this question is one of the quickest ways to find yourself in stress, as you start to feel as though you might be missing something vital at any given moment. And even if nothing is immediately going wrong in your world, not knowing the answer to this question leads to inefficiencies and the nagging doubt that a stressful surprise might be lurking around the corner.

Developing your own productivity system and using the principles of the CORD model allow you to definitively answer this question – not just once a day or once a week, but all the time. The reason it's a difficult question to answer is that it requires a lot of thinking to reach the conclusion. In fact, it requires more detailed and methodical thinking than our lazy, forgetful brains can cope with. But that's OK. Our Ninja unorthodoxy brings us back to the old adage of 'if in doubt, just cheat'. If your brain is rubbish at retaining information, maintaining focus and providing the structure to analyze a wide variety of projects and actions (and remember, we're all human after all!), the answer is pretty simple: get a second brain!

SECOND BRAIN

YOUR SECOND BRAIN

'We shall require a substantially new manner of thinking if mankind is to survive.'
– Albert Einstein

A Productivity Ninja is not a superhero. None of us have superhero brains, either. We also know – usually from our own painful experience – that we're all too capable of forgetting important things, making bad decisions because we're too swamped with other things to think about or just not finding the time to focus on the important stuff. It's time to change all that.

We're going to use the CORD model and the Organize and Review habits in particular here to develop a 'second brain'. Your second brain is designed to replace your real brain when it comes to memory. Your second brain is also designed to support the good decision-making – intelligence and intuition – that our real brain is really good at already, but which we perhaps aren't currently using to its full potential or aren't as able to do unless we're in periods of proactive attention.

WHAT DOES A SECOND BRAIN LOOK LIKE?

The second brain is made up of the following basic elements, all of which we'll be returning to in the coming chapters:

MEMORY

- ▶ A list of the tasks you're working on
- ▶ A 'bigger picture' list of the wider projects these tasks relate to
- ▶ Other lists and reference information – basically, things that could be useful in the future.

INTELLIGENCE

- ▶ A series of questions to help support good decision-making and force the clarity that reduces your stress

▶ Checklists and a routine to support regular review – both daily and weekly – of everything held in the second brain.

INTUITION

▶ Checklist questions designed to enhance mindfulness, self-reflection and the regular discipline of being conscious of your competence – or incompetence

▶ 'Thinking tools' designed to aid ruthlessness, by keeping you focused on the potential impact of what you're doing, rather than just filling the need to be 'busy'.

YOUR BOSS-SELF AND YOUR WORKER-SELF USING CORD

The CORD model's four phases also provide the structure to separate thinking from doing in our work – the separation between the boss and the worker. Again, this is all about promoting consciousness of competence, so that in future you develop unconscious habits that are even more powerful. Broadly speaking, you can think about the 'C' and 'D' parts of CORD as being for your worker-self and the 'O' and 'R' habits being for your boss-self. Organize and Review are where the thinking happens, where the psychological heavy lifting takes place. You're a knowledge worker after all, so think of 'O' and 'R' as being the hardest part of your work. The CORD model is designed to strengthen your decision-making, increase your awareness and leave you feeling more in control.

The worker part of you just wants to get on with the work. You just want to put cherries on cakes! The last thing you want is to be presented with loads of difficult thinking to confuse or distract you just at the point where you need to get some serious work done. So the 'C' and the 'D' habits are to help you to trust that the second brain has it all under control and will be doing that thinking in due course, so that you don't have to worry about it right now.

TRUST AND YOUR SECOND BRAIN

Your aim in the next few chapters, as we look in more detail at the CORD model and the various habits and practices here, is to focus on developing a second brain that you trust. If you trust it, you'll use it. If you use it, you'll trust it. Without that trust, you're putting time and attention into developing something that only serves as a distraction. For your real brain to relax, it needs to know that the second brain is taking care of all of those stressful decisions and things that need remembering.

Once you trust your second brain, what you're left with is a profound feeling of Zen-like calm. You're able to be present and in the moment: focused on the current thing you need to do, not worried by all the other possible things that you know you need to work on. Such a level of preparedness and control is difficult to contemplate if it's something you've rarely experienced; just like not believing that you could get your inbox to zero! And, like getting your inbox to zero, the act of getting to a place of trust is the hardest bit, whereas maintaining trust once you've established it becomes an easy habit to maintain.

For your brain to truly relax and let the second brain's system take control, you need to ensure that each phase of the CORD process is being taken care of as much as it needs to be. This differs from person to person, from role to role: if you're a receptionist for example, you probably deal with a lot more inputs than you do

projects – your work is all about dealing with the immediate, organizing your actions and making decisions as they come in, on the spot. If you're a CEO, you of course still have emails and calls, but actually much of your work is about leadership and management – tracking the things you're committed to seeing happen through the network of people who are down in the trenches actually doing that work. What is clear is that while different people may focus more time or attention on different parts of the CORD model, it's vital that whoever you are, you develop these four distinct habits and watch them come together under one coherent system. So as we talk through the four phases here, don't ever think, 'Oh this bit doesn't apply to me'. It does. The only variable is to what extent.

I'm not going to pretend that the exercises in the next few chapters will be easy. Nor will it all be fun (although I hope you will find it liberating!). But developing a fully functioning second brain that you trust *will* change your life. Everything we're going to do in the next few chapters are things I've learned the hard way for myself and coached others to do through our workshops. I know what a difference this stuff makes – and I also know that getting conscious about your competencies and trying to change old habits can be really tough. But trust me, the end result will be worth it.

It's time to experience Ninja-level preparedness and Zen-like calm while you leave the hard work to your new, second brain.

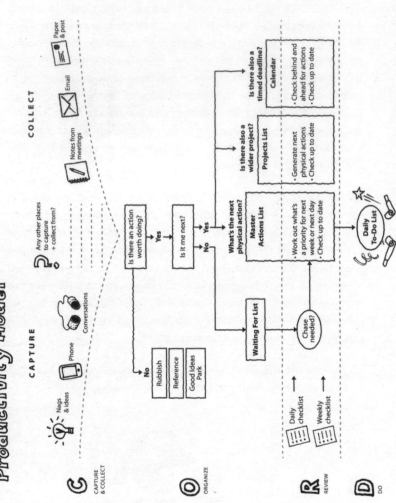

6. THE CAPTURE AND COLLECT HABIT

'Ideas come from
everywhere.'
– Alfred Hitchcock

In this chapter I'm going to show you the first stage of the CORD model: the art of capturing and collecting. This means bringing together every stress, nag or creative idea that tells you that something needs to be done. It also means collecting together every piece of paper that lands on your desk, ends up in your wallet, accumulates on your kitchen table and so on. We'll also deal with every digital input – from emails, to notifications, websites and so on.

Each of these items are captured and collected so that we can apply sharp, focused thinking and use our second brain as the 'memory' that will keep hold of each of these things and remind us again when the time is right.

On the CORD Productivity Model diagram in the previous chapter, you'll see the various elements of Capture and Collect at the top. During this chapter we're going to talk through each of these in turn and then give you the chance at the end of this chapter to reflect on your own Capture and Collect habits. Obviously our first job in our quest to get everything under control is to work out what 'everything' means! Potential inputs and commitments lurk in every nook and cranny. We'll look at what you do already, work to define where your capture and collect points are and focus on what you need to improve on.

Many people find they have a natural resistance to the idea of capturing information. This is because our brains confuse 'Capture' with 'Organize', and we can feel like even writing something down gives us some kind of commitment to actually doing it. So before we begin, I want to emphasize that capturing isn't about committing; it's about gaining clarity. We need to give ourselves permission to have many more thoughts than actually turn into actions, and capturing even the most insane or inane ideas is an important part of this process. So don't try to censor yourself, and let the Capture and Collect phase do its job without interference: you are free to reject any of the ideas captured during the Organize phase, but not before then. If it's on your mind, capture it!

CAPTURING IDEAS

'The ancestor of every action is a thought.'
– Ralph Waldo Emerson

One of the biggest keys to good attention management is staying one step ahead of our brains. Getting a good handle on turning our vague thoughts into solid thinking is a priceless skill for Ninja knowledge workers. Yes, it's estimated that our brains have on average 65,000 thoughts per day, and while a good number of these are primitive things like, 'Hungry. Need food', or 'That person walking along the street is *hot*', we're constantly evaluating and re-evaluating our work in our minds. So unless we capture the actions or issues whizzing through our brain, we risk a number of things happening:

▶ We can't be sure we're making the best choices of where to put our attention, as there could be potential value and even potential commitments we haven't clarified.

▶ We get stressed.

▶ We keep having the same thought over and over again rather than moving on and directing our precious, proactive attention onto focused doing. This stifles our creativity and is plain inefficient!

To capture our thoughts and ensure they're in our trusted second brain is usually all that is needed to finish the thinking and move us back on to focused delivery. The phrase 'I'm just collecting my thoughts' is usually associated with people calming down after a period of stress. You will find a Zen-like calm in the knowledge that you've captured and collected everything that was on your mind: primarily because you've now compensated for your horrendously bad short-term memory with a much more reliable one and are now ready to make decisions about *all* of those things, not just the ones you can remember at a given moment.

'The best way to get a good idea is to get lots of ideas.'
– Linus Pauling

NAGS

NAGS

I'm sure you know what I mean when I use the hugely technical term 'nag'. And no, I don't mean your husband or wife! I'm talking about all of those stressful, panicky, anxious little thoughts. Rather ironically, nags are ridiculously skilled at parachuting their way to the front of your attention at exactly the moment when you can do nothing about them.

> *'I'm worried about the budget!'*

Well guess what – being in the supermarket and worrying about the budget you need to finish back at the office tomorrow doesn't actually help you finish the budget. The nag doesn't really care.

> *'Oh that reminds me, Lucy and Rohan's party is coming up soon and I haven't even* thought *about the fancy dress costume.'*

Well, you haven't thought about it usefully now, anyway. You haven't clarified why it's a nag and what you can do to move things forward. You just know there's something to do. And because you haven't done the required thinking, chances are you have had the same nag several times before. The less you deal with them, the more they follow you around!

Nags are a Ninja's enemy. They're stressful, unsettling and annoying. Worse still, they distract you from the thing you could be usefully doing at that moment, whether that be completing the shopping, working on something else or enjoying a relaxing evening catching up with your family or friends and wanting to give them your fullest attention.

MANAGING YOUR NAGS

Everyone gets nags. I don't think you can cut them out of the picture completely. But by developing a comprehensive system, where your second brain has a good handle on every single thing and where you're following good checklists that keep you focused on the right things at the right time, you can cut down on the number of nags that pop up in your brain. Nags are really a product of your subconscious and an indication that your survival instinct is kicking in. Perhaps our lizard brain is trying to tell us something: 'Deal with this, or else …!'

Or else what? Or else we'll look foolish, miss a deadline, forget to do something we want to do, miss an important commitment, lose money, lose respect, lose *everything*! (Well, no one said nags were rational or measured.)

A nag is us realizing we need to give this anxiety some attention. If we subconsciously start to feel that we have the potential danger cleared, or at least under control for now, the nag will go away. There are two ways to get rid of our nags. We can either use Ninja decision-making to turn them quickly into actions, stored in our second brain to be revisited when we have some time. Or we can simply just capture and collect the nag, knowing that our systems will ensure we return to it later. This second option is only possible if you trust that you're going to return to the nag in good time. Do you see why trust in our second brain plays such an important part in helping us stay calm and in control?

WHAT TO DO *WHEN YOU'RE OVERWHELMED WITH NAGS*

As we talked about, meditation is a fantastic way to move from worrying unproductively about the future to being more focused and present in your thinking. Mindfulness is a skill If you're unsure about meditation, or if you're stressed in the office and just need some immediate relief from the nags, try picking up a pen and paper and writing whatever comes into your head. You may write whatever and however you like – and you may decide to shred the piece of paper in a few minutes. The act of externalizing the nags – getting them out of your mind and onto the

paper where they can be managed more objectively – can in itself be extremely meditative. It's a simple technique that helps you understand what's on your mind, what your worries are, what your instincts are. It also provides that important first step to acting on those things and creating the change you need.

UBIQUITOUS CAPTURE

David Allen, in his book *Getting Things Done*, talks about 'ubiquitous capture': the idea that wherever you are, whatever you're doing, you need a place to capture thoughts at the moment they arise. When thinking about how to implement the CORD model and develop your second brain, this is something to bear in mind. It is often said that our creativity is unleashed when part of our mind is also engaged in repetitive activities. I have a lot of my best ideas while driving, in the shower, on the treadmill in the gym, and so on. I tend to use either a paper notebook or my phone to capture these ideas as soon as I safely can! Your second brain is useless if you just leave it in the office. To truly become a part of you, you need to have it with you at all times. That could be as simple as saving things on your phone or writing things down on bits of paper. The point here is that you do need to think about how you're going to capture things wherever you are.

PLACES TO CAPTURE YOUR IDEAS AND NAGS

MOBILE PHONES

▶ For most of us, our mobile, our wallet and our keys are the three items that travel with us everywhere we go, making the idea of ubiquitous capture so much easier than it once was. What's great too is that you can synchronize the tasks function on your phone with your Outlook, or sync between a web-based to-do app and your phone's version of the same app.

'TO-DO' APPS

▶ Pretty much every phone on the market these days comes with some kind of task management or to-do app built-in. If you don't plan on using the app for the Organize and Review stages of CORD, then the chances are the native to-do app is all you need.

DICTATION APPS AND VOICE RECOGNITION

▶ Dictation feels so very 1970s! But most smartphones now have voice recognition or dictation apps, which some people find very useful. My own experience is that they are great for saving me a few seconds looking up contacts ('Call Gareth!'), but leave me frustrated and excited in equal measure when it comes to its capturing possibilities. But I am sure this will change, and fast!

MICROSOFT OUTLOOK, LOTUS NOTES AND SIMILAR PROGRAMS

▶ Back at your desk, you still need to capture ideas to come back to later on. In the UK, Outlook is almost as ubiquitous in offices as pen and paper! It's always a shock to us when we get off the phone to a new client and someone utters the words, 'They *don't* have Outlook!', because we're just so used to seeing it wherever we go. But most of these systems allow you to combine Mail, Calendar, Tasks and Contacts and swiftly move between them.

PEN AND PAPER

▶ You may assume that with all this talk about information productivity, pen and paper is a doomed thing of the past. I think sometimes there's an aversion to using pen and paper as tools because there seem to be much more sophisticated tools out there these days. I think this is the wrong approach. My focus is always on what gets the job done with the least setup time, resistance and drag. A lot of the time, especially for capturing and collecting, pen and paper wins hands down.

CAPTURING *CONVERSATIONS*

A great deal of the ideas and inputs that we need to deal with arrive in disguise and our stealth-like Ninja skills will be put to work here to make sure they don't escape capture. It is very easy to miss or forget ideas, nags or actions that arise during conversations with our bosses, colleagues or friends – precisely because we don't want to break off from the conversation to capture something, so we tell ourselves we'll come back to the job of capturing once the conversation has finished – and then, being human, sometimes we just forget.

So wherever possible, capture things during the conversation. If capturing on your phone, make clear to your colleague that you're capturing so that they don't think you're just sending a text to someone else! Here are a few of the situations that you'll need to look out for:

CONVERSATIONS IN THE OFFICE WITH YOUR BOSS

▶ If you're chatting to your boss, they probably expect you to do something as a result. There might be actions that are discussed, or more vague discussions that still require you to do some further thinking, research or follow-up. Take a moment after any conversation with your boss to reflect and literally gather your thoughts – chucking them into your second brain for organizing later!

MEETINGS

▶ Make sure any actions relating to you are consistent with the minutes of the meeting, to ensure your version of what's been agreed is the same as everyone else's. Where you are writing your own notes from a meeting and relying on them, think about developing a key so that you can quickly access any actions or other follow-ups without having to read all of your notes. I use a simple star mark to separate my notes from the actions, ideas and nags that need to be transferred into my second brain.

SOCIAL MEDIA

▶ So many of our conversations happen electronically. While email is easy to collect, organize, review and do – all directly from within Outlook or whatever program you're using – due to the volume we receive in one place, social media can prove trickier. The distinction between work and social can be much more blurred on something like Twitter than it might be on email, so we may not be in the habit of capturing the commitments we make to others here and we may be in danger of missing things.

VOICEMAIL

▶ Our phone's voicemail can be one of the places where things get stuck, particularly if you're like me and listen to voicemails on the run and don't always have the time to then capture any actions that come as a result. This remains, despite all my Ninja skills, as one of the weak points in my own system. However, in recent years I've learned that these kind of 'fall between the cracks' weaknesses are easy to combat – using the checklists we'll cover during the Review habit a bit later on.

COLLECTING

As well as the proactive capturing of ideas, nags and potential actions, we need to ensure we gather together all the bits of paper or digital inputs that we need to organize. All of us have a pretty consistent set of 'collection points' where inputs will be landing regularly and automatically. The most obvious and commonly used two or three of these for most professionals are their email inbox and incoming bits of paperwork and letters on your desk. For your email inbox, we've already looked at how to use the main inbox space in your email software as the collection point: the landing pad on which new inputs wait to have their fate decided. Happily, almost every piece of email software comes with an inbox and therefore an inbuilt collection point from which we can begin the CORD process. Having got this far, you'll have heard about the power of keeping your email inbox at zero, and for an obvious reason: it gives you peace of mind that you're on top of the decision-making that's needed around these inputs (the decision-making is really the basis for the Organize habit).

COLLECTION *POINTS*

For paper letters or bits of paperwork such as forms that float around the office, many people will have an 'In' and 'Out' stack of trays on their desks. If yours is currently acting as just an extra shelf for files, then you can learn how to make them useful again in the 'Organize' chapter. If you don't have an actual in-tray, just take a minute to think about where you or others might put new letters or paperwork when you return to your desk – chances are, there's an area that you instinctively already use as a collection point without labelling it formally as such. Your collection points don't have to be ordinary – I have had people use their fridge door at home, cigarette papers and of course a great many people who still insist on using the backs of their hands and a black pen! But here is a quick run-down of some of the most helpful.

DESK IN-TRAY

▶ Paper in-trays work well as a collection point for letters, forms and other kinds of paperwork as well as an 'organize point' for all the thoughts you've captured on pieces of paper.

▶ Likewise, it's worth investing in some kind of in-tray for your home. While this may feel like overdoing it, you'll find that having one actually reduces the number of 'collection' piles that tend to develop in any place in the house with a clean and flat surface! There will be work stuff that you bring home, receipts and notes that you need to take back to the office and of course, you may have things in your home-life that you want to apply the same Capture and Collect principles to as well. Having an in-tray per person is doubly recommended and I can personally testify that it leads to happier relationships! Finally, placing your in-tray somewhere close to the front door will encourage you to empty it regularly: junk mail or recycling will flow more quickly to its proper place and the stuff needed back at the office will return there more quickly too.

WALLET/PURSE

▶ If you're like me and some of your work takes place away from your own office, you'll probably have travel tickets and receipts to claim back as expenses. You need to collect these too. As most of us have learned the hard way, it's easy to lose receipts or forget what each one was actually for, especially if you leave it a long time between getting and organizing them.

A4 PLASTIC FILES

▶ When I'm out and about, I carry two very important A4 plastic files with me in my laptop bag. One is labelled 'To Office' and the other 'To Home'. If I am collecting paperwork while out and about, these effectively serve as my temporary paper in-trays – in my bag – until I reach the destination on the front of the folder. Over the years I've found these files to be invaluable. Firstly, they help me avoid the danger of putting loose paperwork into my bag and it getting at best, crumpled or at worst, lost. Secondly, they give me easy access when I get back to base, so that I can load the right things into the right in-trays wherever I am.

COMPUTER DESKTOP

▶ Do you have a million little icons of old Word documents on your desktop screen, or just a beautiful image of a peaceful lake and a mountain range? The computer desktop is a veritable treasure trove for two types of files or folders: the ultra-useful and the ultra-useless. Our laziness sees us save important documents here rather than risk – wait for it – saving it in a reasonable location instead! And heaven forbid having to use the search function to relocate the file if we don't find it immediately! So, our computer desktop suddenly becomes another collection point. It requires a bit of organization though. Try setting up a folder called 'Desktop Inbox' and regularly sweep all of those random documents inside it. Once you have a good pile in there, you can spend a few minutes filing them all back into the right place, or of course getting delete-happy with what you don't need!

MINIMIZING YOUR COLLECTION POINTS

When designing your productivity system and thinking about where your collection points are, it's worth remembering that your job is not just to collect, but also to empty! Try to design your system in such a way as to encourage the least resistance to using it: for example, if you know you have to check three more email inboxes other than your current professional one just to know that they're at zero, you're less likely to do it. So perhaps you could have all of your email accounts forwarded to one place so that it feels easier and you eliminate setup time and psychological drag. And while we're at it, you can set up social media messages to be forwarded to an email address too, so spend a couple of minutes on each of these sites looking through the settings. Only do that in instances where it will genuinely save you from checking social media though – you don't want to just create more distractions in your inbox!

EXERCISE: MINIMIZING MY COLLECTION POINTS

What you'll need:	Pen and paper, active/proactive attention
How long it'll take:	10 minutes
Ninja mindset:	Weapon-savvy

Before we get started on implementing your own CORD Productivity system, we need to make sure we're clear on getting the design right. For this exercise, write a list of all of the collection points in your own system. These might be tools you use already, new things you're going to put in place, or new ways to use old tools. The important thing to know is that you've answered this question:

> 'How will I know that I've captured and collected everything where there might be a potential action that's worth doing?'

On the CORD Productivity Model diagram, you'll see we've got paper-work, post, email, notes from meetings, things from conversations, things in your phone and wherever else you might capture your ideas and nags.

There is a huge difference between knowing it's all there and thinking there might still be something lurking despite your best efforts. So make your list on the next page.

My collection points:

1. ....

2. ....

3. ....

4. ....

5. ....

6. ....

7. ....

8. ....

9. ....

10. ....

11. ....

12. ....

13. ....

14. ....

15. ....

Now that you have your list of collection points, are there any changes you could make to your habits that might mean you have fewer collection points to regularly empty? Could you start using a new tool? Or could you combine some things together? Remember that you'll have to not just check but also empty every one of these collection points on a regular basis, so you probably won't want to end up with more than about ten. Write your final list of collection points here, complete with any changes you've just made or intend to make now as a result of this question.

My final list of collection points:

1. ....

2. ....

3. ....

4. ....

5. ....

6. ....

7. ....

8. ....

9. ....

10. ....

CAPTURE

Nags & ideas   Phone   Conversations

Any other places to capture + collect from?

COLLECT

Notes from meetings   Email   Paper & post

EXERCISE: THE BIG CAPTURE AND COLLECT!

What you'll need:
An in-tray or box able to act as one, pen,
pile of scrap paper, boss-mode proactive/
active attention. Access to all unfiled
paperwork, receipts, vouchers, Post-its,
print outs and so on

How long it'll take: 20–60 minutes

Ninja mindset:
Ruthlessness, Agility,
Preparedness

We want to get your system up and running now, so let's start with an exercise to do the first part of that. It's an exercise we do on some of our workshops and one we've done with everyone from senior executives to secretaries to landlords to youth workers to web designers to teachers. It's universally met with two reactions: one group of people find it cathartic and wonderful to be emptying their minds; the other find it stressful because it throws up all kinds of resistance as well as feeling like, temporarily, things are out of control. If you feel the latter, just trust me. I know what's coming next and I know you'll feel a whole lot better once you get there! This exercise can take over an hour for some people, so make sure you have the time available for it – preferably with probably five minutes of recovery time at the end, as it can get quite intense! I also recommend only doing this exercise at home or in the office, or certainly somewhere where you can replicate those conditions (i.e. don't try this on a crowded train!).

STEP ONE

Find yourself an in-tray, either at home or at work. If you don't have one, find any box or receptacle that can at least hold things the size of an A4 piece of paper.

STEP *TWO*

Grab a pen and a pile of scrap paper or a writing pad.

STEP *THREE*

Tear a small strip of paper and write something on it that's on your mind because it's not currently getting done. Once written, add the piece of paper to your in-tray. At this point, this could be something nagging you, a task at the back of your mind, or even just a vague idea that there's some action needed on a certain project or issue.

STEP *FOUR*

Repeat step three – again and again and again ... and again.

THERE ARE ONLY A FEW RULES HERE:

▶ Write only one thought or idea per piece of paper.

▶ If you have an existing to-do list (which hopefully you're currently discovering is wildly incomplete!) then you can simply add your to-do list to the pile – you don't need to rewrite every item on there on little strips of paper.

▶ If there are emails in your @Action folder which are reminders of things that need doing *outside* of email, you can delete the emails and use bits of paper to add these to the tray instead

▶ Once written and added to the tray, do not return to the pieces of paper, even to touch them.

▶ Be aware of the resistance against writing more.

▶ Write more.

▶ *Don't* try to prioritize, organize or otherwise 'manage' what you're capturing. At this stage, we're practising the art of capturing and collecting only.

▶ If it seems like a good idea, write it down.

▶ If it seems like a bad idea, write it down anyway.

▶ If it feels more like a worry or a nag than a truly actionable item, write it down anyway.

▶ The winner is the person with the most items in their in-tray, so don't feel inhibited, try not to feel stressed and … write.

At some stage you might find yourself running out of ideas about what to capture. Think about the different roles you play in life (parent, partner, child, employee, manager, coach, household head chef, household head finance manager, landlord, volunteer, etc). Most of us play many different roles in life and perhaps you've focused more of your attention to some and less to others.

How will you know you've finished?

When you really feel that there's nothing left that you could write down, you're ready to move on. If you've had a couple of minutes of pondering and nothing's coming to you, you can call an end to this exercise and feel free to capture anything else that you think of later on.

STEP FIVE

Right now, you should have an in-tray or box filled with lots of bits of torn up paper, each filled with a thought or nag about something that isn't yet done. But in real life, once you put this book down, there are many other things that need to be captured and collected. So if you're at home right now, take a walk around. Find anything that's lying around because it's waiting to have something done with it, bring it back and add it to your in-tray. Items might include the vouchers that you need to redeem at the supermarket, the book that needs to go back to work, the consent letter that needs to go back to your child's school … Likewise if you're in the office, there might be a whole host of piles, or faded Post-it notes, or expense receipts hidden away in murky drawers. As before, don't pay any attention to priority of the tasks that might lie beyond these bits of paper or items.

STEP SIX

Finally, you need to consider all of your other collection points, which may be harbouring valuable information. Is there anything else you can add to the tray from these places? Are each of these collection points set up ready to be used straight away? Take a few moments to do whatever you can now to ensure that they are. For any that require setting up in a separate location that you can't do now, capture what needs to happen on a piece of paper and add it to the tray!

And you're done! Every thought, every nag, every vague idea, is now captured and collected, ready to be dealt with. Again, I want to emphasize that it's not unusual for people to feel stressed at the end of this exercise. The mind has a powerful hold over our ability to take action so if you do feel stressed, move swiftly on to the Organize section now, where we'll put that right. And if you feel pretty elated at what you've just done, that's quite natural too – it's time to take some skilful and ruthless action to cut through that big in-tray like a true Ninja!

Are you a Ninja?

▶ A Ninja's agility comes from being able to capture and collect ideas as they arrive, keeping their mind focused on the task at hand.

▶ A Ninja is prepared: by capturing and collecting everything on their mind, they ensure that they're ready to enter the Organize phase. A Ninja knows how to achieve Zen-like calm: it comes from being ruthless, prepared and mindful.

▶ A Ninja achieves Zen-like calm as a consequence of clear thinking. Everything is out of their mind and stored inside a second brain they can trust to deal with it.

7. THE ORGANIZE HABIT

'In my youth I stressed freedom, and in my old age I stress order. I have made the great discovery that liberty is a product of order.'
— Will Durant

By now, you've captured and collected everything that you have. It's time to unleash the power of the second brain as we move on to the Organize habit. The aim here, much like we did with your email inbox, is to get your tray down to zero. Of course, this time there will be a more varied mix of things inside your tray than there was in your email inbox, but the principle is exactly the same.

THE THREE LEVELS OF LISTS

The Organize phase is a boss-mode phase, so of course the Productivity Ninja has one eye on their worker-self (in Do-mode) and will therefore prepare everything here to be as conducive as possible to playful, productive momentum and control. The primary aim of the Organize phase, then, is to ensure that our worker-self is prepared and that we're clear and confident on what we're committed to. Here, we will first talk about the structures that are required and then go on to discuss the best tools to use (paper, apps, Outlook and so on). A standard to-do list just isn't enough to give us the agility to manage the various levels of complexity we encounter in our knowledge work – from immediate actions through to those things we *could* be doing, through to the wider, project-level tasks. In fact, one of the reasons our standard to-do lists don't work is that they're often trying to do what we will separate here into two or three different lists – and they're failing at all three. We're going to set up three different levels of list, as the cornerstones of our second brain:

▶ **PROJECTS** LIST

▶ **MASTER** ACTIONS LIST

▶ **DAILY** TO-DO LIST

In this chapter we're going to focus on these three lists and other key components of the Organize habit. Next, we'll look at how we utilize asking the right questions in a logical order to make organizing easier and more intuitive. Towards the end of the chapter, we'll then start to look at some of the practicalities of setting up your second brain. And of course, in the exercise at the end of the chapter, it's over to you!

THE **PROJECTS** LIST

Let's look first at the highest of the three levels. We're going to use a single 'Projects List' to keep track of all the projects we're working on. I would define a project as a collection of actions that is designed to achieve a particular aim. Therefore, a project is any piece of work that requires more than a couple of action steps to complete, regardless of how big or small.

For example, getting a replacement phone when your phone contract is up is often treated as a thing to do when of course it's not. The desired outcome is to have a new phone, perhaps on a new network, up and running. But to get there, we might have a range of actions from researching phones on the internet, calling our current provider, comparing price plans and thinking about our current usage, speaking to friends about their experiences, visiting the local phone shop, buying the phone, activating it and getting the direct debit payment form sent off. That's a collection of actions making up one project.

Even with only a couple of action steps, if the desired final outcome will take more than one week to achieve, I would still classify this as a project. One of the problems we often face with the standard to-do list is the fact that, with only one list there is no sense of scale. We therefore mix the tiniest of actions with the largest of projects, all on one list, and then wonder why we feel overwhelmed! Separating your projects in this way is the first stage in regaining control.

Your Projects List is really just a checklist of all the current projects you're working on, which you won't need to use on a daily basis, but which we will return to when we talk about the Review habit in the next chapter. Your Projects List doesn't need to be hugely detailed. Its function is primarily to ensure that you have something to focus on at a more strategic level at least once a week.

The Projects List generates actions. From each project will come one or more current actions and obviously as projects move forward, new actions are generated and added to the Master Actions List, ready for completion.

Naming a project

When thinking about defining and naming your projects, it's important to help your mind visualize a successful final outcome. So think about the following questions:

▶ What is the successful outcome I'm seeking?

▶ How will I measure success?

These two simple questions not only help us to define a project, but also name it. It's a great tip to make the name of the project reflect the measure of success. So for example, rather than talking about 'Conference', talk about 'Conference with 100 delegates' or instead of 'Car MOT', talk about 'Car MOT passed by March 21st'.

Organizing your Projects List

Within your Projects List, you may wish to group or organize the projects into sections so that it makes the list easier to read and easier to navigate around. You can organize or group the projects any which way you like.

The most obvious way is to organize it into some simple categories. For example ...

Work projects:

Home projects:

You may require a little more complexity, so how about breaking down the work projects into some simple sub-categories? Here are a few examples of Work projects:

Work – Sales:

Work – People:

Work – Financial Management/Budget:

Personally, I have a number of different categories of projects that relate to the different 'departments' within Think Productive (Clients, Backstage, Workshops and so on) as well as categories for personal projects, charity projects and so on. It helps to maintain a Projects List with some methodical sections such as these, so that when you come to the Review stage, it's easy to view all of the sales projects in one place, then all the people projects, then the finance projects and so on.

If you're using some kind of list management software or to-do app, you can sometimes be quite limited by the fact that the names of your projects appear in alphabetical order. I get round this by using letters and numbers to ensure that my projects appear in the right order in the list. For example, for managing the process of producing this book, my to-do app (Toodledo – more of which later!) contains a number of different projects in my Projects List, each listed with a letter and a number to ensure they're kept together on my Projects List (so the 'B' here just stands for 'book'!) and that they're also in the most logical order:

> **B1 – writing**
>
> **B2 – editing**
>
> **B3 – proofing**
>
> **B4 – graphic design**
>
> **B5 – website live**
>
> **B6 – marketing and PR**
>
> **B7 – launch**

I keep all of my personal projects in one place by using the letter 'P' before them:

> **P** – Car service and MOT by March 21st
>
> **P** – Family visit to Brighton in June
>
> **P** – Flat-hunting (decide on area by February 1st)

There are lots of other ways of categorizing project lists. Matthew, one of our Productivity Ninjas at Think Productive, uses a nice ABCDE categorization to his Project List:

A	=	**Acquire**
B	=	**Broker**
C	=	**Contract**
D	=	**Deliver**
E	=	**Extract Payment**

The ABCDE method mirrors the process of business, so whatever you do, you'll probably find that your work fits into one or more of these categories. I personally have a good spread of projects falling into each of these. A is for 'Acquire', so finding new clients. This would include things like marketing activities, outreach, networking, promotional events, conferences and so on. B is for 'Broker', the specific stage where you're discussing a deal with a potential client and working towards them signing on the dotted line. C is for 'Contract' and covers the process of actually sealing the deal. D is the work itself – delivering on what that contract has committed you to. And finally E is for 'Extract Payment', making sure your invoices are sent off and that the cheque is paid in to the bank. It's a nice way of grouping projects. You might find this useful or you may have something more suitable in mind. A good place to start when thinking about how best to organize your projects is to take your job description (if you have one!) and look at the section headings. Now, you may think your role these days is much broader and deeper than what was written on that original job description, but it's still not a bad place to start from – you can adapt, edit and add from there.

Don't worry too much about the finer details of what should be on your Projects List right now, or indeed what the ordering or numbering should look like. We will come back to this during the exercise at the end of this chapter.

The point of making a projects list is to spend a few short moments each week forcing yourself to do the requisite thinking that brings extreme clarity, by working out what you're actually committed to doing. Most people I work with might have a shared team project list that details *some* of their personal responsibilities, but chances are that they haven't recorded the rest of their projects in any kind of structured format at all. In fact, what then happens as a result of this is that people capture projects in the same way they capture actions and blend the two together on a standard to-do list, which then has everything from five-minute actions to five-month long projects mixed together side by side. This makes tiring reading, especially when so many of these projects require more thinking time rather than being things that you can actually *do*! Projects can't be done at all – only actions can be done! And that's what your Master Actions list is for.

Breaking these bad habits and separating the projects from the actions, the thinking from the doing, does take a little bit of getting used to. But once you're in the habit of it, it's easy to maintain and super-useful. A complete checklist-style list of projects helps with boss-mode thinking, but also crucially helps to keep this thinking separate from our worker-self in Do-mode. We're no longer distracted by that bigger picture when we're trying to crack on.

THE **MASTER** ACTIONS LIST

The largest, most important, most dynamically changing and most used list is your 'Master Actions List'. It's similar to the kinds of to-do lists you might have intuitively created or read about in some of the old time management books, but there are also some fundamental differences:

1. It's a *Master* Actions List. As such, it contains every single action you could currently do, for each and every project. It doesn't map things out for months in the future, because guess what? Things change.

2. It's easy to break down the Master Actions List into lots of different categories so that you have super-quick access to only the most relevant information you need to make really quick decisions.

3. The Master Actions List is where you can tell, at a second's glance, what you should be doing with your current period of proactive attention and what you should do later when your brain is completely fried and your attention is about as inactive as it gets. It will also manage actions based on where you are: whether in the office, working from home, out and about, and so on. Finally, you

may want to keep track of any actions that have an element of collaboration, so perhaps actions that involve conversations with your closest colleagues or items for the agenda of a forthcoming meeting.

4. You get to decide what those categories look like and ultimately tailor it as a system that will work for you.

Your Master Actions List can be as complex or as simple as you need it to be. It might reflect your job role or the fact that you work across multiple roles. It might just reflect what you feel most comfortable with.

In the 70s, 80s and 90s, time management courses culminated with the 'free gift' of a sophisticated looking, often leather bound planner or diary. Inside it was the perfect framework for time management. Your job was to fit your working life into this perfect framework. Well, what most people found was that either the system was too complicated or it didn't fit all that well. The point is that your system – and especially your Master Actions List – is the most personal of interfaces between your boss-self's brain and your worker-self's hands. Getting exactly the right kind of Master Actions List to suit you is the difference between struggling through or just getting a fair bit done and the kind of playful, productive momentum and control we're looking for.

5. It's action-focused. The language of the Master Actions List is deliberately designed to encourage action rather than the need for more thinking.

Each action should describe exactly what you need to do next. This sounds so simple, but as humans we tend to focus on a vague idea of an outcome rather than what actually needs to happen next. You want to remove all uncertainty at this point so that your worker-self feels just like they're putting cherries on cakes: no thinking, no uncertainty – just Zen-like calm from a position of preparedness, and ruthless, in-the-moment doing.

THE NEXT *PHYSICAL* ACTION

The words we choose to put on our list matter. It's important to have a clear idea about what should – and even more importantly should not – be stored on your Master Actions List, and the language we use with ourselves is crucial here. Imagine each and every decision you make as a conversation between your boss-self and your worker-self. Allow your worker-self the luxury of screaming at your boss-self, 'Be more specific!' or, 'What *exactly* do you need me to do?!' Unless you can picture the activity, it's not really an action. Think about the next physical action you could take. There may be several actions you could take, simultaneously, with no need to follow a particular order. These are the things to add to your Master Actions List. You need a Master Actions List filled with the thing you can actually do when you next have some time, in order that you can make the most informed choice when that time arises.

VERB, OBJECT, SUBJECT

If you're unsure about whether your action is specific enough, think about whether it contains a verb, an object and a subject. If you have all three, you'll avoid uncertainty and create momentum further down the line. So it's worth just spending a few seconds forcing yourself to be really clear and use clear language.

GOOD AND *BAD PRACTICE* ACTION PHRASES

Good Practice Action Phrases	Bad Practice Action Phrases	Really Bad Practice
Call Geoff about ideas for conference venues	Contact Geoff	Geoff
Schedule a meeting in Outlook w/ Elena re: pay rise	Sort Out Elena's pay rise	Elena pay rise?
Email Rob and ask his advice about next steps for social enterprise funding	Look into funding for social enterprise	New social enterprise idea
Print out draft of report and write down final changes to make	Finish report	Report deadline today!!
Google options for skip hire companies and give to assistant to get quotes	Arrange for skip to clear out garage	Garage

KEEP FUTURE ACTIONS THAT YOU CAN'T DO NOW AWAY FROM THE MASTER ACTIONS LIST

What you don't want on your Master Actions List are a whole bunch of actions that are either not actions at all (because you haven't yet defined them properly!) or that you can't do next because there are interdependencies. For example, if I were organizing a conference, I could call the six venues I know and ask them if they're free to host my conference. I could also at the same time be drafting ideas about the conference programme or marketing plan, but until I have the venue in place, I can't send out the invites. So in this scenario, try to keep the action of sending out the invites away from your Master Actions List. Remember, we're trying to eliminate the need for too much thinking when you want to just get on and do things, and this would quickly create vagueness and uncertainty.

The 'physical' part of the action is what turns it from a noun into a verb! So 'Chase Virginia about the programme' is really a noun – it's a thing that needs to be done. Calling Virginia, now that's a different story. It's physical! You can picture yourself doing it. As soon as you have the words and the picture in your mind that describes what you need to do, you probably have the right words for your Master Actions List. This may feel too detailed – lots of people we train find this pernickety or annoying – but the power of this habit is encouraging clearer thinking, and as you write those words onto your Master Actions List, you're encouraging clearer thinking that aids more powerful doing later on.

ORGANIZING YOUR MASTER ACTIONS LIST

As you start finding things to add to your Master Actions List, it's important that you start to think about the structure of this list and how it should best work for you. Here are the three main structural elements, in order of importance. The most important – Places – is first.

'The thinker needs information
– at the right moment.'
– Nancy Kline

PLACES

This is really the cornerstone of the Master Actions List. Where do you need to be in order to get each specific action done? For many people, this is a simple answer: the office. Their work is pretty consistently in the office. By far the biggest part of my list is my 'Office' category list, but I have a few other places, too:

Home:

> Either working from home, or managing home-related or personal tasks which I do at home.

Out and About:

Being a trainer, I often find myself in the middle of cities with an hour to kill before my evening train home. So this list comes in very handy for me as I can always find a local bookshop, stationery shop, or whatever else I need.

Online Banking:

Yes, this happens in the office, but the big setup is getting through the Fort Knox-like security systems, so once in there, it makes sense to have a list of all my other online banking tasks that I can access in an instant and clear from my list.

Calls, Thinking/Decisions:

These are two lists that aren't really places as such, but they indicate that the tasks can be done anywhere – so even out of the office or on a walk somewhere, I can make decisions; I can still make phone calls.

Other Office:

If you work across multiple office sites, you may choose to separate out this way, especially for actions that require specific software or paperwork that's only in that location.

Other Job:

So many people these days freelance, work two part-time jobs, have other strings to their bow and so on. You never know what's going to need your attention and when, so just as you start to get stuck into writing Monday's report, ideas for Thursday's meeting in a different job pop into your head. You need to be able to keep track of your other places of responsibility, as a tactic to keep that stuff off your mind right now.

Even if 95% of what you do can be stored on one 'Office' list, you'll find the 5% you store on the others really useful! Having comprehensive, location-based information on hand wherever you are is crucial for making the best, in-the-moment decisions.

ATTENTION

This is where things get extremely Ninja! The other way of breaking down and splitting up your lists is by an estimate of the attention level that different tasks will require:

Office – **Proactive** Attention

Office – **Active** Attention

Office – **Inactive** Attention

By splitting into these three sub-lists, you can then easily schedule periods of attention to ensure that you're using your proactive attention to get to the difficult stuff! It might appear like hard work having to record everything in such detail, but it needn't be any hassle at all. I tend to use my standard office list to mean 'Office – Active Attention' and then siphon off the other tasks to 'Office – Inactive' and 'Office – Proactive'. If you're using task-management software here, it could just be an optional category or tag. (More of which in a few moments.)

PEOPLE & *CONVERSATIONS*

The final potential sub-list idea you can use is to sort them by people. This is particularly useful if you have a boss or an assistant who is always asking you questions about a lot of things, or if you want to turn unavoidable interruptions like phone calls into priceless moments for productivity (someone interrupting you and knocking you off your flow is your cue to keep them on the phone and pull up your relevant sub-list to run through with them!).

There are a couple of different techniques for organizing your tasks by people and they may or may not be relevant to you:

'Lisa' and 'LisaWaiting' –

I have two sub-lists for my assistant Lisa in my system. I have the same for other people I line manage directly. The first is just called 'Lisa'. This is a list of all the actions I have stored up for her to do, but haven't yet delegated to her. We run through this list whenever I'm in the office. The second, 'LisaWaiting', you can now probably guess! It's the list of all the delegated tasks I'm waiting for her to finish. I move tasks to this list once we have discussed them and she's taken them on. Sometimes individual items bat back and forth between Lisa and LisaWaiting, sometimes also over to my own 'Office' list if the next action to move it along is then back on me.

'Lee Conversations' –

Lee is one of our top Productivity Ninjas. He keeps a 'Graham Conversations' list and I keep one for him. Whenever we get together on the phone, this is the list that we both run through. Most of the things on here aren't really actions, but it's a list of the conversations that I need to have with Lee – things to check, ask advice about, float as ideas and so on. Storing these separately from the Office lists is great because it means whenever we get ten minutes on the phone, it's more productive than us both sending each other hundreds of emails. Again, these can be separate lists, or could simply be tags or categories if you're keeping your lists electronically.

If you don't line manage people or if there aren't a small number of people that you need to constantly keep in check with, you may not need to use any form of 'People and conversations' sub-lists at all and that's fine. Having just two variables – places and attention – is often a good foundation from which to build your system anyway. Again, only use this technique if you feel it will add some value. You may not need it.

THE *TWO-MINUTE RULE* AND SHORT ACTIONS

One of the key tenets of many productivity systems and time management books is the two-minute rule. Popularized by David Allen in *Getting Things Done*, it was also used earlier by Dean Acheson in his *Time/Design* system. The rule is pretty simple: *anything* that you decide needs to be done and that you decide can probably be completed or moved forward in less than two minutes should be done straight away instead of a reminder being added to your Master Actions List.

This is a useful technique to develop as part of your wider Organize habits. It reduces the number of items that need to be held on your Master Actions List and allows for habitual decisiveness and efficiency. Efficiency, because *not* doing those two-minute actions straight away would probably then involve two minutes of writing them down, reading them again later, trying to remember exactly what needs to be done and … spending longer than two minutes on the thinking rather than having just got it done!

THE CHANGING NATURE OF THE MASTER ACTIONS LIST

If you're on top form, your Master Actions List will be growing and shrinking all the time – after all, it's a dynamic list of all the things you could be doing at any one time. So too, will the main sub-lists. As things happen, they get crossed off the relevant list. As more new inputs arrive, these are converted into new actions and added to the Master Actions List. Be aware which parts of the system are working well and which less so. When you're in Review-mode, make a point of consciously reflecting on this. Perhaps you need a new sub-list or category, or could you even delete two or three to streamline things? It's both natural and useful to keep freshening your system to reflect the ever-changing world that is your priorities, your commitments, your life.

AN EXAMPLE MASTER ACTIONS LIST – *SIMPLE*

A simple Master Actions List could involve the office, home and the places you visit in between! The only kind of categorization is 'Places'. This is sufficient for lots of the people that we work with. As long as none of these three sub-lists are filling up with dozens of items, this will be all you need to track what you need to do:

Office	Home	Out and About
Draft ideas for Thursday's meeting	Research skip hire companies and get three local numbers to call	Pick up prescription from the chemist
Call Susan about New York hotels	Check what's in the fridge/cupboards ready for shopping list	Look at laptop bags to get ideas/check quality
Finish typing monthly finance return and send to Nick in finance department		

It's worth noting that what I'm trying to do here is give you the *structure* of a Master Actions List. You'll probably find that you're keeping quite a few different actions under each category rather than the one or two or three things I've added to each category on the example. But hopefully what's more interesting to you here are the structures and categories being used. As you look at these, you might get some ideas about how to structure your own Master Actions List. We'll be returning to this to help you get set up in the exercise at the end of this chapter.

AN EXAMPLE MASTER ACTIONS LIST – *AVERAGE*

A more average Master Actions List might look something like this. Again, we have the split by 'Places' (office, home, out and about). But if you have more than say a dozen office tasks to complete, you might find it helpful to group them by the level of attention you'll need (proactive, active and inactive attention). We've also added two sub-lists that reflect things that you can do from anywhere: 'Thinking/Decision' and 'Calls'. This provides a bit more flexibility and allows you to be more specific about how and where things should best get done.

Office – Proactive Attention	Home	Out and About
Draft ideas for Thursday's team meeting	Research skip hire companies and get three local numbers to call	Pick up prescription from the chemists
Spend half an hour reading through sales proposal and make any final changes before sending	Check what's in the fridge/cupboards ready for shopping list	Look at laptop bags to get ideas/check quality
Office – Active Attention	**Calls**	**Thinking/Decision**
Email Chris about the transcription project next steps	Call Susan about New York hotels	Do I want to go to Peru with my sister in September? (Decide this week)
Finish typing monthly finance return and send to Nick in finance department	Call customer services re new phone	What kind of person are we looking for when we recruit for the new role? (Draft some thoughts)
	Call Lee re agenda for Bristol training day	
Office – Inactive Attention		
Scan credit card statements and email to Nick		

AN EXAMPLE MASTER ACTIONS LIST – *COMPLEX*

Below is an example of a more complex Master Actions List. This reflects someone working in different locations, working closely with staff and assistants and managing a heavy workload. At this point, don't worry about whether these exact categories are what you could or should be using. You also need not worry about where best to keep your lists ('Paper?! iPhone app?! I'm confused!'). Don't panic, we will focus on the implementation later. For now, just start to marvel at the second brain at work. Don't forget, what we're looking for here is clarity and Zen-like calm. Knowing your second brain is holding everything tightly in its memory means you don't have to hold it all in yours!

Office – Proactive	Office – Active	Office – Inactive
Draft ideas for Thursday's team meeting	Email Chris about the transcription project next steps	Set up council tax direct debit
Spend half an hour reading through sales proposal and make any final changes before sending		Finish typing monthly finance return and send to Nick in finance department
Online banking	**Lee Conversations**	**Calls**
Transfer £40 to Nathan for Ronnie Scott's ticket (s/c 089186 a/c 13356599)	Skype call Lee to finalize agenda for upcoming company training day	Call Susan about New York hotels
Check if Joanna paid back my loan		Call customer services re: new phone
		Call Lee re: agenda for Bristol training day

Other office (Fridays)	Out and about	Thinking/Decision
Introduce myself to the new tenant In the office downstairs	Pick up prescription from the chemist	Do I want to go to Peru with my sister in September? (Decide this week)
Pick up the train tickets for next week's Bristol trip (on my desk)	Look at laptop bags to get ideas/check quality	What kind of person are we looking for when we recruit for the new role? (Draft some thoughts)
Lisa Actions	**Lisa Waiting**	**Home**
Lisa to scan credit card statements and email to Nick	Waiting for Lisa to book travel tickets for Birmingham trip next Saturday	Research skip hire companies and get three local numbers to call
		Check what's in the fridge/cupboards ready for shopping list

THE DAILY TO-DO LIST: A NINJA'S DOUBLE-EDGED SWORD

Once you've got all your projects and actions mapped out, it's useful to have a plan at the start of every day. The Daily To-Do List becomes a big part of this plan. Sitting down, coffee in hand, writing out the list of 'Things to do today' is a regular ritual for many office workers. But while many people do this already, most create lists that don't really work: they try to plan their day from their own memory or from the scraps of paper they left on their desk before leaving last night because they don't have the second brain of a complete Master Actions List. So they scratch around trying to remember the two or three most urgent things to be getting on with and then fill the rest of the Daily To-Do List with whatever else springs to mind first.

This is a big mistake. Most of the time, working without the back-up of a Master Actions List veers us more towards the urgent and loudest rather than the important and subtle.

A Productivity Ninja sees the Daily To-Do List slightly differently. At the start of the day, with the Master Actions List to scan, you can make some much clearer and cleverer decisions about where to put your limited time and even more limited attention.

The Daily To-Do List provides focused selection. Think of the Master Actions List as like a wardrobe full of all your clothes and your Daily To-Do List as the things you're going to wear today.

My Daily To-Do List is usually a Post-it note. And while I will undoubtedly go back and look at the larger Master Actions List at points during the day, the simple Post-it note helps me focus on a very small number of items and keeps me on track. If you prefer not to use a Post-it, it could be as simple as underlining or marking in pen certain items on your Master Actions List. Or if your Master Actions List is in a digital format (such as a to-do app or Outlook Tasks) creating your Daily To-Do List could simply mean marking as 'high priority' or 'to do today' certain items and then viewing only those on the screen. This small step, practised at the start of every day, will increase your focus and help you say 'No' to a myriad of distractions that are just about to come your way!

But Daily To-Do Lists are a double-edged sword. They do indeed provide focus, but they can also quickly fall prey to what psychologists label 'the planning fallacy'. At the start of the day, when you're feeling fresh, it's all too easy to be overambitious and fill your Daily To-Do List with far too many things, underestimating not just how long each item would take, but the ebbs and flows in our level of attention and, critically, the potential new inputs that may show up and need managing during the day. It's very easy to start the day with a great plan and great motivation, only for that to be destroyed by 11am by an urgent email from Josie in accounts wanting urgent figures in some unknown or annoying format and with the three line whip of the CEO cc'd in there to ensure you drop everything. Under such circumstances, how do you imagine you'll feel at 5pm when you look at that Daily To-Do List again, into which you haven't made a single dent?

RENEGOTIATING YOUR DAILY TO-DO LIST

If surprise hits at 11am, you might blindly carry on with the day. Occasionally you'll look at your Daily To-Do List but now instead of providing focus, it will just remind you of your perceived failure, as other things supersede what you had planned to spend your precious attention on. So perhaps at lunch time, or at choice moments throughout the day, it's worth renegotiating what's achievable. Productivity is so determined by momentum that you can ill afford to let your own lists become a source of stress! So change the rules and win.

Promise me this solemnly. Never, ever forget that you are *not* a superhero. You are a Ninja. You're human. You must realize that the world changes, but that you're as prepared as you can be, that you're making intelligent decisions, you're on top of new inputs and their potential impact, you're working on the most appropriate stuff and you're getting into the Ninja work groove whenever you possibly can … And you know what? That's all you can ever do.

THE 'WAITING FOR' LIST: A NINJA'S SECRET WEAPON

OK, OK, I know I said there were three lists. Actually there's a fourth – but it's a quick one. By now, you'll implicitly trust your own second brain to manage your own actions. The trouble is, well … everyone else. While you beaver away getting everything done, you can be sure that half of your colleagues are messing around on Facebook, gossiping in the kitchen and generally not behaving like any self-respecting Productivity Ninja.

So the 'Waiting For' List is a cunning, stealth-like little tool that helps a Ninja get around the problem of other people and their unproductive mess. The idea is pretty simple: just keep a list tracking all of the people who are off doing things that you want to make sure actually get done. This allows you to track these items during the Review phase and chase as appropriate. The @Waiting folder in your email inbox, as featured in our earlier chapter on email is simply the email equivalent of this. I use my Waiting For List to keep track of a whole myriad of items such as …

▶ Sales enquiries ('John said he'd get back to me by the second week of January.')

▶ Outstanding payments ('Waiting on expense claim from client X.')

▶ Personal reminders ('Waiting on tickets for Wimbledon – being mailed in early May.')

The 'Waiting For' list can be stored in the same place as your Master Actions and Projects Lists. Again, you won't need to focus on this list very often, but later on we'll look at a couple of checklists that will act as a reminder to make sure you do check your Waiting For List just often enough.

THE **OTHER THINGS** YOU NEED TO BE ORGANIZED

With your three levels of lists, the Projects List, Master Actions List and a Daily To-Do List, you're well on your way to having everything you need. However, there are a few other components we need to consider before we get into the task of organizing all of the items in your tray. These are:

▶ Waiting For Tray

▶ Digital and paper reference systems

▶ Good Ideas Park

- Calendar

- Checklists (which I will show you how to make in the next chapter)

- A large rubbish bin.

Let's look at each of these in turn.

WAITING FOR TRAY

One of the missing elements of many people's personal organization is the place to 'park' all the physical things you can't currently do anything with, such as the tickets for the conference next week, the printout of the letter you're waiting on a reply from or the forms you're waiting for someone from another office to come and collect from you. Your physical Waiting For Tray can be in the same stack as your In-Tray that we discussed during Chapter 6 on Capture and Collect. My own personal preference is as follows:

- In (top)

- Waiting (middle)

- Out (bottom) – Out filing is all the paper work you've dealt with that you're saving up to file into your reference files.

REFERENCE SYSTEMS: DIGITAL & PAPER

Like many people, I use paper reference systems less and less these days and would love to reach a point where I was truly paperless but there are times when only paper filing will do. For that reason, I will focus here first on digital filing and its growing importance before offering some tips about paper files.

There are three components of digital reference:

1. The Server (work files such as Word and Excel files, shared among the team or organization): these days, there's less of a need for servers in smaller organizations as services like Dropbox and Google Docs gain in popularity.

2. Personal Digital Reference (the place you personally keep passwords, customer reference numbers, snippets of text, recipes and perhaps photos of mind maps and other things to help with particular projects): over the years I have used Outlook's Notes function, One Note and now Evernote for this. The great thing with Evernote is that it goes wherever I go – I can access my files via the Evernote website, but also on my laptop, iPad and mobile phone. It's a fantastic way of keeping lots of useful information at my fingertips.

3. Website bookmarks: many people use services like Delicious to keep track of websites they've visited that they want to come back to in the future. If you're not someone that needs to save a lot of website bookmarks, I suggest incorporating this directly into Evernote or into your preferred web browser for simplicity's sake, but it's certainly worth keeping a separate account with one of these services if it's something you'll use regularly.

The looming death of paper reference

Keeping a simple paper reference system these days is still a must, but I certainly see this changing. However, some bits of paper (certificates from the Government about your car or tax, for example) are irreplaceable and the idea of achieving a 'paperless office' to me seems like the wrong goal to aim for. Rather than seeking to achieve 'paperless', just start with 'a lot less paper'. Here are a few ways you could do the same if you already have a couple of filing cabinet drawers or shelves full of old paperwork:

▶ Throw away or recycle any piece of paper reference material easily available on the web. Nowadays, so many forms, reports, newspapers and magazines are archived and available either for reading online or downloading.

▶ Emphasize the keepsakes, where it truly matters to hold an original document rather than looking at a scanned copy.

▶ Thin out existing files down to only the bare bones of what you need to keep (it's good practice to do this once a year or so, anyway).

There are also some seriously quick scanner devices on the market these days, which make the job of dealing with paper reference materials and uploading them to your server or into a personal digital reference program like Evernote really quick and easy! If you currently deal with a lot of paper reference materials, filing cabinets and archives, you might find that investing in such a device pays for itself given the time and money it will save your company by you not having to manage so much physical paper work anymore. Having a super-scanner on your desk is also a great way to be more ruthless with throwing things into the recycle bin: not sure if you really need it? Just take a quick scan and chuck the document away!

What's left of paper reference

With the things you have left, usually it's simplest to keep to a pretty standard A–Z structure as the best way to store your files and recall them when you need them. I personally make two exceptions to this rule, storing all of my financial information in a small number of folders for ease of reference and renewal, and because it makes archiving easier at the end of the tax year; anything financial lives in a separate folder rather than in my A–Z drawers. The other exception I make is certificates and contracts, which again I like to keep all in one place for ease of finding them all together. Aside from this, everything is stored alphabetically. A few years ago I had an entire four-drawer filing cabinet; it's now down to two drawers and I aim to go further in the next couple of years.

GOOD *IDEAS* PARK

There will occasionally be ideas or recommendations that seem like they could be really useful, but for whatever reason don't seem to fit into your current set of priorities. These are the ideas that might inform future projects. They also may not, and you might delete them in future, but for now you don't want to lose the idea. This is where the 'Good Ideas Park' comes in handy. My Good Ideas Park currently contains about a hundred items as varied as software to try out, places to go on country walks, business development or marketing ideas, ideas for blogs and articles, a couple of charity related ideas I'd like to set up and so on. It's a dumping ground and it's pretty chaotic there, but every now and again it provides me with just the right idea at the just the right time. One thing that grew out of my Good Ideas Park was a separate list which I call 'Watch/Read/Hear'. I use this list for when friends and colleagues recommend good films to see, books to read or music to listen to. If I'm on Amazon or iTunes and I pull up that list, it's only a few clicks until all of that stuff is on its way to me. My memory for these kinds of things is terrible and some of my favourite films, books and music have come to me through this simple list.

CALENDAR

I recently ran a workshop for a group of 16- to- 18-year-olds from some of the poorest parts of London, who were taking part in a summer programme designed to boost their skills and aspirations. It was a real challenge translating some of the complicated 'work speak' into the kind of language that would resonate with kids, many of whom had never stayed in school long enough to complete exams, let alone set foot in an office. At the end of the project, they invited me back, along with many other volunteers from a range of businesses, for an awards ceremony. One of the kids approached me and said, 'You're the productivity guy, right? Great session. Hey, y'know what I did after your session? I went and bought myself a *diary*, man!'. It was just one of those moments for me. The diary or calendar is something we take for granted, but having never really been told he needed one, it fell to me to be the guy to give him that very simple piece of inspiration.

Far be it from me to prescribe too rigidly how you should complete your paper diary or fill in your electronic calendar. These are tools that take on natural personality. There are, however, one or two pointers that I hope are common sense and can fit alongside your personal preferences:

▶ Don't allow others to book out your entire day with Outlook appointments. Try to keep as much control and autonomy for yourself when it comes to your schedule.

▶ Don't fill your calendar with tasks. Only add tasks to the calendar for today, not for the days ahead unless absolutely necessary. And even then, only add things to the calendar if there is a time-related deadline or meeting. It's more important to keep your calendar flexible and agile because surprises will lie ahead and you need a clear view.

▶ If you use a paper diary, make sure you sync it up with what's happening on your electronic calendar whenever possible.

▶ Since your system is only ever as good as its weakest link, consider for a moment what would happen if you lost your paper diary. Regularly ask yourself this question and use a phone camera or photocopier to spend five minutes making the backups you need to address this question.

CHECKLISTS

Checklists are one of the most underrated tools available to us, and I will explain how to use them when we move onto the Review phase in the next chapter.

In short, though, the purpose of the checklist is to replicate previous thinking so that, for repeated processes, you can get straight to best practices rather than having to try to remember what you've already thought previously. Checklists remove the friction of having to revert to boss-mode before starting tasks so that now, with the checklist, you can remain in worker-mode and just get on with things. You can often maximize the proactive attention required of you, or limit your propensity to make mistakes or miss things out. Here are some examples of environments or instances in which you could consider using checklists:

▶ Regular meetings such as team meetings or supervisions to quickly help set the agenda.

▶ Regular assignments, such as running the same event or shipping the same products over and over again.

▶ Regular trips or annual holidays, ensuring nothing gets forgotten when preparing or packing for the trip.

▶ Regular shopping lists (I have one for my regular online food shop and we have another for our weekly office supplies shopping).

▶ Distribution lists, such as who to invite to events or who to send Christmas cards to.

Checklists give you confidence and reduce friction. The beauty of checklists is that you can update them based on feedback of anything missed and in response to anything new. Checklists sit inside your digital reference library as a secret weapon of productivity. If you're running your own business or working in a team, checklists are the beginning of process and systems design and as a result, are the first step on the road to delegation and automation.

A LARGE RUBBISH BIN

The Productivity Ninja recognizes that one of the most important productivity tools in their armoury is the humble bin. Getting ruthless is much more difficult if you don't have somewhere to throw unwanted paper. Digitally, it's also worth spending a few moments with the settings of your computer's trash or deleted items folder. Ensure that it holds onto such items for a short period, giving you a bit more confidence to delete files and clean up with back up. It's also worth noting that if you're keeping your files on a cloud type service like Dropbox, these services usually keep a week's worth of history too, meaning that you can delete an item and still have time to retrieve it at a later date.

NINJA DECISION-MAKING

The purpose of the Organize phase is to gain clarity about all of the new inputs that you've captured or collected, preventing that feeling of information overload. By making decisions as and when new inputs arrive in your email inbox, in your brain or anywhere else, you'll instantly see if, how and where they fit in with your current projects and actions. The Zen-like calm that this engenders is what leaves you free to direct so much proactive attention towards Doing, free from the need to procrastinate, feel uncertain or frantically remind yourself of the decisions you'd subconsciously made but not consciously confirmed. But this level of calm productivity, while freeing, is not free. It takes Ninja-level preparedness through making decisions – systematically, diligently, ruthlessly – in order to remain calm and create the space necessary to think.

*REMEMBER: THINKING IS THE **HARDEST WORK** THERE IS …*

THE CORD DIAGRAM: STEP BY STEP

We are now going to practise using the CORD diagram that I showed you briefly earlier to get us to the Review stage.

The purpose of this diagram is to provide a constant reminder of how to move through the four different habits – and organizing your actions and other reminders in the middle of the diagram as well as you can is pivotal to its success. The empowering thing is that with any single input in the entire universe, following this diagram will bring it to the point that gets it off your mind, into your second brain and into the right position to get done. Anything. We're going to test this out for real in the next section, but for now, let's walk through the decision-making process.

At the top of the diagram is the Capture and Collect phase, which we've already covered. We now get into the Organize phase. For each of the inputs you have piled up in your in-tray, we'll be asking the set questions as follows. In the beginning you may find it helpful to put a copy of this diagram somewhere visible on your desk and refer to it as you go through the Organize phase. You can also download it from http://www.thinkproductive.co.uk/productivity-ninja-resources/ if you'd prefer a PDF!

If you practise these steps relentlessly, they'll become a habit and in the end you won't even need this diagram. It is certainly possible to train yourself to be decisive, even if you consider yourself to be naturally anything but – I am personally proof of that!

The CORD Productivity Model

CAPTURE

- Negs & ideas
- Phone
- Conversations

COLLECT

- Notes from meetings
- Email
- Paper & post
- Any other places to capture + collect from?

C — CAPTURE & COLLECT

O — ORGANIZE

Is there an action worth doing?

No →
- Rubbish
- Reference
- Good Ideas Park

Yes → Is it me next?

Yes → What's the next physical action?

No → Waiting For List → Chase needed?

Master Actions List
- Work out what's a priority for next week or next day
- Check up to date

Is there also a wider project?

Projects List
- Generate next physical actions
- Check up to date

Is there also a timed deadline?

Calendar
- Check behind and ahead for actions
- Check up to date

R — REVIEW

- Daily checklist
- Weekly checklist

D — DO

Daily To-Do List

IS THERE AN ACTION WORTH DOING? NO

If the answer is 'No', there are three possible options here:

1. Reference

2. Rubbish

3. The Good Ideas Park

Reference:

For plenty of the items you've accumulated on your desk, the Reference option will be the one to choose. If there's nothing for you to do, but it feels too important to throw away, this is where it goes. In dealing with a lot of potential reference material in one go, use the out tray or a designated space on your desk to pile up reference materials as you go – it's just as quick filing 20 things away in reference as filing two or three, so much more efficient to batch them up and do them all together in a time of inactive attention.

Rubbish:

Don't be afraid to throw things away – or recycle them if at all possible. Anything you're keeping just because keeping the paperwork triggers an action can be thrown away and the action added to your Master Actions List. For example, if you're keeping a whole brochure as a reminder to contact a new supplier, all you really need is a phone number and website address. Anything that can also be found online should be recycled. Why would you keep something for future use when it's effectively already kept more neatly inside your internet browser?! You'll be amazed at how much you can throw away.

The Good Ideas Park:

Be extremely choosy about the things you commit to. Saying 'No' to some useful and productive things you *could* be doing is an important part of making way for the really vital stuff either already on your lists or about to show up. Be ruthless, and use The Good Ideas Park to come back to some of these ideas in the future – they're safely parked there for now so you won't lose them. The Good Ideas Park can just be a simple list and you can put as many things on there as you like. After all, there's no commitment to *do* anything about these things.

IS THERE AN ACTION WORTH DOING? YES

OK, so there's definitely something to do here. The next question is whether you need to do something yourself, or whether there's any way you can leave the action to someone else – remember, the more you can stealth delegate to others to do, the more is getting done in the world! It's all about finding potential leverage.

IS IT ME NEXT? NO

THE WAITING FOR LIST

If you're able to delegate the doing elsewhere, you might want to keep track of it via your Waiting For List. You will be checking through your Waiting For List at least once a week, so this is where you'll be reminded to chase up those colleagues that haven't communicated back whether their actions are underway or completed. Obviously, if you have delegated something and don't care what the outcome is, or if you trust your colleague 100%, then you don't need to track it.

IS IT ME NEXT? YES

So is it going to be you doing the next physical action? Right. Time to step up. This is where the Productivity Ninja really shows their prowess. There are three small bits of thinking that must now happen, ideally in this order, to successfully record the action in the system.

1. *WHAT'S THE NEXT PHYSICAL ACTION?*

Add the action onto the Master Actions List, based on the categories we talked about earlier (Places, Attention-level and People). Remember, if the action is less than a couple of minutes, it might be just as quick to simply do it than to add it to your Master Actions List!

2. *IS THERE ALSO A PROJECT RELATING TO THIS?*

As well as adding to the Master Actions List, the second question is a check to see if there is a project here that is not yet on the Projects List. Creating a Project for it will allow you to keep on top of each subsequent action as the project continues. You'll come back to this regularly during the Review stage. Remember to make the project name a measurable target.

3. *IS THERE A DEADLINE I NEED TO CAPTURE ON MY CALENDAR TOO?*

Finally, if there's a deadline for the action, you may want to keep a note of the deadline in your calendar. I suggest if you're using Outlook or a similar digital calendar, that you use the 'All Day Appointments' so that such deadlines are held at the top of the day's section. I also use the colour red to delineate them from other activities. For warnings of upcoming deadlines or where the deadlined point is 'by this week' rather than by a specific day, I tend to use the Sunday of the upcoming week. This is because on Sundays I never manage my life using my Outlook calendar, so in effect the Sunday space is a dumping ground for all the things I'll pick up during my next Weekly Checklist and start to make plans for. A word of caution about this: setting deadlines yourself, *for yourself*, simply doesn't work – we know deep down that there are no consequences if we break it.

SO WHERE DOES IT ALL LIVE?
WHERE SHOULD I MANAGE MY LISTS?

We've talked a lot so far in this chapter about your second brain and the following lists:

▶ Daily To-Do list

▶ Master Actions List

▶ Projects List

▶ Waiting For List

▶ Good Ideas Park

So where should your second brain actually be? Where should you keep such lists? On the fridge, maybe? In a drawer or folder? In your notebook? On some desktop software? It seems like the possibilities are endless, but the answer is really very simple indeed. Keep them wherever you like! Wherever feels comfortable to you. Often, people attend our workshops and see others around them using smartphone apps, iPads and so on. They feel guilty that their lists are kept on pen and paper and start to think about shifting to a more technological approach. While I personally favour technology for managing lists, nothing can beat pen and paper for a lot of my capturing. Below, therefore, is a non-exhaustive list and you are very welcome to choose from beyond these parameters in choosing the best home for your lists!

PAPER NOTEBOOK OR DIARY

If you already manage your lists using your big, black A4 diary or your paper notebook, then this may well continue to be the best place for you. Chances are, you're going from managing a pretty standard to-do list to us now needing to make space for Master Actions List, Projects List, Waiting For List and Good Ideas Park. There are many ways to do this, but this seems to be the best one I've come across and is the one we recommend:

▶ **Use the inside back cover for your projects**

This is because your projects don't change hugely week to week, so if you're using a paper notebook or even a diary, you can bet that most of those projects will last for most of the time that the book is being used. You then use the inside back pages for your Master Actions and Waiting For Lists. For ease, keep the Good Ideas Park list somewhere else, such as in a digital reference file or on a piece of paper in a drawer. If you're using a diary, you can then take things from the Master Actions List and add them to the day in question.

▶ **Use the front of the notebook as normal**

Likewise, for a paper notebook, you still have the front section clear for capturing and collecting. Resist the temptation to capture straight onto the Master Actions List – give yourself the important discipline of going through the Ninja decision-making process, which is as much about saying no as it is categorizing the yeses. This is so that you have permission to have creative, wacky and sometimes bad ideas – without them accidentally ending up on your Master Actions List!

▶ **Tear out the back pages – the Master Actions List – when it gets messy**

You might choose to tear out these back pages once a week and be in a regular routine of doing it, but the trick is to do it just before it gets unwieldy. When a lot of the actions have been done and it's starting to look messy, this will start to prey on your confidence and clarity and will start to stress you out. If you're running out of room, this can sometimes be all you need to subconsciously start resisting adding things to the Master Actions List. It needs to be kept on top of.

WORD DOCUMENT OR TEXT FILES

Much like pen and paper, Microsoft Word is pretty ubiquitous and most people are fairly comfortable using it for basic lists, moving stuff around the page and so on. Word has the added advantage of allowing you to insert tables, select fonts, text sizes and so on, so that you can make your Master Actions List functional, colourful and easy to navigate. If you must save all of your lists in one Word document, use the following order:

1. **Daily To-Do List**
2. **Master Actions List**
3. **Waiting For List**
4. **Projects List**
5. **Good Ideas Park**

Since you want to create the most immediate access possible to your Daily To-Do List and Master Actions List, and need the others in this descending order of frequency, that's usually the best way to do it. Be careful here about things spilling onto the next pages and use the page break feature in Word to ensure that you have a solid line of separation here to avoid confusion. I would also recommend using two or three columns on the page, which will help avoid your Master Actions List becoming a wieldy ten-page document!

MICROSOFT OUTLOOK, LOTUS NOTES AND SIMILAR PROGRAMS

For years, Outlook has been my main program for email, calendar and contacts. I also used it for many years as my main task manager and while I've since moved away from it, I did so quite reluctantly: it's an underrated task manager! The reason so few people really love Outlook Tasks is that the power and flexibility of it is hidden away. What I always see when I work with someone and ask them to show me the Tasks section on their Outlook is the first seven things that person did when they started their job. People start out with the good intentions of using Tasks to keep track of everything; but Outlook's default settings capture everything onto one long list, which quickly repels people because they recognize that it's easy for important things to get lost in a long, amorphous list. The trick with Outlook Tasks is to use the Categories function, which allows you to create categories such as:

▶ **Office – Proactive**
▶ **Home**
▶ **Lisa Waiting**

You can also use Categories in different ways to incorporate more than one kind of sub-list. For example, you could use the '#' symbol to denote Places and an 'at' (@) symbol for People-based lists. This will group types of lists together and make it easier to manage them. It's also a great tool for creating sub-lists – just make sure you make the most important lists the most accessible.

Have a play around with it, and don't be afraid to tailor an unorthodox set of lists to your own requirements: it's your second brain, after all.

EXCEL

If you're someone very familiar with Excel, you may decide that it's the best place for you to keep lists. I've seen some really good uses of Excel, using different tabs for different places and lists. I've also seen it used well with all the information in a single sheet and then using filters to chose whether you're in Projects list view, Master Action List view or Daily To-Do List view.

INDEX CARDS: THE 'HIPSTER PDA'

American productivity writer and speaker Merlin Mann coined the term 'Hipster PDA' to describe creating a set of lists out of a stack of simple index cards – the kind you use to remind you of key points in a speech. These can be a great way to keep your lists portable, accessible and easily navigable. Use a different index card for each Place. Like paper, it's harder to 'slice and dice' the information any which way (as you can with Outlook) so that you always have what you need, at your fingertips. And when a particular card gets a bit shabby, just replace it!

WEB-BASED 'TO-DO' APPS

Probably the most flexible and functional place to keep your lists is in a dedicated web-based list manager. There are a number of benefits to using this kind of software. Firstly, it's purpose built for the job and the good ones come with features that you can easily use to manage sub-lists across Place, Attention and People fairly easily. As well as good categories for your Master Actions List, you can also group those same actions by Project, thereby giving you a really easy way of keeping Projects List and Master Actions List in the same place – just change the view to see whatever you need to see at that time!

For example, if I'm with Jim I can pull up only the tasks tagged with Jim's name. Or if I'm at home but feeling good, I can pull up all those tasks that are on both my 'Home' list as well as marked as 'Proactive Attention'. Or if I'm in Review-mode and I want to look at all my projects, I can just see that.

Web-based apps and their phone and tablet equivalents also give the easiest options for text-based searching and tagging, so it's possible to get straight to the piece of information you need very quickly and easily. In fact, the possibilities to engineer and re-engineer the data into the most useful formats are almost endless. That is a great strength of web-based apps. It's also occasionally a liability; people get distracted by drooling over a slightly better way of managing their lists rather than settling for what's functional and then getting on with some serious doing. It's a fine line!

MOBILE PHONE & TABLET APPS

While many people use web-based apps, very few of them use them without also using the equivalent iPhone, android or tablet app too. When choosing which web-based app to go for, you should also have an eye on the opportunities for taking the same tool mobile and make sure you pick one that seems functional and useful across both computer screen and mobile device. Below, I list the main things to look for when making this decision. My only suggestion really is to check out as many YouTube videos, customer reviews, screenshots and product tours as you can, all of which will give you a good feel for the style, value and functionality of each app.

WHAT TO LOOK FOR WHEN CHOOSING AN APP:

1. Functionality

Above all, you should look for one that has at least the following:

▶ A way to add Projects (often called 'lists').

▶ A way to create sub-list categories for your Master Actions List (often called 'contexts' or 'tags'). They will often have both a tags and a context function, in which case you can use both for different things!

▶ A way to mark priorities, such as high, medium and low (this can either be used as it is intended, or actually used for Proactive, Active and Inactive attention).

▶ Ability to synchronize with your phone – this is where you start to get the added benefit of being able to view your lists or capture new ideas anytime, wherever you are!

Other added extras to look for here include:

▶ Good search functionality and the facility to save some of your regular searches.

▶ Date and alarm functionality – personally I trust my system enough not to need to schedule a lot of things by date and my system is enough of a reminder, but many people find this a good additional facility.

▶ Location/GPS functionality – the ability to have location-specific actions pop up on your screen when your software detects you're in that location (again, not a necessity, but pretty cool!).

▶ Ability to capture straight into the program from other places. (For example, one of the most popular apps, Remember the Milk, allows you to capture items inside it by sending them as tweets on Twitter, through Gmail and through web-browser plugins).

▶ Ability to synchronize with another program such as Outlook (often this is a paid for added extra rather than inherent in the program itself).

▶ Ability to export your data out of that program if you decide it's no longer working well for you. (This is also a nice safety feature if you're worried about one of these apps going bust and your data being stuck in there, which is admittedly pretty unlikely!)

2. Reliability & track record

With any piece of software you're trusting to store a lot of data on your behalf in 'the cloud', there's always a small risk that there may be short periods where their servers go down and all of your lists are inaccessible. While this risk is minimal – and further minimized if you also have the data synchronized to your phone anyway – there's also a small longer-term risk that the software has its brief moment of glory before dying a death, either to be taken out of existence or to continue to exist but in a decaying, unsupported and unloved state. Without any support, you have no way of contacting anyone if things go wrong, and with something as trusted as your ability to stay calm and productive at work, you need to know you're leaving that in good hands.

Read reviews of the software to look for any issues of reliability, notice what's being said about customer support if things go wrong and make sure you're entrusting your valuable data to someone with a track record that suggests they're able to look after it. Reviews count. Again, being an early adopter is fine if you like added risk with no promise of return, but for the rest of us, far better to go with the safety and security of a company with a strong track record.

3. Stylishness

There are one or two newer players on the market that are really starting to ramp up the style stakes. As long as they have all of the above, that's fine. Stylish user interfaces that make it both easy and fun to use are of course a big part of the appeal for the tech-savvy. If something feels easier to use, you'll instinctively use it that little bit more. Anything that makes it a joy to interact with your lists and keeps you coming back for more is certainly to be encouraged. Be careful that it's not just style over substance, though.

4. Price

Last and certainly least in terms of consideration should be price. This is for two reasons. Firstly, at the more accessible end of the market, you have apps that are free on the website version and either free or ridiculously cheap on the phone and tablet app versions. Many are completely free, but don't prioritize the free ones over the ones that cost a small amount – get over that little mental barrier and pay for something if it's going to be better! Paying a couple of pounds for a good phone app that you'll use every day for years should never be an issue when you think how

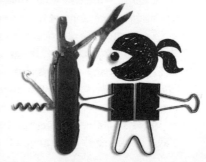

easily you might waste that money elsewhere. The value that the right app generates by comparison is huge. Likewise, at the expensive end of the market, there are a couple of very highly respected apps that cost some serious money and yet I know people who feel so happy using them that the money is just not something that crosses their mind. Think about it – even spending £100 on the perfect app has paid itself back very quickly if you imagine the extra revenue, extra commission, pay rises or reduced stress that it brings. If you think about all the hobbies and pastimes that you're happy to spend money on in order to reduce your stress, it should hardly be an issue spending a few pounds a month on the right app if it really works for you.

WHICH APP?

So if you're convinced that you should look at a dedicated list-management tool, which one should you go for? Here are my top picks. (I have *no* commercial incentive to endorse any of these, so this is completely objective, in case you were wondering.)

Toodledo

This has been the app of choice in the Think Productive office for a while now. It's what I personally use too and I love it. It certainly doesn't have the prettiest interface (especially its iPad app, which is quite dull), but the website interface is very easy to use, it synchronizes perfectly between phone and website and it has everything you need. The web version is free and the iPhone and iPad apps are no more than a couple of pounds to buy. Toodledo keeps it simple and functional and we love it!

Todoist

Todoist has many admirers and works on many different platforms. One of Think Productive's Productivity Ninjas, Lee, is a Todoist obsessive. The website has a clear but colourful drag-and-drop design, and its phone and tablet apps are perhaps slightly better than Toodledo's. It also has a really nice range of other features such as plug-ins to integrate directly with different browsers, email systems and calendars. We often receive messages from people who have been on one of Lee's workshops and are extolling the virtues of Todoist after they were inspired by seeing Lee demonstrate his own set-up! Again, the free account gives you everything you need, and the phone and tablet apps are free too, but there's a subscription of around £18 (around $30) per year for some of the advanced features.

Pocket Informant

One of the favourites among Apple users, Pocket Informant is slick, easy to use and is Productivity Ninja Matthew's app of choice. It has a good search functionality and while it costs a bit more (around £15) here, and $15 in the US, it's definitely worth investigating. It combines calendar and tasks quite nicely too, by synching tasks with a Toodledo account and calendar with Google Calendar. Add integration with Evernote and web access and it's a great all-rounder. My personal view is that this one beats 'Things' which is similar in style, price and Apple exclusivity.

OmniFocus

Another Apple-only app. Omni involved Merlin Mann, creator of Inbox Zero and 43folders.com in the design of OmniFocus and it really shows in how functional it is. It comes with a pretty hefty price tag (around £40 or $80) but has a lot of loyal followers and inbuilt features that help with Weekly Checklists as well as the usual list management. It's extremely slick and is probably what I'd use myself if it was multi-platform. Our Irish Ninja, Keith uses this one and jokes that the cost is a benefit in itself: once you've paid 'proper money' for an app, you're invested in it and less likely to waste time switching around!

Nozbe

Michael Sliwinski, creator of Productive! Magazine, is the guy behind Nozbe. He built it to be the perfect app for implementing David Allen's *Getting Things Done* system and you can see that the software has all the hallmarks of a labour of love. Again, it's not the cheapest on the market – it has a monthly subscription cost of around £10 ($15) but it also has a band of very loyal followers who love it. It's worth checking out.

Evernote

In truth, Evernote wasn't built solely as a productivity tool and its list management capabilities are (currently) limited. But I have seen people customize Evernote to be a great list manager alongside all the other cool things that it does. We're told that the future of Evernote will be the development of more productivity elements to go alongside its status as the best 'digital filing cabinet' out there. There's something really exciting about the thought of managing your lists right in the same program as a lot of the supporting materials relating to those projects and actions and it'll certainly be worth keeping an eye on it in the next couple of years as it could seriously steal the show!

How to choose where to put your lists ...

All the choice available may seem bewildering: not only are there hundreds of apps out there, but you could also choose Word, Excel, paper, Outlook, index cards and a myriad of other options too. So if you're torn, remember two important things:

1. It's much better to go with something you can see yourself using than the thing you think you *should* use. If your boss is chivvying you towards Outlook, or peer pressure is swaying you to explore the technological solution when you're happier with a pen and paper, stick to what you know or feel comfortable with.

2. It's much better to stick with a system than risk wasting a lot of time and attention regularly switching around. While switching every two to three years can be a nice way of forcing yourself to freshen up your lists, avoid any time that feels like additional management of lists. By its very nature, the additional ten minutes spent on lists is ten minutes fewer available for *doing*. Since we're in the business of productivity not simply being organized, be very wary of falling into this trap. Perfection is an enemy; 'just enough to be super-functional' should be your mantra.

EXERCISE: NINJA DECISION-MAKING

What you'll need: Your list manager of choice, your diary/calendar, your in-tray/waiting tray/out-tray, paper and digital reference systems, a recycling bin

How long it'll take: 1–2 hours

Ninja mindset: Preparedness, Zen-like Calm, Ruthlessness

The purpose of the Organize phase is to gain clarity about all of your projects and deal with each of the new inputs that you've captured or collected. In this exercise, we're going to replicate the day-to-day art of Ninja decision-making with all of the things in your tray from the previous 'Big Capture and Collect' exercise.

The object of the exercise is to get that in-tray *completely empty*. In doing so, you'll have clarified all of the actions and projects that relate to each of the items in your tray, and will have recorded them on your various lists.

INSTRUCTIONS

▶ Pick up the top item from your in-tray.

▶ Follow the CORD diagram, asking the 'Organize' questions to decide on the next physical actions, projects and any timed deadlines.

▶ Repeat with each item in your in-tray, one at a time, until the tray is empty (and your Master Actions List is full!).

> 'I'm not telling you it's going to be easy; I'm telling you it's going to be worth it.'
> – Art Williams

RULES

There are only a few rules here, but they're important:

1. You can fool others, but you can never fool yourself – never shirk making the tough decisions, as this act of procrastination only leads to increased nags and future stress. There's no escaping here. You're a Ninja. You're going to apply ruthless focus and get this done.

2. No cherry picking the good stuff. Just like we did with emails, work one by one. Pick up the item on the top of the pile and don't put it back down until you're ready to move that piece of paper to your reference pile, the rubbish bin, or wherever else you've decided it needs to go.

3. Do the quick actions there and then. Pile together the things that need filing. Work on the principle that if you can get stuff done in just a couple of minutes, do it as you pick it up rather than recording these on your Master Actions List: better to get some momentum going while the decision is fresh in your mind and save your lists for the meatier, longer items.

4. Ignore all other distractions at this point – turn off your email, put your phone on silent and bury it at the bottom of your bag. Focus on the hard thinking that this exercise will generate and focus on developing the ruthless decision-making habits that these questions are designed to encourage.

HOW LONG WILL THIS TAKE?

It's really hard to predict how long this exercise will take to complete because everyone is different. It's rare that it ever takes less than half an hour. Most people can complete it within an hour or so. Set aside two hours so that you don't feel rushed and you should be able to complete it during that time. It's not a competition though – if it takes several hours to get the first thinking done, that's just because you had a lot to get under control; you'll also be one of the people who benefits the most from the momentum that follows.

AT THE END OF THE EXERCISE, YOU SHOULD HAVE ...

▶ An empty in-tray

▶ A pretty full Master Actions List, broken down into Places and maybe Attention and People too

▶ A rubbish bin full of scraps of paper and perhaps even a big pile of old reports, leaflets and so on

▶ Your emerging Project List, Waiting For List and Good Ideas Park

▶ Maybe one or two deadlines in the calendar.

HOW DO YOU FEEL?

How do you feel getting all of that stuff under control? For many, it's quite a profound feeling. It's not something we usually spend time doing, unless we're in the throes of a major event, like going off on leave, finishing or starting a job, moving to a new city or doing a big spring clean, but why not experience that sense of completeness and clarity much more regularly? The CORD Productivity Model and your emerging second brain will develop the habits to get you back in control at least once a week, if not once a day!

Do you feel a sudden burst of energy? It can be incredibly empowering knowing exactly what's on your plate that needs to be done, and exactly how you need to do it. Such energy brings on periods of hyper-productivity, which helps to build the motivation to keep everything under control, which in turn helps build the momentum to want to get more done. If you've been reading the word 'momentum' throughout this book and not quite understanding why, hopefully now you can!

Are you a Ninja?

► A Ninja is agile and eliminates stress to work in the present moment; their second brain is organized to tell them exactly what they could be doing at any point in time.

► A Ninja is prepared and knows exactly what they have on their plate.

► A Ninja achieves Zen-like calm and is relaxed and confident about what they *can't* do right now because their second brain is up to date and reassures them that what they're not doing is under control.

8. THE REVIEW HABIT

'To make knowledge productive, we will have to learn to see both forest and tree. We will have to learn to connect.'
– Peter Drucker

The sense of momentum when you get on a roll makes the Doing part of the CORD process seem effortless. It comes from the clarity and control you feel, which in turn comes from your new habit of making decisions about your work as and when such inputs and decision points arise. Far too often, we leave this type of thinking – about exactly what needs to be done – until a deadline is looming, risking making bad decisions under pressure. Even if we pull through with the right decisions, we're still cutting it fine, and it's stressful.

However, keeping on top of the inputs and decisions on a daily or weekly basis is difficult. The non-Ninja way of handling this is to constantly flit between worker-mode and boss-mode, convinced that there's still more undefined work to do in the other mode, never reaching conclusions, gaining *some* clarity but also creating stress by leaving many stones unturned.

There is a better way. It would of course be nice if that better way was to 'just get on with doing stuff' and ditch the boss altogether. But the truth is that we do need our boss-selves and we need them to go on a leadership training weekend and learn some better skills! We need total clarity from them, not these fleeting moments of, 'Oh yeah, must do ...' or 'That's a good idea, let's ...'

If you add up all of these small moments of thinking about our work, it would total several hours a week. Yet this time never really gives us any benefit because we don't tend to finish the process of thinking. In fact, it more often results in more stress than in clarity. A Ninja takes thinking seriously and separates thinking from doing.

So, as discussed in the previous chapter, we're going to create two checklists to provide the structure and consistency to aid your Review habit: Weekly and Daily.

To be clear, these checklists are NOT to-do lists. They are simply the lists of the consistent thinking or behaviours that make up your Daily or Weekly review time.

Both of these reviews are the times in your day or your week for your boss-self to take control, which is why we're using checklists – because checklists have been a major secret weapon of bosses and industrialists the world over, from Toyota to Tesco.

Checklists bring consistency to the process. In Michael Gerber's fantastic book, *The E-Myth Revisited* he makes one of the most powerful cases for the humble checklist I've ever come across. One of the examples Gerber uses is the checklists that make up the operating manual to run a franchised business, such as McDonald's.

Whatever you think of the food in McDonald's, there's no denying its consistency – a Big Mac in Moscow tastes the same as one in London or New York or the local place a mile from your house. It's this consistency that is at the heart of McDonald's customers' expectations. People go there because they know what they're going to get. Imagine if you could produce work as consistently and reliably – *and* with as little day-to-day thinking as McDonald's use to produce their burgers and fries! The beauty of checklists is that McDonald's don't need to have trained chefs making the burgers, they just need people who can follow the checklist – which was once devised by a trained chef. So checklists also aid your ability to delegate, help you to share your work or have people cover for you when you're not there. Checklists help produce the clarity that produces momentum and checklists reduce the uncertainty that causes friction.

Think about the Review habit as the time when your boss-self and worker-self sit down together and plan out the work. It's your very own line management supervision, planning meeting and thinking time all rolled into one. Good communication between boss and worker saves time and eliminates mistakes. Likewise, good Review habits promote clarity, reduce stress, increase control and boost productivity.

THE WEEKLY CHECKLIST

A concentrated thinking period of somewhere between an hour and two hours a week is enough to ensure the playful, productive momentum and control we need for the rest of the week. During this chapter I'll show you how to develop your most critical Review tool: the Weekly Checklist. It's the crème de la crème of boss time; time for reflecting, deciding, re-prioritizing, strategizing, visioning and breathing new life into projects and actions in preparation for the next set of battles. It's the ultimate moment for preparedness, mindfulness and occasional unorthodoxy that you wouldn't have harnessed without having time set aside for concentrated thinking. The Weekly Checklist ensures that your Master Actions List is up to date and keeps you familiar with what's on the list for the week ahead.

THE DAILY CHECKLIST

'Beware the barrenness of a busy life.'
– Socrates

The Daily Checklist is a very short piece of concentrated thinking – around five minutes – that sets you up for the day. It's also the moment for you to make a Daily To-Do List, by looking through your Master Actions List and picking out the actions that you're going to work for that day. It's the ideal start to the day – a moment of clarity and calm before all the noise of emails and other inputs come in. The Daily Checklist helps to develop a strong and productive habit. This is a great example of where our second brain provides the intuition and intelligence (the Daily Checklist) and the memory (Master Actions List) to help our real brain stay productive. Think about how your real brain feels on a wet Thursday morning after a bad night's sleep – hopefully you're starting to see here why the second brain is so necessary and so effective.

'The ability to simplify means to eliminate the unnecessary so that the necessary may speak.'
– Hans Hofmann

DON'T THINK, JUST DO. EFFORTLESSLY.

With the Daily and Weekly Checklists, you may think that I've just asked you to add two more hours' work to your week. I have done nothing of the sort. Much of the thinking you're attempting through the Weekly Checklist and Daily Checklist processes is thinking you'd spend far *more* time doing if you weren't using these processes – the difference is that at the moment, you don't consciously separate it from the rest of your work and it takes longer because you have to keep revisiting it, never sure that you've got full clarity.

The really beautiful thing about your Weekly Checklist and Daily Checklist is that they separate thinking from doing. In these couple of hours a week, you cover the thinking, leaving the rest of the week for doing. Your worker-self is given such clarity about what needs to be done that their only decisions are to decide when, not why and how. All you need to do for the rest of the week is trust your Master Actions List, think about your attention levels and stay self-aware to keep on top of your game. Just picture it. No more thinking to do about priorities, politics and possibilities: just unadulterated doing.

Those that question the need for such a formal process as the Weekly Checklist quickly change their minds when they experience the freedom that it provides. Using this process delivers freedom from the need to constantly flit between boss- and worker-modes, freedom to just get on and do your work from the safe position of knowing you're doing the right work in the right way.

SEE THE TIMBER FROM THE TREES

'Thinking for yourself is still a radical act.'
– Nancy Kline

The density and complexity of our overloaded world means that while we spend most of our days in the trenches, we rarely get enough perspective on our overall position to really 'see the timber from the trees'. I describe the Weekly

Checklist and the Daily Checklist processes as the time that you observe your work from *above* your work. It gives you helicopter-level strategic vision, and believe me, is powerful, cathartic and calming. The calming effect of going through a deep, thorough Weekly Checklist is really quite profound. I often finish my reviews feeling lighter, more confident, more comfortable in my own skin, more agile, and more up to the tasks ahead. It's like your boss-self just gave you the greatest pep talk to leave you feeling inspired and re-energized. Doing a Daily Checklist first thing in the morning before all the madness hits helps you to have the agility and confidence to tackle things head on when they come along. Doing a Weekly Checklist on a Friday afternoon means you have the confidence and peace of mind to switch off at the weekend and enjoy whatever you have planned. Or if you choose to do your Weekly Checklist on a Monday, even just knowing that you've got your Weekly Checklist diarized to kick-start your Monday is enough to aid the weekend switch-off on Friday evening! We will look at your optimum time to do your Weekly Checklist in the upcoming exercise.

PALATABLE *PROJECT MANAGEMENT*

Some of the Weekly Checklist items we'll talk about are just common sense, old-fashioned project management. A lot of people confuse project management with project planning. They get obsessed with and dependent on project planning software or intricate charts when what really matters is that someone is managing, checking and re-adjusting the plan on a regular enough basis to keep things agile and fit for purpose. The detailed, upfront style of project management is tiresome: it's characterized by over-thinking, over-planning and ultimately, under-delivering. However, if you've ever been part of a project steered by a really excellent professional project manager, you'll know that there's magic in there somewhere. The Weekly Checklist provides just enough of that to steer things brilliantly, but not so much to make thinking become a burden.

This is the time in your week for your Inner project manager to step up to the plate. It provides the rigour and discipline you need to expertly steer not just one project, but every project on your Project List. You use the checklist to generate the next set of actions for each and every project, keeping you fully aware of dependencies and inter-dependencies ... without the need for all that over-planning. It's not project management in a traditional sense, more a 'project management approach'.

So, let's discuss those two key review checklists in more detail, and then it's your turn to create your own.

THE STAGES OF THE WEEKLY CHECKLIST

Everyone's checklist is different, although there are some consistent themes in a consistent order that characterize the Weekly Checklist. At the end of this chapter we'll go through these stages in more detail and build your personalized weekly checklist, but for now the five key stages are as follows:

1. **Get all of your inputs back to zero**

2. **Get your second brain up to date**

3. **Think ahead**

4. **Get ready**

5. **Questions**

Let's look at each of these elements in turn.

1. *GET ALL OF YOUR INPUTS BACK TO ZERO*

The first part of the Weekly Checklist is to check that you're on top of the Capture and Collect and Organize habits that we discussed in the preceding chapters. In an average week, I may only be in the office for a couple of days, so while I have access to emails 'on the run' and can continue capturing ideas and organizing, it often takes that quiet time back at base to truly catch up on capturing, collecting and organizing. One of the strengths of the Weekly Checklist is that it gives you a level of consistency in knowing that no matter how chaotic your world becomes, you have time set aside to catch up and get back in control. If I know that things are particularly out of control after a few days on the road, I may initially work on getting these stages back towards zero and clarity before I officially get into boss-mode and start the checklist process. It's difficult to move on to the later stages of reviewing and thinking ahead if you still have inputs lurking around in need of attention. So this first stage is about getting everything back together: emails, the notes from your meetings, the new nags and ideas that have come from a busy week, the remembering actions or ideas from conversations with your boss and anything else in between.

2. *GET YOUR SECOND BRAIN UP TO DATE*

OK, so you've cleared the decks again. You're now ready to enter full on, Ninja-level boss-mode! I liken this next part to deep-sea diving. It's like diving into the depths of your second brain; you check what your second brain says is on your plate and make sure it's accurate. This is about listening to yourself. Are there any 'unconscious projects' that you

haven't named and recorded? Any that you've been thinking about or contemplating whether to do, but haven't started consciously managing in your system? For your lists to truly become part of your second brain, you need to trust they have everything covered. As soon as you start to feel that there's a whole other series of projects that are not part of this system, the system is no longer the source of clarity, but another source of stress. So stage two is really about reorientation: going back through the calendar for the last couple of weeks, checking what's ahead, remembering the projects you are still working on but perhaps haven't given much attention to this week – in fact getting a good grip on your current situation, so that your second brain has a complete 'memory' and so that you continue to trust in it.

During stages 2 and 3 of your Weekly Checklist, the thinking you do here is crucial to your entire week. It's the time when your main lists interact with each other: the Projects List, Master Actions List, Waiting List and Calendar. Each of these four components is fine on its own, but it's bringing them all together that generates the confidence, trust and control. Doing this thinking well now allows you to forget about almost everything other than just your Master Actions List and Calendar for the next seven days. Everything you need is on your Master Actions List for you to look at each day and your Calendar provides the guide to any time-specific things you need to think about.

3. *THINK AHEAD*

The Think Ahead stage is where you start to visualize the coming week and ensure that your Master Actions List does indeed contain all of the necessary actions you can be working on. Remember we talked about the idea of 'next physical actions'? This is a time in your week to generate the new actions for each and every project you're currently committed to working on. You'll be looking through everything that is on your Projects List, Master Actions List, Good Ideas Park, and also looking out for input from the wider world that might affect how you work on them. The aim here is to stay ahead of the game. What are the new things that need to happen with each of these projects over the next week or so? And what are the obstacles that could stand in the way? This is also the time that you start to do the important thinking about what gets prioritized and what gets deliberately neglected.

4. *GET READY*

Getting ready is like preparing your kid's bag for school the night before to avoid early morning panic, or preparing a great packed lunch to take to work tomorrow – we know it's a better way to be, but we still rarely prepare in advance when there are better things to do the night before! But in the quiet calm of your Weekly Checklist, a Ninja creates the time and space to think about what to do to make things happen as effortlessly as possible in the week ahead. You need to think about what you'll need for the week ahead, who you'll need to talk to, and when your periods of proactive attention are likely to be. These are important, stress reduction tactics, and especially important for those of us who don't spend our working weeks in just one office: so if you travel around or spend different days in different places, this stage is all about removing residual panic about places, things, documents, tickets and the like.

5. *QUESTIONS*

The final stage of the Weekly Checklist is really designed to promote mindfulness and allow us to revisit the idea of 'conscious competence' so that we continuously improve. It's where your boss-self and your worker-self have a quick reflective and preparatory conversation with each other, recognizing jobs well done and also  what might be hard in the next week. It also promotes ruthless focus on what really matters. Design your own Weekly Checklist questions carefully – practised properly, these will ensure continued focus on the things that might otherwise get forgotten in the humdrum of everyday life. I like to make sure mine cover topics like focus, ruthless-ness, resistance, health and happiness, but everyone's will be different. Asking the bigger questions regularly helps to develop self-awareness, and encourages a mindful approach to both productivity and life in general.

In the exercise that follows, we'll build a tailored checklist for you. The feeling at the end of the Weekly Checklist can be pretty euphoric. That euphoria is built on consistent hard thinking and the result of having made so many of the decisions you'd been putting off or were sub-consciously not even aware of. As such it's also likely to be one of the more tiring parts of your week. So at the end of a Weekly Checklist, give yourself a reward for finishing it – it's such a useful process and your worker-self will thank you tenfold in the coming days. After all, it's so rare and so thrilling to work for a boss-self that gives such clear instructions! For now, celebrate a vital job well done. Your reward could be as simple as a walk in the park, a slice of cake with your after-noon cup of tea, half an hour of rest and relaxation, some new music or whatever you fancy. It doesn't really matter what you choose, it just matters that you build a positive state of mind that recognizes the importance of getting clarity and control – and the occasional dif-ficulty in getting there.

WHEN SHOULD YOU DO THE WEEKLY CHECKLIST?

'Until we are distracted, solitude is a thinking environment.'
– Nancy Kline

The Weekly Checklist is, as you've probably realized by now, a critical element of your productivity. Doing it consis-tently and well really is the key to successful knowledge work. How, then, should you give yourself the best possible chance of making this important habit stick? When is the best time to schedule it so you're most likely to see it through? Well, there's no one specific time that's universally the best to be in Review-mode, but there are a few general principles you can follow here:

TIME *AND ATTENTION*

Find time in your week where you are able to schedule two hours and where you are also likely to have proactive attention and good energy levels. If, when that time comes, your attention feels much less than proactive and you're less than raring to go, reschedule the checklist for some time in the next couple of days rather than trying to struggle through it.

SPACE

As well as sufficient time and attention, you'll need space. Choose somewhere where you can lay out your papers easily but also a space where you're unlikely to face interruptions, distractions and other attention threats. Many people whose work is 100% office-based get permission to spend the Weekly Checklist time away from the office, perhaps in a meeting room on a different floor, in a coffee shop or at home. A good Weekly Checklist feels like the rest of the world stands still and allows you to catch up. Think about your ability to screen out everything else that might get in your way.

ROUTINE

The final factor to consider is trying to get into a regular routine so that you make your Weekly Checklist a habit. Having your 'checklist time' at the same time every week turns it from being another thing to think about to being part of your regular routine, a ritual that over time you don't even think about the need to do; you just do it.

My personal reflections on this are …

> **Mondays suck.** There are too many other people in the world that want a piece of my attention on a Monday morning and by lunchtime I'm in flows I find difficult to break.

The office sucks. I can't guarantee the right kind of protective wall around my attention, unless it's a day when I'm there on my own or a lot of people are away.

I love trains. The psychological and physical space I get from a long train ride is perfect review territory. I travel a lot, but also do a regular trip by train to watch Aston Villa. Living in Brighton, the train ride from Brighton to Birmingham is my default review time and plenty long enough to complete my Weekly Checklist (at least two uninterrupted hours and a nice 'change of pace' break in the middle to cross London on the tube!).

Fridays are great. If there's no Villa game on, I tend to opt for Friday mornings at home. I have more energy early on a Friday than I do by mid-afternoon on a Friday and if I get it done before lunchtime, there's a whole series of chase-ups and actions from me reviewing my lists that hits everyone else's inboxes before they leave for the weekend.

Early mornings are great. Getting into the office an hour before everyone else, or staying at home for the first part of the day and focusing in without the surrounding noise is a great way to complete a Weekly Checklist.

THE DAILY CHECKLIST

If the Weekly Checklist is mental deep-sea diving to ensure your system and your brain are on the same page, then the Daily Checklist is dipping your toe in the water to remind yourself of its temperature. The Daily Checklist is a very short process designed to kick-start your day. It's not compulsory: if you have a day out of the office, out of the normal flow of things then it's not even that necessary to do a Daily Checklist at all. However, if you're going to spend a good proportion of the day working through items on your Master Actions List, then this process will turbo-charge the day.

FIVE QUESTIONS, *FIVE* MINUTES

The Daily Checklist comprises five questions that you should ask your-self. In total answering all of these questions should take no more than five minutes.

1. **Calendar:** what's in my calendar today and are there any deadlines looming in the next three to five days?

2. **Big Rocks:** what would a good day of actions look like today? What would I have ticked off? What's the one or two or three 'big rocks' that need some focus and mental heavy lifting?

3. **Resistance:** out of those tasks, which am I most likely to resist wanting to do? And why? (Once you've decided this, move this to first on your list for today and do it while you're feeling fresh! How nice to know that once done, the day is easier from then on in, having done the hardest thing first!). We'll talk more about big rocks and resistance in the next chapter.

4. **Attention Management:** out of those tasks, which of them requires the intense concentration of my proactive attention, and which can be done during inactive periods? (Use this question to start to shape the schedule of your day.)

5. **Dependencies:** are any of the things I've chosen time-dependent, people-dependent or resource-dependent? (In other words, is there a necessity to *when* any of these tasks get done?)

At the end of this brief process, you can then create your Daily To-Do List, perhaps by marking some items on your Master Actions List as today's 'Daily To-Do's' and then setting the software to view only these, or you might have created a separate Daily To-Do List on a piece of paper or Post-it note if you find that easier for added focus.

You might also like to decide as you do your Daily Checklist process to schedule the times or frequency during the day when you'll deal with your email and do other Capture and Collect phase and Organize phase activities, so that you're really clear about how much of the day you'll be able to spend in Do-mode. Time, attention, priorities, tactics and mindfulness – all in a fabulous five-minute burst of thinking!

HOW TO PRIORITIZE YOUR REVIEW TIME WHEN YOU'RE UP AGAINST IT

It can be so easy to try and skip Review altogether and get out of the habit of doing it. Coming into the office and immediately turning on your emails is a sure-fire route straight to everyone else's priorities rather than taking that Daily Checklist time to think about your own. And likewise the Weekly Checklist can slip down the pecking order if it seems like there are a hundred things that you need to get off your desk by five o'clock and you're under real pressure to deliver. Never see the Review phase as a luxury or a burden. It saves you time, it reduces stress, helps you manage your attention and makes your whole job feel like putting cherries on cakes again. It's a necessity, an asset and the time invested in it pays off in spades.

WHERE TO KEEP YOUR CHECKLISTS

The main part of this exercise is going to be you choosing suggestions from the above lists for each of the five stages of the Weekly Checklist. However, before we get into that, let's have a think about where your checklist should actually live. There are several options:

▶ Inside a to-do app – some of the to-do apps we looked at, such as OmniFocus or Nozbe, feature dedicated sections for review checklists. You can also set up recurring tasks in most to-do apps that will mimic this, but make sure that in doing so, you have a sense of the 'journey' that a Weekly Checklist takes – you will want to develop your own very particular order in which each of the elements of the checklist are ticked off.

▶ If paper-based, use the inside front cover of your diary or notepad.

▶ Microsoft Word or similar. This is a great option, enabling you to print out a fresh checklist each week and then physically tick the items off, one by one.

▶ Wherever you keep your digital reference materials (Evernote, OneNote, Outlook, etc). Again, this can be printed weekly and can also sit next to any other checklists that you're using.

Personally, I use a Word document and print a stack of new Weekly Checklists every 10 weeks or so, which I carry with me in my laptop bag everywhere I go. That way, if ever I feel the spontaneous need to get deep into Review-mode, I have a printed Weekly Checklist close to hand, whenever and wherever that happens. I keep other check-lists, such as my Daily Checklist in Outlook and Evernote. Your Weekly Checklist doesn't need to be comprehensive or complex. In the exer-cise below your job is to pick those elements that matter to you, not reproduce all the possibilities.

As time goes on, you'll also find that you can tweak your checklist, add new and more creative questions in there, or cut out some of the parts that are proving less needed or useful than you first imagined. I tend to review and tweak my checklist every three to six months as my work and life change. Reviewing your review time is the ultimate geek activity, but well worth it once in a while!

EXERCISE: DEVELOPING MY WEEKLY CHECKLIST

What you'll need:	Boss-mode proactive thinking
How long it'll take:	1 hour
Ninja mindset:	Weapon-savvy, Preparedness

Below are the five stages of the Weekly Checklist, complete with some suggestions to help you with designing your own. You can also go to http://www.thinkproductive.co.uk/productivity-ninja-resources/ and download a template for your Weekly (and Daily) Checklists. Design your very own checklist by choosing what you need to focus on during your weekly review time. Once you've done this, you might like to transfer the final Checklist into a Word document, or type it into your calendar. Again, remember you don't need to use everything here! Make this just about what you need and don't overdo it.

THE FIVE STAGES OF MY WEEKLY CHECKLIST:

STAGE 1. GET ALL OF MY INPUTS BACK TO ZERO

Collect:

> Post, internal paperwork (check my desk, drawers, bag and anywhere else at this point)
>
> Notes from meetings
>
> Any expense receipts in my wallet/purse/bag? Get them into my in-tray
>
> Any other items? Add them to my in-tray.

Capture ideas, thoughts, nags, worries and anything else. Think about:

What's been happening over the last week?

What have I been working on?

What projects are on my mind? Why?

Conversations with my boss

Conversations with my colleagues

Conversations with my clients/customers/stakeholders

Any family events or personal issues I need to manage.

Organize. Get back to zero, and go through the Ninja decision-making process to get new actions recorded on my Master Actions List. Make sure I'm at zero on:

Email

My paper notebook

Voicemails

My in-tray

Social media direct messages

Any other inputs?

STAGE 2. GET MY SECOND BRAIN UP TO DATE

Calendar/Diary:

Go through each appointment in my calendar for the last two weeks – are there any follow-ups I need to do?

Go through the next three weeks of my calendar – any new actions here?

If I have a paper-based calendar, make sure it has all the same appointments in it as my Outlook calendar!

If there's also a wall planner for the team in the office, do the same with this.

Think further ahead in the diary and look for initial conversations, or where I need to make advanced travel plans like booking flights, booking rail tickets in advance, and so on.

Master Actions List:

Check for completed items and cross them off.

Read and ensure I have clarity about each action listed.

Waiting For List:

Are there any items on here that I'm no longer waiting for and can remove?

Do the quick one- to two-minute emails to chase up any items that are now becoming urgent.

Add anything that is going to take longer to chase to my Master Actions List.

Projects List:

Any projects that are finished or simply no longer *need* to happen?

Any new projects to add?

Do I have any additional projects kept somewhere else (such as a team project plan)? If so, add these to my Projects List so that I have everything in one place.

STAGE 3. *THINK AHEAD*

Projects List:

Go through each project in turn and make sure I have added new next physical actions to my Master Actions List. At the very least, ensure that I have one action on my Master Actions List that relates to each project.

Think about the strategic-level with each of these projects. What more is needed?

Master Actions List:

Decide on the main activity areas for the next week.

Think about what my big priorities will be.

What items need to be crossed out for next week to be judged a success?

Make a reminder note in my calendar or mark the high priority tasks.

Which items will present a big challenge to my proactive attention? Schedule these in the diary specifically.

Good Ideas Park:

Anything here that I need to renegotiate and decide is now worth doing?

Any new ideas to add?

The Wider World:

Check trade press or internal communications to see if there are any events or opportunities coming up this week.

Anything interesting to write about or tie into?

Any school holidays or religious festivals coming up that might present opportunities or schedule changes?

STAGE 4. GET READY

Packing and preparing:

What documents do I need for the next week? Get the printer running now!

What files do I need for upcoming meetings?

What reading materials do I need access to?

What travel tickets do I need? If they're already in the office, find them and add them to my bag, wallet or purse. Can I check in online right now? Can I look up the train times and make a quick note of them?

People:

Are there any conversations I need to have with people to ensure that *they* are prepared for the things happening next week?

Drop quick emails to people confirming meetings or ask for more information in preparation for next week.

Is there anyone (boss, assistant, colleague) who needs to know more about my schedule for next week?

Attention management:

When are going to be my best periods of proactive attention?

When am I likely to be exhausted, stressed or not at my best?

Is there anything I can do now to support those times or minimize hassles?

STAGE 5. QUESTIONS

Focus:

Is anything on my Master Actions List so big or that will take so long that it would be better if broken up into chunks?

Is there anything on my list that's been hanging around for a few weeks? Do I need to redefine the action to give it more clarity?

Ruthlessness:

Delete three things from my Master Actions List simply because they're not mission-critical. Let anyone else relevant know that I'm doing this (and my reason!).

Delegate three things from my Master Actions List that someone else could just as easily do.

Resistance:

Is there anything here I'm resisting?

What makes it/them challenging?

What is going to give me the momentum I need?

Could I cheat or move the goal posts? (Remember, unorthodoxy that gets the job done is fine!)

What's the smallest step forward I could take? How about just committing to that?

Health & Fitness:

Am I eating well?

Am I drinking enough water?

Am I getting the exercise I need? If not, where does this fit in to my routine next week?

Did I meditate or find time to completely switch off this week?

When are my best opportunities to do that next week and how can I ensure they happen?

How do I feel physically and emotionally? Are there any problems or issues I need to think about?

Relationships:

Am I spending enough time with family and friends?

Am I happy when I do? If not, what would change this and how can I work towards it this week?

Hobbies:

Am I making time for hobbies?

What's coming up in the next week?

Happiness:

Am I happy, at least most of the time?

What would make me happier right now? Listen to my soul here!

So now you have your first Weekly Checklist! Congratulations! A question that often comes up when we run workshops on this is whether there are any elements here so crucial that they should be compulsory. I think there are a great many elements here that you shouldn't do without, but make sure you definitely have the following in your checklist before you continue:

1. Get back to zero on each of your collection points, and go through the Ninja decision-making process to get new actions recorded on your Master Actions List.

2. Go through each project in turn and make sure you have at least one action on your Master Actions List for each.

3. Make sure you read and have clarity about each action listed on your Master Actions List.

4. Go through the next three weeks of your calendar – are there any new actions?

There are a great many other steps that I know that I can't live without, but these are the truly universal ones that everyone should have on their Weekly Checklist.

EXERCISE: DEVELOPING MY DAILY CHECKLIST

What you'll need: Boss-mode proactive thinking

How long it'll take: 20 minutes

Ninja mindset: Weapon-savvy, Preparedness

Again, write out a Daily Checklist, choosing the elements that most apply to your role from the list below. Feel free to add in additional questions or themes if there are things that you naturally do at the start of a working day. One thing though: try to keep this to thinking and planning, so hence avoid 'processing email' as part of the Daily Checklist. If you do this checklist at 9am, you can process your email at 9.05! Don't panic!

Calendar:

What's in my calendar today and are there any deadlines looming in the next three to five days?

Any other schedules to check? Paper diary?

Big Rocks:

What would a good day of actions look like today?

What would I like to have ticked off?

What are the 'big rocks' that need some focus and mental heavy lifting?

Resistance:

Out of those tasks, which am I most likely to resist wanting to do? And why?

Attention Management:

Out of those tasks, which of them requires the intense concentration of my proactive attention, and which can be done during inactive periods?

Dependencies:

Are any of the things I've chosen time-dependent, people-dependent or resource-dependent?

Are you a Ninja?

▶ A Ninja uses stealth and camouflage to create the space and thinking time needed to review.

▶ Your Weekly and Daily Checklists are your regular opportunity to remain agile and renegotiate your priorities.

▶ Reviewing promotes mindfulness, preparedness and Zen-like calm.

9. THE DO HABIT

'The realisation of the self is only possible if one is productive, if one can give birth to one's potentialities.'
– Johann Wolfgang von Goethe

This is where things start to get very interesting. Remember the worker putting cherries on cakes at the start of the book? Having already completed the boss part of your job, whatever you have to do, however complex, is now as simple as sitting in the factory, putting cherries on cakes.

You've captured and collected everything, organized it and have gone through the review processes of the Weekly Checklist and the morning Daily Checklist. Now you're fully prepared. You have everything you need. From here on in, you can develop momentum, make the doing part of your work as effortless as possible and experience hyper-productivity on a scale you've never known before.

Having already done the hard parts of the thinking, the decisions that follow are really more tactical than strategic. You already have clarity over what to do; your job is just to decide the order in which you'll do the various tasks on your Daily To-Do list (which at the start of the day, you've chosen from your Master Actions List), and schedule each one appropriately to your time, attention and sense of impact.

THE BEAUTY OF THE '*DO*' PHASE

Being on a roll in Do-mode is a wonderful feeling, as you experience playful, productive momentum and control. Part of what makes it so satisfying is that it's so incredibly simple. The Do phase requires much less interaction with and management of information.

THE *WORKER* NINJA DASHBOARD:

▶ Master Actions List or Daily To-Do List

▶ Calendar

'All serious doing starts from within.'
– Eudora Welty

THE *BOSS* NINJA DASHBOARD:

- ▶ Master Actions List
- ▶ Calendar
- ▶ Projects List
- ▶ Waiting For List
- ▶ Good Ideas Park

Having put so much of the boss work behind you, you can focus your attention onto just one or two areas. If necessary, you can refer to your calendar or diary but really the bulk of your time and attention is just spent immersed in the Master Actions List and getting things finished. A powerful rhythm emerges: choose an action, complete the action, choose an action, complete the action. So little thinking is required, with so little friction or resistance.

DO HABITS

There are three broad sets of what I call 'Do habits': the approaches, techniques and best practices that aid playful, productive momentum and control:

1. **Managing Attention**

2. **Decision Tools**

3. **Do tactics**

MANAGING ATTENTION

PROACTIVE, ACTIVE AND *INACTIVE ATTENTION*

Realizing the need to get beyond time management and manage

your proactive and active attention to their optimum capabilities is a huge step forward. A Productivity Ninja is constantly checking in with themselves, 'Do I still feel good?', 'Can I sneak some more proactive attention in here before I get tired?', 'Do I need a break?', 'What will get me back up there?'. So few people are conscious of this to the point that it starts to influence scheduling. Develop a good sense of your daily attention flow so that it dictates the rhythm and difficulty of your work at different times of the day. Time might be spent, but attention needs to be paid in order to move something to done. Give yourself permission to handle the easy tasks when you're flagging at inactive attention lows, but equally be sure to bite off the most difficult tasks when your proactive attention has you salivating for results. Before you even think about things like priority, make sure you're factoring attention levels into your tactical planning.

PROTECTING ATTENTION *FROM INTERRUPTIONS*

Remember, proactive attention is your most precious commodity. The vultures of interruption and potential distraction will circle you, trying to make you a victim. Stay in control. Aggressively and ruthlessly defend your attention.

SELF-AWARENESS *AND AGILITY*

A Ninja is agile. The plan for the day at 1pm may be entirely different from what that plan was at 9am. With access to such brilliant information on your Master Actions List, it's easy to change the plan, move things around and be nimble. Since in Do-mode all you need to work from is your Master Actions List, it's easy to stay agile and alert to changes going on around you. You can react quickly to new inputs while confidently knowing the exact consequences of doing so (because you know what *won't* get done as well as what will). You can also give heed to your attention levels and change your plan if you're having one of those 'hitting top form' kind of days, or of course if you're fading faster than you expected. Again, such agility doesn't come for free: you have earned it by putting in the necessary hours on the Capture and Collect, Organize and Review phases.

MINIMIZE **SETUP COST**

With any new activity, whether email, writing a report, online banking, creative thinking or attending a conference, there's a high setup cost in terms of time and attention. For email, you have to fire up Outlook, let the program load and synchronize with the server and open your emails. If returning to a report, you have to re-read all the bits that you've forgotten you wrote last time, you have to navigate back through the document ('Where was I?' and so on). Online banking requires a seemingly endless list of codes and passwords before you can actually *do* anything at all. All of these are the setup costs of doing. The cost is twofold: it takes you time and it also takes attention and energy. Working in larger 'chunks' (such as writing the whole report in one go, rather than trying to split it over several days) is a great way to minimize the time and attention spent in setup mode. Despite being ultra-aware of this fact, I attempted for a long while to write this book on a designated day each month. Needless to day, after six months of me failing to ever really get beyond the setup cost of getting immersed in what I'd written so far (which, for a book, takes me several hours!), I decided to take a month out to immerse myself fully in the writing of it. On the first two days I added no more than a dozen words but did lots of useful thinking. And on the third day, it all kicked into gear.

MIX **AND MATCH**

Potential distractions are around every corner. Don't even create the temptation to get distracted because you're bored. Keep your days and weeks fresh by giving yourself variety. So if Monday is very much a solitary thinking day, perhaps Tuesday will be full of interesting people and conversations. Wednesday might be out of the office, but allow Thursday to focus back onto admin and getting your in-tray back to zero. Variety is the spice of life. Bad news if you're looking at your entire Master Actions List and seeing only boredom ahead: it's probably time to get a new job. And if you're happy being bored at work every day for the rest of your life, it's probably time to get a different book!

DECISION TOOLS FOR DO-ERS

There are a number of other well-known productivity tools and techniques I've used over the years. I'll quickly run through my favourites below. Of course, they won't all appeal to you, but if one takes your fancy, give it a go!

PARETO'S LAW

Pareto was the Italian economist who once walked around his garden and noticed that 80% of the peas in his garden came from just 20% of the pods. Being a good economist, he didn't just discard this as an interesting observation; he wondered how he could turn it into a law of world economics. Pareto's Law is a reminder that not all actions are equal. Some of the things we do create profound and lasting impact. Other things we do are instantly forgotten. Meetings are great examples of this: 80% discussion for 50 minutes, with the ten minutes at the end set aside for actions, clarifications and the things that will be remembered in two months' time. The rest will all be forgotten. The rule of 80–20 is worth keeping in mind.

A few years ago I created a charity from ten pieces of A4 paper. I had been to Uganda and worked on an HIV education project there, while on a sabbatical from my job as the Student Volunteering Manager at the University of Birmingham. On returning to Birmingham, we created a poster, photocopied it ten times and placed it around campus. The poster had various facts about HIV and was really a 'call to action' asking for volunteers to help some of Uganda's leading charities address the issue during the summer holidays. About 80 people packed into the meeting room we'd booked to give a talk about what they could do to help. When they arrived, I spent about ten minutes talking passionately about what I'd seen in Uganda: a country ravaged by a virus spreading through lack of information; the refusal of the education system, religions or communities to address taboo issues; and some good news that there were some under-resourced yet innovative Ugandan charities that were doing their best to address these issues. I could see lots of the students listening intently, waiting to hear the details about the volunteering programme we'd put together to send them to Uganda, how much they might have to fundraise to go and so on. But, as I told them, we hadn't prepared anything at all. It was up to them to make it happen. Cue half the room getting up and leaving. Oh dear.

But actually, that was an important moment. As the remaining 40 or so people sat there, looked around at each other, looked at the people leaving the room and looked back at me, a collective understanding grew that this was very possible. They could create this. It was going to happen. Sure enough, about twenty students helped create a charity called Intervol and flew to Uganda that summer. It has continued to this day, and currently they send around a hundred students to a dozen or so countries around the developing world each year, offering their skills, energy and passion. They're branching out to help students in other universities do the same. All it took was for me to create that poster. Sometimes from the smallest of acts can come the largest of impacts. Every piece of paper represents a wonderful opportunity to add infinite value.

The reverse is also true. We can easily get sucked into the 80% of activities that add only low-level value. So much of what we think is our real work is just fiddling about, changing font sizes from 10 point to 12 point, or hankering for perfection. Worse still, it's refilling the kettle, waiting for Windows Updates to load or answering the phone to annoying sales people who cleverly disguise the fact that they're selling you something for an annoyingly long time. Real impact isn't created through these activities. Move on as quickly as you can.

PARKINSON'S LAW

Parkinson's Law states that work expands to fill the time available. Put simply, we rarely work at our optimum speed. Think about when you're trying to finish a piece of writing such as a report or, thinking back even further, a school or university essay. As you feel the deadline looming large, your hands type the words a little bit quicker. You think that little bit faster too and while you might be prone to mistakes, the sense of urgency produces profound productivity. If you think you have a week to do three essays, the three essays take a week. Yet, they always seem to be written on the last night of your half-term break. So if you'd have just been given one day to do three essays, you'd have produced exactly the same thing. Work expands and contracts depending on the time available. So next time you have a two-hour report to write, consider what might happen if you were only given one hour to do it. Probably the most important 20% of it – the stuff that adds 80% of the impact – could easily be done in an hour. In many ways, the less of a perfectionist you're able to stomach being, the more you can push your productivity to higher levels than you thought possible.

Parkinson's Law is also a good way to think about why the second brain works – the Daily To-Do List, created from the Master Actions List and the habitual thinking of the Daily and Weekly Checklists ensure there's constant focus and minimize the chances of 'drift'.

HOFSTADTER'S LAW

Perfection is a dangerous disease. So much of what we do has the potential to unravel way beyond what is even necessary (think 80–20) and way beyond what we could find ourselves drawn to do (think Parkinson's). Hofstadter's Law states that, 'Work takes twice as long as you originally anticipated, even when taking into account Hofstadter's Law'. Wake up and smell the cappuccino. Everything you do has the potential to unravel and require more effort than you think.

So use Hofstadter's Law as your reminder to commit to less. Use Parkinson's Law to dare yourself to be different and work to firm boundaries or time constraints. And in all of that use the 80–20 principle to remind yourself what matters. Life's too short.

BIG ROCKS

In his book *The Seven Habits of Highly Effective People*, Stephen Covey tells a story he had heard many years earlier of a teacher in a classroom who pulls out a large jar and several big rocks from underneath a table. He fills the jar with the big rocks, screws the lid back on the jar and asks his students, 'Is the jar now full?' 'Of course,' say the students, 'you've just filled it with those big rocks.' The teacher then reaches back underneath the table and pulls out a bag of small pebbles. Unscrewing the lid of the jar, he pours the pebbles around the larger rocks and fills the jar with the big rocks and the small pebbles. 'How about now?', asks the teacher, 'Is the jar full?' While a number of the students reply yes, a fair few are now suspicious of what else the teacher might have underneath his table. Sure enough, the teacher reaches down and finds a tub of sand, which fills the jar in between the big rocks and the pebbles. Finally, even though the jar is filled with rocks, pebbles and sand, the teacher pours water in and fills the jar to the brim.

The teacher then asks his students what they think the lesson might be here. What might this teach us about managing our time? One of the students raises his hand and suggests it means that, 'Even though we thought our day was full, there's always more that we can cram into every day'. The teacher replies by saying that while that may be the case, the real lesson is that if you are going to have any hope of fitting the big rocks into the jar at all, you need to start with them.

So much of our day is taken up with the pebbles, sand and water of our attention. Emails and information inputs are really all just pebbles. The big rocks – those things on our Master Actions List that require proactive attention, lots of energy, potentially awkward conversations and a whole raft of other things that make them difficult – are the things that need to be scheduled first. Start every day with the question, 'What are my big rocks today?' and focus on them ruthlessly, especially during periods of proactive and active attention. Let the pebbles, sand and water flow around the big rocks, rather than spending your day filling the jar with water alone.

SHIP

'Real artists ship.'
— Steve Jobs

In *Linchpin*, Seth Godin talks about 'shipping' – the idea that there's no value in what you're working on unless it's actually being used. Completing something means 'shipping it' to the customer. We all have the power to ship. In recent years, the literal act of shipping has gone from a pretty exclusive activity, only practised by large mail order companies to being something we all have certainly the power and opportunity to practise and experience: eBay, Etsy, Amazon and so many other places open up the world for us all to be tiny businesses and know what it feels like to wrap up the goods, write a thank you note and send them off through the postal system to a customer. It's possible these days to build websites, create eBooks, design customized T-shirts, write and record music, make TV shows, and organize events – all with such fantastically low barriers to entry. All of these things would have been, to our grandparents, things that required prior approval from some kind of middleman: publishers, manufacturers, record company executives, managers and so on. These days it's all right there for us. We can ship without them.

So the choice is yours: sit around waiting for approval, or just ship. Sit around trying to make something that little bit closer to perfection (which is currently being used by no one!), or just ship. This is a fantastic mindset to have more generally. The focus should not be just on doing, but really on homing in on answering the question, 'What would this look like when it's finished?' We can sometimes get so carried away with how much better something can be that we forget that the whole purpose is to put it out into the world. Even if what you're working on is something as simple as a report, thinking about the shipping stage of that might allow you to come up with a creative customer service idea or might just motivate you towards that elusive final stage in the process with more confidence.

At the final stage, we're often caught in a high level of resistance to finishing the thing – we're worried about how other people might judge our work and whether we'll look foolish in some way. We worry about whether it's perfect rather than whether it's going to have the desired impact. We get caught in self-doubt and it's so tempting without anyone to help us ship to take the easy option and either ditch the whole project or apply more delaying tactics. It's not about how much you do, but ultimately how much you ship.

MONOTASKING

DO TACTICS

MONOTASKING

> *'Action is eloquence.'*
> *– William Shakespeare*

If there was a worse invention in old-school 'time management' babble than the idea of 'multitasking' I'd love to know. Multitasking was long heralded as the ultimate badge of honour for a knowledge worker. You're good if you're getting things done, but you're more efficient if you're multitasking and doing two things at once. Wrong, wrong, wrong. Let's be clear about what people are actually talking about when they use the term 'multitasking'. Multi-tasking is really about juggling two or more actions at the same time and requires your brain to switch onto one thing, make a small amount of progress, switch to the next thing, react to something else, come back and make minimal progress on the first thing again, switch to a new thing and so on. In trying to manage our attention in this way – or more accurately, falling into the trap of letting our attention be used in this way! – we expend a lot of energy and attention on the costly mental setup time ('Where was I again?') and create constant drag away from actual doing and completion. If anyone tells you they're great at multitasking, what they're really telling you is that they don't have their full attention on what they're doing!

I once had someone in one of my workshops who completely disagreed with me about this. She was a classic professional multitasker and she revelled in this identity. As I approached her desk, I asked her to show me her emails. She had a bulging inbox among the largest in the company and then nine separate windows open on the screen. In each of those nine windows was yet another incomplete email. She looked at me and smiled.

A much better idea is 'monotasking'. Once among the most unfashionable words in the business lexicon, it should be celebrated. Let's raise a toast to monotasking, the art of doing one thing to its natural conclusion and without interruption. When you've done that, move on to the next thing, do that to completion and without interruption and yes, don't move on until it's finished. Regular and sustained monotasking is like putting cherries on cakes. You feel more present in your work, more engaged, calmer and more at ease with the world around you. That world might feel like it's burning with urgency, noise, panic and stress but you're locked in a kind of cocoon. You're quietly doing what a Ninja does best: you're shipping and clarifying, completing and organizing – one thing at a time.

Multitasking is somewhat of a default mindset in the cultures of many of the big companies we work with. This is more out of chaos than conspiracy – it has simply evolved as the various forms of technology and the main components of knowledge work have developed. You may recognize your own working environment as being full of interruptions and noise: pressured, challenging, open and frustratingly frenetic. There may be little you can do to change this. What you can do is recognize that perhaps your best proactive attention work might need to take place outside of this location. It's a mystery to me why some bosses are so closed off to this idea – perhaps as if raising an idea that might boost your productivity and lower your stress levels is in some way only meant as an indictment of the company's current working environment. Or worse still, they'd have to *trust* you! If you have a boss like this, I sympathize. You might need to get into stealth mode and choose your moments to 'break the rules'. Sneaking off to a meeting room to get some calm thinking time so that you can do your job better or clear a backlog should hardly be considered a crime.

CAPTURE TO CONTINUE

Monotasking is hard for a whole series of reasons. One of these is that we are constantly trying to derail ourselves without even realizing it. As we sit down ready to monotask our way through something important or useful, we're reminded of nags, ideas and other actions. And we're tempted into checking our email or succumbing to external distractions. Yes, our own brain is trying to make us multitask! This is precisely why we need to be capturing and collecting any potentially useful Ideas, even if some of these ideas later turn out to be less than useful. Capturing these ideas and knowing they're part of our Ninja System allows us to return fully to what we're working on, without the need to switch programs, take our brain too far into the other thought process or disrupt our flow too much. Capture and Collect becomes the critical habit for encouraging the art of monotasking. To support this habit, make your capturing as easy as possible. Capture into your phone or onto a piece of paper rather than change what's on the screen if you're working on a Word document. Experiment with finding the quickest, easiest, most friction-free ways to capture. Think of capturing not just as a useful act in its own right (for the potential that these ideas might generate), but as a piece of emergency correction to keep your mind focused on the (mono)task at hand.

THE *POMODORO* TECHNIQUE

Invented by university student Francesco Cirillo in the late eighties, the Pomodoro Technique is named after those stylish kitchen timers you can buy in the shape of a tomato. Essentially a tool for managing attention and focus, Pomodoro has at its heart two extremely simple but powerful observations. Firstly, that short bursts of attention (25 minutes) followed by short breaks (five minutes) are the best way to preserve your proactive attention throughout the day. And secondly, by splitting the day into lots of 25-minute chunks and using a timer, you spend the whole day with the constant buzz of being up against a clock. Time is counted backwards, counting down from 25 to zero, rather than forwards indefinitely until you take a break. It is a great tool for splitting much larger tasks down into more bite-sized chunks, it can help provide an important sense of focus and can help you resist the temptation to give in to distractions. You can download Pomodoro timer apps for your phone, or download a desktop timer for your computer: they are quieter than using a real kitchen timer. I've used both over the years, but I'd advise against using a real one if there are other people in the office!

Pomodoro is also an interesting technique to ensure you don't focus too much attention on any single area of your work. Used over a day or a week, you can start to view your schedule in terms of Pomodoros spent – and see exactly how little of your time is spent on the stuff you like the least.

SCHEDULED *PROCRASTINATION*

One of the good things about Pomodoro is knowing that after every 25 minutes of work there's a five-minute comfort and distraction break. This is really useful as it creates a boundary between temptation and virtue by making you consciously aware that a five-minute period to give in to temptation is heading your way. You can take this idea a step further. If you find yourself procrastinating, checking Facebook, doodling and daydreaming, realize that all have their place. Rather than beating yourself up for doing these things (which adds more drama to what you're ultimately trying to resist and hence reinforces the resistance to it anyway), simply create the right boundary. So if you catch yourself procrastinating, your boss-self is allowed to decide, 'OK, five more minutes of this procrastination and then we're moving on to this specific thing'. In creating this, what you've done is demystify and disempower the procrastination and you'll often find that such a boundary moves you along at the end of the five minutes and into what's required of you now that you've 'had your share'.

POWER *HOURS*

The Power Hour is something I developed for myself a couple of years ago and I use it if avoiding a particular important activity. The idea is simple. Schedule an hour of your most proactive attention to work on what you're avoiding. After all, it's just an hour of your day. I'm not asking myself to work on that thing for the whole day. Adding it to the diary changes it from being a possible option for the day (which I'm likely to ignore in favour of easier, noisier work) to being a commitment, hard-wired into my day. It brings focus and by the end of one Power Hour I've usually delved deeply enough into the activity to know that it's not quite as scary or difficult after all. To make choices about what to schedule as a Power Hour activity, I use a question on my Weekly Checklist: 'What are the big rocks that are either difficult or that you might be avoiding?' If that throws up an answer, I'll schedule Power Hours for the following week, right there in my review. It's such a relief knowing that I have a commitment and a plan to move forward on the things that are stuck.

The other way to use Power Hours is to think about this question:

> 'What's the one activity that, if you did it consistently for an hour a day every day this year, makes a person in your job successful?'

If you were a sales person, that activity might be cold calling. If you don't enjoy cold calling, you'll always find something else to do in its place. Developing a habit, though, that every day between 9.30 and 10.30am you cold call, will, over time, yield results. Of course, this isn't rocket science. But if you have a clear idea in your mind right now about your one activity, the chances are that you're not actually practising that for an hour a day or more. The Power Hour can be a way to find consistency, develop muscle, turn a conscious choice into an effortless, unconscious habit and ultimately meet your goals.

You'll also find Power Hours easier if you can tell your colleagues you're doing it and ask for their co-operation in not interrupting you during that time. Perhaps put that china cat out on your desk, as Elena does in the Think Productive office. This public pronouncement will also firm up the commitment in your mind. Anything else you can do that might subconsciously create a signal that this hour is special and different from all the rest will really help, too. This could be something as simple as changing your desktop background, putting on your favourite music or drinking expensive herbal tea instead of the usual 'normal' tea. You could also do something more physical, like work from a different desk or take your work outside to enjoy the view.

EXERCISE: CREATING MY POWER HOUR

What you'll need: Access to your calendar, awareness of when your attention levels are proactive, boss-mode proactive thinking

How long it'll take: 15–20 minutes to set up, one hour per day to implement

Ninja mindset: Mindfulness

You're now going to schedule your very own Power Hour. Start with these two questions, and see what ideas are sparked in your mind about what your Power Hour should focus on:

▶ 'What are the big rocks that are either difficult or that I might be avoiding?'

▶ 'What's the one activity that, if I did it consistently for an hour a day every day this year, would make me successful?'

Next, establish when your attention is at its most proactive and the time in your days that's most conducive to scheduling in an uninterrupted hour of pure productivity:

The only two rules are:

1. Once you've committed to a Power Hour, you can't change the time or reschedule it (you wouldn't reschedule a meeting at short notice with your boss, so why be more willing to let yourself down than you are to let down others?).

2. You can only have one Power Hour each day. The focus on consistently doing one thing well is what counts here. Trying

to schedule seven Power Hours a day just leads to stress and disappointment, so don't even try.

Finally, can you tell your colleagues and ask for their co-operation? Do you need a way to indicate that you're in Power Hour mode and you're not to be interrupted?

Is there anything else you can use or implement as a personal signal that you're entering 'the zone'?

MORE **DO** TACTICS

BATCHING

One of the smartest things you can do to avoid wasting a lot of attention and energy on setup time is to batch up similar tasks and tackle them all in one go. Getting 'in the zone' with something takes some time, so if you're already in that zone, it's a good idea to keep going. That's precisely why I recommended 'batching' all of your emails into just a few periods each day. It's particularly useful if you're working on something that requires a lot of background paperwork or files to be available since half the time and hassle is in finding the right bits of information to refer to. Doing all of your sales or client development work in one go also gets you into the right mindset to make better in-the-moment decisions about the language you use or your general approach – you may even be able to cut and paste snippets of information from one email or report to the next. Handling a whole series of calls at the same time not only means you're in the right mode to make calls, but you can also use it as an opportunity to get out of the office and get some fresh air. Batching enables you to generate a sense of flow that gathers its own momentum; you'll find that you're far more productive than if you were simply moving from one task to another.

What we did earlier in Chapter 4 on Ninja email was to increase efficiency by batching email rather than having email constantly in the background and done in tiny, distracting chunks. Do you know how many Pomodoros it takes you every week to keep your inbox at zero? Well, over the next couple of weeks you should find out!

MODELLING & ***MENTORING***

We deal with a whole lot of tasks where it feels like we're the pioneers. Perhaps we're taking our work into an area the organization has never been before or developing a completely new product or

'It always seems impossible until it is done.'
– Nelson Mandela

idea. When we're doing this it can feel like all we have to call on is our own imagination, but this is rarely the case. Look around within your organization and outside of it and you probably won't have too much trouble finding someone who's taken on a similar challenge and won. It's much easier to 'model' their behaviour than try to reinvent the wheel. Look for opportunities to pick these people's brains. Perhaps ask them if you can buy them a coffee, or drop them an email with a couple of key questions that would move your own work forward. Look for opportunities to ask for advice, learn from the mistakes of others and be generous with the advice that you could offer to someone else on their way up the same ladder as you.

Quite apart from being immensely productive, mentoring also provides you with a friend or two in high places, which certainly has its career advantages.

HACKING

A lot has been written about 'LifeHacking' and now 'TravelHacking' is becoming a blogging phenomenon too. When the website www.lifehacker.com first started, it was a bit of a phenomenon and full of genuinely useful 'hacks'. A hack is really anything that allows you to shortcut the conventional way of doing something, cheat the system or generally be a little bit unorthodox in your approach. Hacks are often presented as well kept secrets that, once unlocked, will allow you to boost your productivity.

Websites like LifeHacker.com are great places to find nuggets of useful information. However, beware of the tendency in your brain to confuse reading about productivity with actually being productive! Avoid getting sucked into a loop of 'productivity porn'. And furthermore, there are a lot of sites out there that will post a mixture of genius productivity solutions alongside fairly mundane advice about how to clean bird poo off your car windscreen. Nevertheless, an occasional browse through posts on sites like Lifehacker may help you improve your use of particular tools, or help you find new ways to do things more efficiently.

A great tip to find any hack or shortcut, particularly concerning software like Outlook or Toodledo is to put the exact question you're trying to solve into YouTube or Google. You'll be amazed at how many helpful geeks are sat at home making step-by-step tutorial videos to solve your exact problem! Blessed are the geeks, for they shall inherit the earth.

DO STUFF YOU **LOVE**

'Nothing great was ever achieved without enthusiasm.'
– Ralph Waldo Emerson

This moves us neatly on to my final observation in this chapter. Doing what you love and loving what you do used to be seen as some kind of pipe dream. I would argue that as we firmly establish the information age, it's easier than ever to make this a reality. It's possible to make the connections with people all around the world who can help us get where we want to be in our careers or develop the relationships with those who can help us *create* what we want to do. The barriers to entry are low, yet so many people stick it out working long hours in jobs they hate and try to make themselves happier at weekends by buying more stuff they can't afford. The debt that this creates keeps people firmly stuck, unable to take risks or make changes. I want to be clear here that I am not advocating that the only way to do something you love is to leave your company, but it is certainly true that you'll be a bigger asset to your company if you're doing something that you're fully engaged in and actually enjoy doing. I believe passionately that one of the true secrets to productivity – and the best 'Do tactic' of all is not sticking around doing stuff that you hate for too long.

EXERCISE: DO TACTICS, DECISION TOOLS AND MY HABITS

What you'll need:	This book to refer to, your calendar/diary
How long it'll take:	15 minutes
Ninja mindset:	Unorthodoxy, Agility

Review the Do tactics below and indicate whether you already do them, which one(s) you'll start and when, what you might do in the future, and what seems crazy and definitely won't be appearing on your Weekly Checklist any time soon.

	DO CONSISTENTLY ALREADY	COULD DO MORE	WILL TRY	MIGHT TRY	WILL NEVER TRY
Monotasking	☐	☐	☐	☐	☐
Capture to continue	☐	☐	☐	☐	☐
The Pomodoro technique	☐	☐	☐	☐	☐
Scheduled procrastination	☐	☐	☐	☐	☐
Power Hours	☐	☐	☐	☐	☐
Batching	☐	☐	☐	☐	☐
Modelling and mentoring	☐	☐	☐	☐	☐
Hacking	☐	☐	☐	☐	☐
Do stuff you love	☐	☐	☐	☐	☐

Are you a Ninja?

▶ A Ninja is ruthless with what they choose to do and takes an unorthodox approach to find the quickest, easiest and most efficient ways to do their work.

▶ A Ninja does their work from a place of relaxed, Zen-like calm.

▶ A Ninja is agile and nimble because their well-prepared second brain allows them to do their work in the most efficient way possible.

10. NINJA PROJECT AND MEETING MANAGEMENT

WHAT IS A PROJECT?

'Let our advance worrying become advance thinking and planning.'
– Winston Churchill

So, you've got your inbox down to zero, organized all of your information, cleared the decks, prepared your to-do lists and checklists, and are ready to start putting some cherries on some cakes. There is, however, a problem: other people. Working with other people can be one of the greatest joys of a job, but it can also be one of the most frustrating parts. So in this chapter we're going to look at techniques to manage this, first in terms of how it can affect your ability to complete group projects, and then, in more detail, at how you can harness the power of other people to have more productive, Ninja-like meetings that get results.

Simply defined, a project is anything that you have a commitment to finish or do that will take more than a couple of individual steps (actions) or where the completion date is more than a week away. This is indeed a broader definition than most, and deliberately so. Anything that is classed as a project gets managed on your Projects List, so the wider this definition, the closer your Projects List becomes to truly being a complete list of everything you're working on.

We've given much emphasis in this book to the managing of actions and with good reason. Focus on actions ensures focus on delivering things and making things happen. However, managing projects is an important skill in its own right. Projects give our ideas and actions a sense of structure and purpose. Actions on their own can be chaotic; actions as part of projects create progress.

Look around you. Everything you see has the potential to be a project. It can be extremely empowering to think of small pieces of work and even leisure activities or resolving personal relationship disputes as projects. A Ninja

is always on the lookout for new projects, too: capturing and collecting ideas and working out at the Organize phase whether there is indeed a project here that can be managed. Everything around you is an opportunity to create a project and make magic happen.

The truth is that our more traditional definition of what constitutes a project is born from old and painful experiences. Projects are seen as the complicated things judged by others. We think of them as a chore, perhaps recalling school projects that were boring and cumbersome, where the thinking and planning that went into the project seemed to outweigh the doing and achieving that took place. We think, too, of professional project managers, so often the professional busybodies whose job seems purely to chase, hassle and annoy.

As well as a wider definition of what a project actually is, I'd like to propose a much simpler approach to dealing with most projects. The behaviours we've already discussed in this book and particularly those of capturing and collecting, organizing and reviewing mean that you have a greater capacity to regularly apply a very effective but light-touch management approach to each project during your Weekly Checklist. Every week, your job is simply to steer the project, by establishing the next physical actions that are required and adding them to your Master Actions List. As you do so, you also check up on the health of each live project and make changes to your Projects List as new projects are added, completed or removed from the list because they're no longer relevant.

HAVING A PROJECT MANAGEMENT APPROACH, *WITHOUT BEING A PROJECT MANAGER*

Much like the old style of to-do lists, old-style project management rarely works well for day-to-day projects. It is synonymous with uber-detailed planning and not enough regular monitoring; thus, when the world changes (which it is wont to do, and often), delivery falls behind schedule and your hours of detailed planning go awry. Quite simply, people get in the way! It's easy to plan great projects in theory, but then other humans blunder along, putting blocks in the road, not doing what they say they're going to do and causing confusion and conflict. Through your regular weekly project surgery, the Weekly Checklist, you'll be given enough of a steer to keep projects on the right track. It is more important to be ultra-agile than to be over prepared. Do very little *planning* and lots of checking back and monitoring.

Of course, there will be complicated projects with hundreds of interdependencies, where you need to find the 'critical path' through all of the detail and complication. In those instances, I'm not suggesting you ditch the idea of project planning there, but I would certainly recommend hiring an experienced project manager to help steer you through!

THE *FIVE-MILESTONE MODEL* OF PROJECTS

But for the day-to-day projects, we should think in terms of 20% planning and 80% regular management, re-alignment and steering. It is possible for one person to manage a complex project plan that they themselves have put together, but as soon as other people get involved, things can quickly get convoluted. A perfect project plan for regular, light-touch steering should contain no more than five milestones. Milestones should be the tangible moments when you answer the question, 'How will we know we're on track?' Too often, milestones become micromanagement or seem to provide complication and confusion rather than clarity. So in each of your projects, you should look for between one and five milestones. Never more than five, never fewer than one.

A SIMPLE PROJECT IS *LIKE A GOOD STORY:* IT HAS A BEGINNING, MIDDLE AND END.

Occasionally when you involve other people in delivering your project, you may need a little bit more detail at the beginning of the project to really make sure the project is travelling on the same journey that you envisaged. Again, think about the fact that the more detail you try to delegate, the more confusing it's likely to get, despite all the good intentions and skill that you and others bring to the table. That's just what happens. So avoid the temptation to overcomplicate your projects. The five-milestone model of projects is all you ever really need:

1. **Establishment**

2. **Underway**

3. **Mid-way**

4. **Completion**

5. **Celebration**

Let's look at the five stages in turn:

1. *ESTABLISHMENT*

Establishment is getting your resources lined up and deciding what the overall project will look like. It's the act of communicating what you think or jointly agree are the milestones to aim for and delegating the responsibility for each stage of the project to the relevant people.

2. *UNDERWAY*

Underway is really just checking the direction of travel. I often use this as a way of creating an opportunity or excuse for me or someone else to check on the progress of the first few days of the project or on the first few actions that have taken place. It's a useful stage if you want to provide an extra steer or if the person in charge of the project lacks a bit of experience and you want to give them some extra support. An example would be a design project where you're creating a new brochure or website, and you use the Underway milestone as a chance to discuss initial ideas with the designer, plus the likely sticking points that you couldn't have anticipated before you started.

3. *MID-WAY*

How will you know that you're on the home straight towards completion? Is there a halfway point to the project? The mid-way point in a project can be extremely motivating. Again, use it to check on progress and revisit the end goals to make sure what you thought was the final conclusion is still what you want to do – after all, the world has changed since you started the project!

4. *COMPLETION*

Completion feels like the easiest to define, but so often this is the one that people get wrong. Make sure during Establishment or at least as things get underway that your definition of complete is the same as everyone else's! How will you know it's done? What does that completion look like? What are the measurements of success? Is there a financial measurement? A specific or estimated number of people who have been involved? A quantity of products produced, bought or sold? Define success carefully at the beginning, or your vagueness may return to haunt you!

5. *CELEBRATION*

The final stage is celebration. Celebrating success and reflecting on the things that went well is something that we Brits are not in the habit of doing enough. We often let such opportunities to celebrate success pass us by. In using this model, you can develop opportunities for positivity, reflections, acknowledgements and learning points. I'm not suggesting here that you celebrate every client report being delivered with some kind of expensive wrap-up party, but even just a short email or conversation with the main people involved can be enough to provide an important 'thank you' and some useful dialogue. This should be as true if the only person working on the project is yourself as it is when there's a whole team involved!

There are a huge number of books out there that are specifically about project planning, so I'm not going to go into any more detail here. But the key thing to remember is this: you are a *Ninja,* and while group projects can be stressful, if you follow the way of the Productivity Ninja you will be equipped with the agility to deal with whatever obstacles are thrown in your path. It's not about avoiding curveballs, it's about catching them.

MEETINGS

Invariably, running projects will, at one time or another involve one of the most dominant mediums of productivity and one that is both loved and loathed: meetings. When talking about meetings, it's important to shift our focus from the individual to the group. We arrive at meetings as individuals and we leave as individuals, but the work of the meeting is done in a group. So this section will look at both the micro-level and the macro-level: what do we personally need to change and what could our organizational culture look to change?

THE ATTENTION TENSION

At both the individual and group level, there exists an important tension. It's the tension between listening and doing.

High listening, low doing therapy	High listening, high doing productivity
Low listening, low doing bureaucracy	Low listening, high doing ignorance

LISTENING

DOING ⟶

Treading the fine line to ensure sustainable, longer-term, maximum productivity isn't easy. We need to consciously spend some of our time and attention on understanding those around us, understanding what's happening strategically and listening to how others perceive the things we think are valuable. Likewise, there are times when we just need to get on with it. Learning to understand this tension, and gauge how to best use it will help you figure out whether a meeting is the most useful tool to use in this instance, or whether you need to apply some Ninja stealth tactics to avoid other people dragging you into unproductive meetings.

How would you describe your own time and attention in relation to the others around you? Are you spending all your time in 'therapy' meetings – focused more on listening and detached from doing – and wishing you could just be left to get things done on your own? Or are you stuck in the 'ignorance' phase, all guns blazing, but failing to gain the support, reassurance and feedback to ensure maximum productivity and impact?

And how would you describe your organization's culture with regard to meetings? Are you in the 'bureaucracy' wasteland, craving more communication and feeling like no one is listening to you? Or are you regularly finding yourself bored out of your skull having more 'therapy' in meeting room 3? Or perhaps you think your organization is treading the 'attention tension' pretty well, getting the balance just about right? This is the 'productive' box that we want to make sure all our work falls into.

We're going to look at both sides of the attention tension. First, I'll help you cut down on the time spent in meetings by eliminating some of the unnecessary ones and offering suggestions of alternatives. This will play into your newfound Ninja characteristics of ruthlessness, stealth and camouflage, and unorthodoxy. And then we'll look at the most important part: how to make those meetings you're left with productive, efficient and valuable. This will allow you to create a meetings environment that promotes Zen-like calm, preparedness and agility.

HOW TO REDUCE THE *TIME WASTED* IN MEETINGS

Meetings are *so* twentieth century

Back in the days before computers, most meetings were formal, slow-paced affairs. I had a glimpse of this when I spent a year teaching at a rural Ugandan primary school and attended a staff meeting that was chaired and conducted in the style passed down to my teaching colleagues from their British colonial masters a hundred or so years before. The first half hour involved lengthy, ego driven introductions and 'opening remarks' followed by an excruciating two hours where little was actually decided. The main decision points were the allocation of additional roles and duties for the teachers. These were dished out by the head teacher, with lengthy discussion on each one, but in reality, no questioning of the head teacher's authority or judgement. As a result, I couldn't help feeling that the whole meeting could have been replaced by the head teacher pinning a note to the door saying, 'Here are your new roles. Any questions or problems, just let me know'. The outcome would have been exactly the same – except fifteen of this village's most intelligent and well-trained minds could have spent that same time giving over 30 hours of additional tuition to the children of one of the poorest villages in the world. There really are better things to do with our time.

TIME IS MONEY. AND THEN SOME.

Have you ever thought about the cost of a meeting? I mean, really thought about how much it costs. I don't mean the room hire and biscuits. I don't even mean the hour of your life and the cost of that time to your boss. I'm talking about the cost of getting *all* of those people in a room for an hour. On top of the financial cost of being there, there's the opportunity cost of not doing something else with that proactive attention. That hour could have been spent on the biggest rock on today's Daily To-Do List. Finally, multiply your opportunity cost by that of all the other people sat around the table and you start to get the idea. What seems like a casual hour of giggling, biscuits and a semi-serious ten minutes can actually be a pretty sinister force for evil.

SO **WHY** HAVEN'T WE CHANGED IT?

Considering that the way that information can be accessed and communicated has changed radically in just the last fifteen years let alone the last 30, isn't it somewhat surprising that meetings have hardly changed? I would argue that there are a couple of very good reasons for this and that understanding these reasons is important if we are going to make some progress:

1. We're social animals and coming together in a community is a pretty natural thing to want to do.

2. Some people enjoy biscuits and inefficiency more than they do productivity.

3. As a culture, we face a collective inertia: it's much easier to moan about inefficient meetings than be the one who boldly and energetically tries to change things.

DON'T SUBSTITUTE MEETINGS FOR DECISION-MAKING

'Meetings are indispensable when you don't want to do anything.'
– John Kenneth Galbraith

I realized a while ago that our company was beginning to hold quite a few more meetings than usual and that my diary was littered with little 'half an hour to discuss this issue' type of meetings. Sometimes, by the time my assistant had found half an hour in our collective diaries, all we had was the title of the meeting and a pretty vague recollection of what the meeting was *for* in the first place. The diagnosis was pretty straightforward: I had had a busy couple of weeks and my energy levels were running on empty, so when people asked me questions I was deferring decisions because I simply didn't have the energy to make them on the spot. So I'd say, 'I need to think about this some more, why don't you book me in for a half-hour meeting and we can make a decision then?'

On the surface, this may seem like a fairly smart move: keep the meeting short, impose a deadline to force a decision, get back to whatever you're doing. In reality, this was such a waste of time and energy. So while it may be painful, it's always easier to cut straight to the decision-making and remove yourself as the bottleneck as quickly as possible. Listening to your team in the room, as things come up, is a much better habit than deferring listening until the meeting comes around.

DON'T ORGANIZE MEETINGS, DO SOMETHING ELSE INSTEAD

'The difference between creativity and innovation in the world is the difference between thinking about getting things done in the world and getting things done.'
– Michael E. Gerber (author of The E-Myth Revisited)

This will immediately make you significantly more productive. Just say no. Let's tackle this addiction and feed our cravings for a bit of social contact some other way. We meet for a variety of reasons, but below are some alternatives to spending anywhere from half an hour to half a day draining your time and attention, stuck in a meeting you don't honestly really need.

GETTING ON WITH IT

If it's possible to just get on with something rather than hold lots of meetings before getting on with something, just get on with it. Remember, it's usually better to apologize than to ask permission.

EMAIL

While our first instinct when trying to co-ordinate a group of people is usually to get them all into one room, it is, in fact, easier to use email to get everyone onto the same page. This has added advantages too: when trying to build a consensus or seek permission for action, the decision-maker is more likely to come up with an answer if it's harder for them to faff around thinking of reasons not to proceed.

Email is also an underrated tool when you are seeking ideas. Brainstorming works because it gets the best ideas from a wide range of people, and is at its best when it develops these ideas into an idea or a shape that is greater than the sum of its parts. Email can play a role here too: you can use email to quickly gather everyone's best ideas – it takes five minutes to do this instead of an hour's meeting, and everyone will be happy about that. If at the end of that round of email responses you haven't got the solution you think is needed, you can always send a second email, summarizing the best ideas and asking everyone for further thoughts. As a third – last resort – stage, you can of course bring a few people (those that seem particularly engaged in the topic) together for a short, more focused meeting.

CONFERENCE CALLS

Even though it does the same job of essentially getting everyone in the room, a well-run conference call is almost always over in half the time of a well-run meeting: the topic can be more focused, and the difficulty in judging at what point it is appropriate to jump in and add your thoughts makes it surprisingly effective at filtering out duplicate or valueless comments and ideas. The onset of services like Skype mean that conference calls are set to challenge the dominance of the conventional meeting in the next few years. This can only be a good thing.

COLLABORATIVE TECHNOLOGIES

Technologies such as Google+ and wiki sites are going to become much more common in the future too. The advantage to these options is simple: if you're working on a document or idea, you can collaborate on the final document from day one, with those people who you would normally ask to attend a meeting for their specific expertise – the head of finance, for example – being able to skip hearing the rest of the discussions and focus purely on the financial element to the project.

DESK HIJACKING

Learn the art of desk hijacking! It replaces all those one-on-one meetings in which you ask someone's permission or ask for an opinion. Desk hijacking is done in two ways, planned or unplanned. Planned is more polite: fire off a quick email saying, 'Hi, I'm doing this project that I need to pick your brains about. Are you in the office today or tomorrow? I'll pop up and see you for a quick chat.' If they don't respond, or if it's someone you think might be avoiding you because they're not delivering on a project, go for the unplanned way and just turn up at their desk.

Once you reach their desk, the efficiency of communication is beautiful. You hover over them, in a deliberately uncomfortable position and probably distracting one or two of their colleagues too. They know this, and will do all they can to get rid of you as soon as possible, since right now, neither of you are particularly comfortable. The end result is often an email with everything you need, which they'd much rather spend ages typing, from the comfort and quiet of their desk when you're gone, and you've saved the need for a half-hour meeting where at least half the time is just 'padding' to string it out.

ROUND-UP EMAILS

It's important for good communication and morale that teams are up to speed with what everyone else is working on. There's a genuine need for this in most business environments, particularly as it means everyone has their 'new opportunity radar' constantly plugged in and on full power. Again, much of this communication can be done via email. Having an internal communications person collate the best of the week's news and then ensuring everyone reads it is much quicker than asking everyone to sit in a room hearing it for an hour or more. Besides, they'll hear the bits they're interested in when they bump into colleagues in the corridor, or go for a drink together on a Friday.

CORRIDOR CONSENSUS BUILDING AND MBWA

'MBWA', or 'Management By Walking About' is a fantastic tool for any manager with basic social skills and a limited time. It's no more complicated than it sounds, although its effective implementation is a fine art. By setting aside some time to walk the floors, either once a day or certainly two or three times a week, you make yourself available to your team, and to those outside of your direct line management but with whom you may need to collaborate. I have seen great managers do this without a notebook or any form of capture tool, but if you're like me and have a memory like a sieve, resist the urge to try to be ultra-smooth: take a notebook and capture any actions or ideas that turn up along the way. More importantly, with time set aside during the week to do this, you can even set up a 'People' list of those people and issues you are hoping to meet and make progress on when you're doing the rounds. This can be a regular part of your Master Actions List. Done well, this can be good fun, very sociable, and also cover off half a dozen or more issues in no more than half an hour.

DAILY HUDDLE

This one is cheating slightly, as although it's very short, it is a meeting! There are various books that talk about the idea of short, daily meetings. I particularly like Verne Harnish's book, *Mastering the Rockerfeller Habits*, which talks about how leadership in growing businesses should focus on '1% vision and 99% alignment'. One of the forms of alignment, to keep everyone in the business reminded of what the main goals are that they should be focused on is the idea of the 'Daily Huddle'. The Daily Huddle takes no more than fifteen minutes, yet cuts out the need for a lot of other meetings and communications because of its simple and repetitive format. I run a huddle meeting every day with my team (we usually do ours sitting down, but with a larger groups, the idea is to 'huddle' together in a corner of the room, a corridor or wherever else there is enough space). The Daily Huddle asks five questions, which are the same each day:

1. What's your good news?

2. What are you working on today?

3. What's our progress towards achieving the key numbers in our business?

4. Where are you stuck?

5. Are you OK for tomorrow's huddle?

There aren't many rules here, but a couple of useful guidelines would be firstly to make sure any issues that crop up that are going to take longer than one minute to resolve are dealt with outside of the huddle meeting, and secondly that the meeting runs at the same time every day (at Think Productive, we use 9.40am, primarily so that on days when I'm delivering workshops that start at 10am, I can be set up for the workshop, dial in to the huddle and be back in the workshop room with a good five to ten minutes to spare). We rotate who in the team chairs the meeting, as a way of creating ownership. The huddle, or 'The 9.40' as we call it, takes five minutes on a good day and never more than fifteen minutes.

HOW TO AVOID OTHER PEOPLE'S MEETINGS

'When you say "yes" to others make sure you are not saying "no" to yourself.'
– Paulo Coelho

All of the above are great ways to avoid scheduling attention-sapping, time-wasting meetings. But what happens when the meeting is not yours to call? When someone else invites you to a meeting, it can often seem like you can't say no, and such situations can make you feel guilty about letting other people down. But if you know the meeting is going to be unproductive for you, and sap attention and time you could better use elsewhere there is a Ninja way out of them: avoidance.

'I HAVE BETTER THINGS TO DO'

This is, of course, true, but don't say it like that. 'I'm on a deadline with project X', or 'My boss has asked me to work on project Y exclusively for the next few days.' It's not rude, but it is ruthless.

'I CAN'T MAKE THAT DATE'

A useful line, particularly when you're invited to the meeting as a 'nice luxury' rather than an essential ingredient (which, by the way, is most of the time – since the person organizing the meeting is firmly fixed on their task getting completed and not on protecting your time and attention).

'I CAN'T MAKE IT BUT ...'

Instead of attending the meeting, which may be an hour or two long, spend five minutes reading about the issue at hand, and add a few thoughts to an email. This allows you to contribute without wasting time, and most of the time the meeting organizer will appreciate that you have engaged with the question.

'MAYBE'

This works particularly well with Outlook, where you can use the 'I might attend' option. Don't feel you have to explain yourself – you'll appear as 'tentative', which is usually interpreted as you doing your best to be there; in reality, it might actually be you doing your best to avoid being there. Verbal or email equivalents of this special button can also be employed to similar effect.

You may read these avoidance tactics and say, 'Well if everyone did all this, we'd never have any meetings, but we'd also never have any co-operation in the team and the whole organization would fall apart.' There is certainly some truth in this, and these avoidance techniques are designed to be used only when necessary. Remember, though, that encouraging a culture that questions the status quo is actually a very healthy thing to do. And anyway, if you employ the Ninja technique of stealth you'll be surprised how rarely anyone notices you've avoided a meeting in the first place!

GREAT MEETINGS CAN CHANGE THE WORLD

All of that said, there *are* some times when only a meeting will do. Here are a few ways to think through when a meeting might actually be the best option. Then – and only then – you can plan the most productive meetings of your life.

> '80% of business professionals believe that the outcome of a meeting can be positively influenced by the choice and quality of biscuit on offer.' (Holiday Inn survey, 2008)

MEET IN THE SKY, NOT ON THE GROUND

What usually goes wrong in meetings is that people use them for getting promises on the detail rather than promises on the higher-level questions, such as:

- ▶ 'What's the general approach?'
- ▶ 'If it's this vs. this, what wins?'
- ▶ 'Who are we most out to satisfy here?'
- ▶ 'What's more important here, quality or cost, and where is the line before that answer changes?'

These are the sky-level questions, built on strategic thinking and the knowledge of the bigger picture – find the answers to these, and the action will follow without the need for another meeting to decide the finer details.

> 'A camel is a horse designed by committee.'
> – Alex Issigonis, designer of the Mini

MEET WHEN THE **EMOTIONAL FALLOUT IS IMPORTANT TO MANAGE**

There's definitely no honour in hiding behind an email when communicating the kinds of decisions where someone really deserves the right to look you in the eye. One word of caution here though: only manage emotional fallout if it's important for you to do so. So if John has worked for the company for 27 years and you're having to make his role redundant, that's important. If Bill is going to throw a hissy fit because you've chosen a different design to his preferred choice, perhaps that's something you don't need to see, so let him have that hissy fit somewhere else. Preferably at home.

MEET TO ESTABLISH **MOMENTUM, FLOW AND ENERGY**

Start projects with 'kick-off meetings'. The aim here is to gel a team together so that they're well set up for the next stage of the project. Establishing a good energy, flow and momentum is great because it makes future collaborations easier and smoother. Since the purpose of these meetings is about personal chemistry and light-touch interaction with the issues, it's often a good idea to  hold these kinds of meetings in unorthodox settings. So be brave, and take them tenpin bowling or for a nice meal outside the office.

HOW TO MAKE A MEETING MAGIC

After you have made your excuses and avoided 60–70% of meeting requests and also reduced the number of meetings you personally organize by about 90%, what you're left with are the ones you need to make great. The stakes are suddenly high for these rare occasions. I've been in a few of these in my time. I hope I have even run one or two of them myself, but that's for others to judge, not me!

Some of those great meetings I've attended were conducted by Martin Farrell, Think Productive's meetings magician and a much-trusted colleague. It was Martin who introduced me to the most powerful meetings principle I have come across. This was developed by Lois Graessle and George Gawlinski, who worked with Martin on the book *Meeting Together*. The principle is the '40–20–40' continuum.

THE 40–20–40 CONTINUUM

If you ever need to hold a meeting and you want to make it a success, use the 40–20–40 Continuum: focus 40% of your attention for each meeting on preparation and getting everything right before you meet, then 20% of your attention on the meeting itself – the time you're all together – and then spend 40% of your attention on the follow through.

Like all golden rules, it appears to be simple and even a little obvious on first view, but in reality it's rarely practised and can be difficult to stick to. Our temptation is to spend all our attention on the meeting itself: what the agenda will be, how it will be structured, and so on. In actual fact, more important than these are getting the venue, personnel and 'framing' right. Crucial to the meeting having any impact is, of course, following up to ensure that things actually happen afterwards.

40% PREPARATION

Get the preparation right – and I mean really right – and you'll make the meetings you hold seem like magic. This means thinking through every aspect of preparation, which I am sure will actually take longer than you are used to. As a matter of course you'll need to print agendas, bring background papers or information and, most

importantly, provide biscuits, but this is also about doing all of your thinking long before the meeting begins. The point here is not to spend the least amount of attention and time possible, but on the contrary, to get the highest payback for your investment. Here are a few ways that good preparation can pay itself back in spades:

BEGIN WITH THE *END IN MIND*

Here is another example of where upfront decision-making can really help. Rather than waiting until halfway through a meeting to work out what you think the outcome should be, start there. You'll usually know. You can even add this to the agenda, and as a chair, make sure it is part of your introduction too. An example would be a statement like this:

> 'By the end of the meeting we will have agreed a scheduled plan, with delegated actions so that we can achieve our target of ten new clients by the end of March.'

A more unorthodox, Ninja method is to begin your meeting with the *answer* to your question, not just the question, you then open up the meeting for a more focused gathering of ideas. For example, if your meeting is to set the budget, have someone draw up a draft budget before you start, so that you have something to disagree with but also a general direction set.

FLOW

When you're planning a meeting, think about it as a journey. Work out where you feel you might get stuck, work out where you feel people might need a rest or to stretch their legs, and work out the best route to take. Great meetings provide a sense of a journey. With most meetings, the starting point is setting the scene: introductions to each other, to the topic and to the end point we have in mind. The middle stage is the exploration: discussion, questioning and beginning to form some agreements. The end of a meeting should be where you've clearly gone beyond discussion, and you're into decisions, actions and agreeing the next practical steps forward. It's easy to blur these boundaries without some good 'markers' to signpost the way.

SCHEDULE DIFFICULT AGENDA ITEMS *IMMEDIATELY BEFORE COFFEE OR LUNCH BREAKS*

A great tip with managing flow is to strategically use the natural breaks in the day: a lunch break, a coffee break or the specified finish time. When I am writing agendas I always try to schedule the bits where I can predict things might get a little heated to be just before a coffee break if possible, and better still, immediately before lunch. This means that rather than just being focused on the issue, participants' attention and collective enthusiasm for the fight are diverted towards their collective enthusiasm for a coffee or a nice sandwich and a piece of cake. The person who delays everyone's lunch, even over a matter of principle, is brave indeed. And if it does get a little heated you have the natural break in proceedings to calm everyone down, rather than that heat getting in the way of other agenda items.

ALLOW TIME FOR *'WIGGLE ROOM'*

There are points in a meeting where difficulties and complications will arise from the oddest of places, and there's just no way you can predict these. Rather than trying to predict where this might happen, make a couple of agenda items nearer the end of the meeting slightly longer than you expect will actually be needed. This will give you the necessary wiggle room when other circumstances mean you are running over time. It's like your secret little stash of time. Be aware, though, never to reveal this to others in the room – even those who you trust explicitly – because if they know it's there, it becomes their secret stash too and they will feel equally at liberty to delve in and fritter it away. Use your stealth Ninja techniques and keep it to yourself.

LENGTH

Think carefully about the length of the meeting. The chances are, if you're a disciplined chair, you can probably get it done in a shorter time than would be expected. But what you cannot do is become known for meetings taking longer than planned or needed, so you need to be sensible and realistic at the same time as providing yourself and others with the necessary challenge towards brevity. Just because your Outlook Calendar schedules things in slots of 30 or 60 minutes doesn't mean you can't have a 15- or 45-minute meeting instead – or even a 21-minute meeting if you want to! This is a fine line to manage, so tread carefully by ensuring you have thought it through. An extra five minutes' proactive attention on this could potentially save a whole heap of people's time.

LOCATION AND LAYOUT

How the room is laid out says a lot about the kind of meeting you want to hold: theatre-style with a lectern at the front suggests a didactic style, copious note-taking from the participants, and structured times for them to ask questions. Around a boardroom-style table suggests a level of formality and active participation but with the table and its activities as an occasional barrier to active listening. A horseshoe shaped chair arrangement without a table suggests something akin to group therapy: active listening, team working, consensus building and problem solving. None are right or wrong, just more appropriate to certain occasions and agendas than others. The room layout really matters.

There is also a growing trend developing where people hold their meetings away from the office and in coffee shops. Since as a nation, the UK has in the last ten years really embraced the 'coffee culture' of our European and American counterparts, perhaps this is not surprising. Coffee shops can make great locations for meetings – they're informal, yet you don't want to outstay your welcome, so easy conversation and brevity quickly follow. And of course, fuelled by far too much caffeine from those big mugs, we talk more quickly and are more alert in our pursuit of the outcomes we want.

> 'The room should say, "You Matter".'
> – Nancy Kline

CREATE THE CULTURE YOU NEED

I did some interim management work where I had to sit in on a weekly management meeting. What impressed me most was that the Chief Executive of this organization had created a culture where preparation was *absolutely* expected. The chair was prepared, but so were all of the other senior managers. We were expected to have read all the papers in advance, and as a result, the conversations were focused on opinions and actions rather than on clarifications and long explorations. The meeting itself covered more in 40 minutes than a lot of meetings do in three or more hours. This culture was not an accidental one: it was not only planned, but meticulously reinforced by the Chief Executive, who introduced each item with a couple of lines that almost always included, 'I assume that everyone has read the paper' before very quickly getting onto decisions. If you fail to prepare, you're prepared to fail – you might make this mistake once and miss the boat on an issue of importance to your team. The following week, you'll arrive ready to do battle, having done all the necessary background reading. Create this culture in your teams and you'll make life much easier.

20% IS THE MEETING ITSELF

You've prepared meticulously and encouraged others to do the same. You've even bought good biscuits. How do you now ensure that your meeting is productive?

THE WELCOME AND THE OPENING ROUND

For groups bigger than four or five people, where the group dynamic is going to take a bit longer to gel, the challenge is to make everyone feel as comfortable as possible. Feeling comfortable and welcomed leads to people making an active contribution, as their perceived risk of appearing foolish subsides. One of many ways to do this is to try to make eye contact and have

brief conversations with people as they arrive, making sure you use the word 'welcome' and make people feel special. If you think this is petty or an unnecessary detail, think about the times you've either felt welcomed or not welcomed when you've arrived at meetings – it's powerful.

At the beginning of meetings I chair, I usually ask people to contribute to an 'opening round', inspired by Nancy Kline's excellent book *Time To Think*, which describes how to create the ideal environment for great listening and great thinking. This simple tool allows everyone to contribute and feel comfortable in taking the group's attention for a brief period, and therefore contributes to the bonding of the group.

My usual opening round consists of three or four questions, such as:

▶ Name

▶ Your role (and where you work if the meeting is bringing together more than one organization or location)

▶ Why you're here

▶ One thing that's going well (this can be left deliberately vague enough to mean either professional or personal and is a great ice-breaker).

The last question is my favourite. It's where people open up a little bit, take a small personal risk to engage the attention of the group, and feel more confident about engaging more with the group later on when the meaty stuff is happening. There are also all kinds of studies done on the effect that laughter has on group decision-making, and the final question always provides at least one laugh from a member of the group coming up with something entertaining to say. It's a simple but very effective little tool.

PACE

As the chair, your job is to manage the pace of the meeting. You'll want to strike a balance here: avoid the temptation to become too brisk in order to save time, as sometimes you'll save this time at the expense of people feeling involved and committed to what you're trying to get done. This will backfire later when people start reneging on commitments or protesting that they haven't been heard. At the same time, we're here to make things happen, not get involved in some kind of group therapy session, so you don't want to give people so much opportunity to speak that they start repeating themselves for the sake of it. Think about the kind of meeting you need to have, or the kind of consensus you need to strike here: you can only go as fast as the slowest person in the room, so use your judgement wisely in deciding when, if at all, it's possible to leave that person behind.

ENCOURAGE THE IDENTIFICATION AND *DISCUSSION OF ROADBLOCKS*

What's in the way of achieving your aims? Sometimes this is not an easy thing for people to explain. Sometimes *you* are the thing standing in the way. Sometimes it's personalities, sometimes the team members aren't clear on the task, or have different understandings of what is to be done. Provide a window – either in the meeting or with people individually both before and after the meeting – to openly explore and voice their thoughts on what the roadblocks are. In teams, communication is king, so actively encourage it and make meetings the 'excuse' that some people need to raise issues as well as the place where others can't avoid confronting them.

SLIGHTLY UNCOMFORTABLE = *QUICKER DECISIONS*

Slight discomfort can be a great catalyst for group decision-making. Make reference to this as you are chairing:

▶ 'I know we're all keen to get to coffee break so let's wrap this up and move on.'

▶ 'It's a little warm in here I know. I'll get someone to look into the air conditioning as soon as we've finished this item.'

▶ 'Let's spend another five minutes on this and then we can stretch our legs.'

Other more extreme versions of using this slight discomfort as the catalyst for more focused decision-making include holding meetings in unusual locations, or even standing up. Stand up meetings are a useful tool, but remember the attention tension we discussed at the beginning of the chapter – there are times when discomfort and 'just getting on with it' are the best approach, but also times where discomfort reduces our ability to listen and participate fully.

STEERING TO THE DESTINATION

During the meeting, the role of the chair or facilitator is to take the lead role in steering everyone on the road to the destination, ensuring that decisions and actions are clarified as clearly as possible. If it's the kind of meeting that someone is taking formal minutes for (which in my experience is only occasionally useful), you can make reference to the minutes *during* a meeting as a way of gaining clarity on what is being decided ('OK then folks, how should we capture this in the minutes?'). The mere fact that you are agreeing how to phrase something for the purposes of the person writing the minutes allows a more focused discussion, to ensure that everyone really is on the same page.

CREATE A SAFE SPACE TO MAKE MISTAKES

Mistakes are often looked at as inherently bad. But progress often comes from experimenting as much with what doesn't work as what does. As one Chief Executive once told me, 'I have no problem with people screwing up. My problem is always with the people who don't own up or clear up'. Encourage experimentation and innovation, and think instead about how to do this as 'safely' as possible.

ALL'S WELL *THAT ENDS WELL*

It's important to end a meeting well. The final few minutes will be what most people will remember, so leave them with a sense of purpose, group harmony and momentum. Tell everyone what will happen next and make sure everyone is clear on next steps, especially the steps that involve their actions.

PUBLIC *COMMITMENTS*

Public commitments are a great way to hold people to account and ensure that everyone takes on their responsibilities. Ask participants to commit their actions to paper, and share these either in pairs or with the group as a whole. In the past I have also employed an old facilitator's trick of asking everyone to write a letter or postcard to themselves three months or six months into the future, detailing what they will achieve. I literally collect these up and post them on a set date in the future. But more important than actually receiving it in six months' time (which provides a surprising, physical reminder) it means that somewhere at the back of their minds, the participants resolve to commit to their actions, so that they are done before the letter arrives.

CLOSING *ROUND*

It can also be useful to do a 'closing round' similar to the opening round I mentioned at the beginning of this section.

Again, it gives everyone a chance to speak and feel as though they have participated well, but also offers a few moments to turn their attention to reflecting on their involvement and begin planning ahead. I usually use the following questions as part of a closing round:

- ▶ What have you enjoyed most about this meeting?
- ▶ Has anything surprised you during the meeting?
- ▶ What are you planning to do as a result of the meeting?
- ▶ What are you looking forward to?

40% FOLLOW THROUGH

'Talk does not cook rice.'
– Chinese proverb

The follow through from a meeting is not only an important point, it is *the* point. Without follow through and actual action, meetings are meaningless. Commitments to action or good ideas on their own don't make things happen, they don't get things done, and they don't change the world. Think about that for a moment: the most meticulously planned and beautifully chaired meeting can be a complete and utter waste of time without action and follow through. So let's talk about some of the key habits needed to create a culture of follow through and productive action.

DEVELOP AN ACTION SUMMARY DURING THE MEETING ITSELF

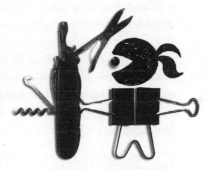

Don't fall at the first hurdle. So many meetings I see get this far, and then the chair commits to taking all the information away, making some sense of the actions, and emailing around later. By the time everyone receives their actions, it's like that old game of 'Chinese Whispers': the words start to lose their meaning. What's more, the memory of the meeting itself is now fading, as there have now been several other meetings on several other topics since, and it's looking less clear what actually needs to be done and by whom. Vagueness breeds procrastination, which breeds fear, and so on and so on.

Follow through starts at the end of the meeting. Don't leave a meeting until you and everyone else has a clear sense of the actions that need to be taken. That means having an action list, preferably visible on a flip chart, already typed into the minutes on a laptop, or on paper somewhere. Use the meeting itself to gain clarity around what needs to be done, and make sure there's a commitment to these actions from all involved.

THE **CULTURE** OF ACTION

Having an action list in meetings is not enough, though. There needs to be a culture of action developing in your teams so that when follow through is completed, it is rewarded but not treated as a complete surprise. It needs to be the expectation and the day-to-day reality not the cause for fuss or celebration.

THE **CAPTURE** EMAIL

The chair should ensure that either they or someone delegated to do this task sends a 'capture' email which includes, either within the text or as an attachment, a complete and clear list of action points. It should also thank the participants for their time and begin to talk of what will happen as a result of the commitments that have been made. Develop momentum, remind everyone of what they are committed to achieving, and do so in a way that can be stored away for ease of reference. Make it clear to read (bullet points, not too long), and clear on the detail of what is involved.

WHO'S DRIVING **NOW?**

Once the meeting is over and you're into follow through mode, it might be easier for someone else to be in charge of driving the actions. Use the capture email as a way of being clear who's now in charge. It might be the same person that was chairing the meeting, or it might be a project manager entrusted to see the project through. But be clear with whom this responsibility lies, who actions should be directed towards, and who will deal with any issues or questions.

CREATE WINDOWS FOR CLARIFICATION QUESTIONS

If you are heading up a team project you need to create windows where the clarification questions can happen without the risk of that person appearing foolish. This might be by follow up emails (more in a moment on this) but could also just be via regular check-ins, desk hijacking, MBWA (managing by walking about) or as part of other discussions. Ask questions such as:

▶ 'Are you clear on what you're supposed to be doing?'

▶ 'Do you have everything you need?'

▶ 'Are you on track?'

And so on, but note that these questions alone don't provide the permission to clarify without the risk of appearing foolish. You need caveats such as:

▶ 'I wouldn't be surprised if you had a few things you needed to clarify. I have some time this week if you want to run through anything?'

▶ 'I know there was a lot to get our heads around so just ask if you need anything.'

▶ 'I've had a few people come back to me with questions already; do you have any?' (Say this one even if you've had no such thing, as it makes people feel they're not alone, and ergo, not foolish.)

▶ 'There are some big challenges in there; what are yours?'

Over time you'll start to notice which people will willingly volunteer their questions to you, which ones will avoid it until coaxed out and which people will avoid any clarifying conversations at all costs, even though they don't have a clue how to achieve what needs to be done.

FOLLOW UP EMAILS

The capture email immediately after a meeting is almost expected these days. What is far less common is a follow up email a week or a month later. This email could simply reattach the original action list, or could provide some updates to give an increased sense of momentum. Above all, it is a reminder that actions are required and it opens that all-important window for safe question clarification at the same time.

DEADLINES

Where possible, have a deadline. We talked about this during the 'Do' part of our CORD process. Deadlines produce rabbits out of hats. Think about that project where you worked into the night to get it finished: seemed impossible when you first started, didn't it? By the same token, when delegating actions from meetings, don't be afraid to work under constraints that place people under tight deadlines, so long as you make yourself available for questions and renegotiation.

MAKE IT MEASURABLE

The action should be measurable not just by the deadline, but by the substance and its impact. Again, these are tools that force clarity and focus in the initial stages, and make the monitoring and follow through much easier as a result. Asking questions about the substance of the action can also be a great way to regularly renegotiate actions if a few weeks after a meeting, a different kind of action is now required.

EXERCISE: MAKING CHANGES AND CHECKLISTS FOR A REGULAR MEETING

What you'll need: Space to think, proactive boss-mode attention

How long it'll take: 60 minutes preparation, 30–45 minutes for the meeting, 60–90 minutes follow through

Ninja mindset: Preparedness

▶ Think about a regular meeting that you chair. It could be a team status meeting or a six-monthly away day review meeting.

▶ Develop a checklist for the agenda items that come up.

▶ Develop a checklist for the actions that always need to happen at the end of the meeting.

▶ If possible include timescales and more detail around the actions.

▶ Map out the process of preparation, the meeting itself and the follow through, spending 40% of time on preparation, 20% on the things you'll do in the meeting and 40% on the follow through

Think about what you're not doing in this meeting right now that would make life easier, and as it's a regular meeting, spend some time right now working on improving these systems so that they can be used more productively, over and over again.

Are you a Ninja?

▶ A Ninja's Zen-like calm comes from regularly reviewing every area of their work – treating everything as a project.

▶ A Ninja takes an unorthodox view of project management and meetings, focusing more on agility and responsiveness than on old-fashioned 'planning'.

▶ A Ninja uses projects and meetings to promote mindfulness and preparedness, and to create trust and develop group momentum.

11. MOMENTUM

'I was already on pole position ... I just kept going. Suddenly I was nearly two seconds faster than anybody else, including my teammate with the same car. And suddenly I realized that I was no longer driving the car consciously. I was driving it by a kind of instinct, only I was in a different dimension. It was like I was in a tunnel.'
– Ayrton Senna (Formula One Champion) speaking after qualifying sessions for the 1988 Monaco Grand Prix

In the last few chapters you have read and implemented the CORD Productivity Model and developed a second brain for managing projects and actions, you've got your email inbox under control and you've focused on managing projects, cutting down on your meetings and making the most of the meetings you do need to attend. All of the tips, advice and approaches we've discussed work. I know that because I've implemented them, I've trained and coached people implementing them and I've seen and experienced the results. Surely nothing can stop you now! Except, well, yourself.

So many time management books fail to recognize that as humans, we're incredibly complex creatures and don't always do what's best for ourselves – even when we know what we *should* do. We make bad decisions and sometimes prioritize low-impact activities when much bigger potential payoffs lie in our unfinished Master Actions List. We also procrastinate, thinking up lame excuses to avoid the difficult things that might well lead to greatness but might also risk making us look foolish or involve confrontation or just intense concentration along the way. We give in to many temptations, interruptions and distractions.

Even when we're ready to 'Do' – even with all the knowledge, tools and systems in the world – we can somehow still find a plethora of reasons *not* to do. As Ninjas, we have yet another enemy to fight: our own resistance.

RESISTANCE

Living somewhere deep inside your soul is a nasty, evil little creature. It's cunning, it's invisible, it's spiteful, it's needy, it's reckless, it's jealous and worst of all, it knows you better than you know yourself. This awful monster is your resistance. No one quite  knows what motivates resistance and why it bothers your conscience at times when all you want to do is get on with your day and get on with being productive. What's certainly true is the more personally invested you are in the work that you're doing, and the more you have riding on the outcome of the actions you're managing, the more your resistance will do its very best to sabotage, destroy and derail.

'You don't need more genius. You need less resistance.' – Seth Godin

Stephen Pressfield's *The War of Art* is a book about your internal resistance and how to beat it. It tells the story of creative people battling their internal monologues of despair, doubt, jealousy, fear and everything else that resistance throws at them to stop them from doing what they need to do. You may not think it, but you too are a 'creative'. If your job involves creating value out of information and ideas, then you're exactly who Stephen Pressfield was describing. Whether you're conscious of it or not, whether you choose to acknowledge it publicly or not, we all experience our own resistance. The Productivity Ninja must use self-awareness to win battles against resistance and use every stealth trick possible to temporarily out-manoeuvre it or build up enough of a head of steam in your work that not even the resistance's best attempts can derail you now. Resistance becomes powerless only in the face of serious momentum. This chapter is about understanding your resistance and creating momentum to use against it.

THE LIZARD BRAIN

THE LIZARD BRAIN

There's a very good reason our resistance exists, despite all the pain and stress it can cause us. Such thoughts come from the oldest part of our brains. The amygdala, part of our brain's limbic system, is the part of our brain that controls our most basic of survival functions: self-defence, hunger, fear, sex, anger and escape. Keep still and the predators will go away. Keep still, don't stand out and we'll live safely to see another day.

Any form of creativity – and I use that word in the loosest and broadest possible sense to include much of the work that you do – will be a battle between two different instincts inside your brain. Your smarter, more developed, human brain craves success and the delivery of your work and your ideas to the wider world. The lizard brain – the source of all of your resistance – is scared by what might happen if you do something it's never seen you do before. It worries about survival, status and safety. It chooses comfort over a shot at the big time.

Anything that your resistance thinks might provoke reaction or change, it will try to disrupt. At the merest hint of a risk that you might look foolish, it will scream, shout, bite and hassle. Anything to survive. Just blend in, keep quiet and look busy.

RECOGNIZING YOUR RESISTANCE

Resistance is simplistic and has just a few core emotions. But never underestimate its force, creativity and deviousness. It can manifest itself in so many different forms. Here are some common forms of resistance for you to look out for. As long as it is, this is far from an exhaustive list:

▶ Being a perfectionist

▶ Arranging a meeting about doing the work you could just do now

▶ Spending ages changing fonts, styles or titles when the rest of the work is already done

▶ Spending hours on research or data collection

▶ Leaving out the controversial or interesting bits

▶ Over-organizing

▶ Being afraid of change

▶ Criticizing people for trying to be innovative or different

▶ Worrying more about the word count than the words

▶ Obsessively checking your work

▶ Asking others for reassurance disguised as feedback

▶ Making a cup of tea instead of starting a courageous conversation

▶ Playing with productivity apps on your phone rather than being more productive.

What you'll notice is that so many of these hit straight to the heart of our proactive attention and distract us with powerful emotions and ingrained habits. Recognizing resistance is the vital first stage. Once you recognize anything resembling resistance, the battle begins.

BATTLING – AND OVERCOMING – RESISTANCE

There are really two ways to deal with resistance at any given moment:

▶ *FIND A WAY OF **IGNORING IT** OR SILENCING IT*

▶ ***CHEAT IT** SO YOU DON'T NOTICE IT*

1. SILENCING RESISTANCE

ACKNOWLEDGEMENT

Our resistance scuttles around inside our brains, rarely showing its face and disguising itself as other thoughts wherever it can. You have to regularly dig it out. A number of the habits and behaviours in this book are designed to flush out resistance:

▶ **Capturing and collecting** what's on your mind allows resistance its little moment in the sun. It nags, blurts and screams. And you get the chance to organize each and every one of those thoughts. The nags and noises are tossed away and given short shrift.

▶ **Meditation.** We rarely delve deep enough into our own minds to really listen to what's going on in there. Meditation is a great way to explore, to notice and to recognize. It's also a great way to *slow down* and detach from the frantic trail of thoughts racing through your mind all day long. In doing this, you become much more able to focus, concentrate and be present.

▶ **Nutrition and physical exercise.** Good physical health can actually reduce the power of resistance. Fitness sessions produce positive endorphins, leaving us feeling on such a high that while we know resistance is there somewhere, we also feel like we're stronger.

▶ **Relaxation.** So many of resistance's most powerful moments happen after the event. We finish work, go home to bathe our child or to a theatre show and just as we're trying to relax, we hear it.

▶ **Reviewing** the Weekly and Daily Checklists. The review stage is crucial. Because you're in the midst of taking stock and seeing the wood from the trees, your review times will stir your resistance and it'll do its very best to disrupt and disturb you.

▶ **Mentors.** A mentor can help you realize that you're not alone and that even the most seemingly cool and calm people have periods in their work and in their lives where they're the swan: graceful on the water's surface but paddling furiously underneath.

RIDICULE

As powerful as it is, resistance is essentially a small-minded idiot. One of the best things you can do – one of the things your resistance hates more than anything – is to show it up as the puny little weasel that it really is. You have more sophisticated reasoning to throw at it. Here are a few ways to really embarrass your resistance:

▶ Change the paradigm from, 'What if it goes wrong?' to 'What if it doesn't?' Our fear often points us towards imagining only our possible failures, in such a way that we fail to realize that the consequences of our actions could in fact be unbridled and wonderful success! On the other hand, if we imagine every task as potentially the thing that our ultimate success depends on, it becomes overwhelming because the stakes are high! So pick yourself out of the quagmire of negative thinking and imagine a world where what you're working on right now isn't going to make you a millionaire, but certainly isn't about to bankrupt you either! It's all going to be fine.

▶ Bust yourself. Say it out loud. Tell someone in the office, perhaps a close and trusted colleague, that you're struggling to finish this PowerPoint presenta-

'I feel I'm in a "downloading" period, right now. I used to call it writer's block but there's no such thing.'
– Erykah Badu

tion because of the resistance. As soon as you say it out loud, you'll realize just how silly it is that this little lizard-brained idiot holds any sway with you. Watch your resistance back off the minute it knows that it's been spotted.

BRAVERY & RUTHLESSNESS

It's rarely the easiest option to actually battle resistance head on. It takes courage, strength and major self-awareness to outwit resistance for any significant length of time. However, if you want to try, here are some ideas that might help:

- ▶ **Create space to force the resistance to battle with you directly.** Don't allow it to disguise itself in websites and other temptations. Create the space where it's just you and the resistance. That way the little critter is easier to hear and easier to trap.

- ▶ **Stare your resistance in the eye** (resistance hates face to face conflict), so you'll anger it, making it louder and more powerful. While you stare, laugh at its puny body, its silly ideas, the useless tactics that you've sussed out, keep laughing and smiling and realizing the power you really have over it. Wait until you feel it scuttling away for the bushes.

- ▶ **Let the resistance out to play.** Take a piece of A4 paper and toy with your resistance. Let it write a 'cons and cons' list of all the reasons not to do the thing that your resistance is shouting at you to avoid. Exhaust the resistance this way. Once done, write a simple list of pros underneath, as you quietly assume control.

- ▶ **Out-negative your resistance.** Think of all the times that things have really gone badly for you in the past. Anything that the resistance throws at you from here is a step up, a victory, and therefore a level of comfort for the resistance that might just force it to surrender … for now.

2. CHEATING RESISTANCE

Of course, much easier than acknowledging, ridiculing or battling the resistance is not having to deal with it at all. Here are some ways that you can sidestep, cheat, outwit and generally out-stealth the resistance. For now, anyway.

DROWNING OUT RESISTANCE WITH A BETTER NOISE

In Stephen King's love letter to his craft, *On Writing*, he talks passionately about his morning routine that empowers him as a writer to get started. One of the scariest things in the world if you're a writer is a blank page. On a blank page, you have nothing but your resistance for company and it's unsettling. King talks in that book about his love of heavy metal music and strong coffee. Both, he says, are things that help him write. They drown out any possible noise of resistance and create the illusion of momentum, which can be replaced by the real stuff as those first words come out. I have three or four pieces of music that always work for me. One of these is Michael Jackson's *Don't Stop 'Til You Get Enough*, the first track on his breakthrough album, *Off The Wall*. It's an explosion of disco energy, optimism, and abandon – you can almost hear his star break through in the minds of everyone listening to it for the first time, it's so bold; and as such, it's the perfect antidote to resistance.

ROUTINES

Routines can distract resistance for just long enough to get you into momentum. Following a particular pattern at the start of your day, where the fifth of six elements happens to be doing a piece of work that your resistance would usually shout and scream about is a clever way of nipping in with the work before your resistance notices. For a long time when I worked from home, my morning routine was deliberately regimented:

1. Drink water
2. Ten minute run
3. Shower
4. Breakfast
5. Worst task of the day
6. Daily Checklist

Hidden inside so many positive, comfortable tasks was doing something truly dreadful. With the endorphins from my run still pumping around my body, the resistance didn't know where to look. These days, every morning is different but those that start with good routines tend to continue on into more productive days.

THE *ILLUSION* OF COMFORT

Remember that your resistance craves comfort and safety. Doing your most challenging work in beautiful, luxurious surroundings can trick resistance into realizing everything is just fine rather than fearing for its life. I work in Brighton and try to do most of my writing on beaches gazing out over the sea. I find it calming and I also find it eliminates the day-to-day distractions and interruptions that give the resistance its hiding places. Try to find an environment that works for you . And if you can't, you can borrow an idea from the world of Neuro-Linguistic-Programming and learn how to develop 'states'. If you're about to make a phone call that you're dreading, or are about to walk into a terrifying meeting, take a deep breath and smile. Use your body positively to send positive signals and reduce fear. Walking tall really helps.

CREATE A *BIGGER FEAR*

This is one of my favourites. Your resistance will rattle around its perfectionist nonsense for as long as you let it, but the fear of looking foolish and losing status is a powerful one, and it unites you and your resistance in a battle to ship on time.

▶ Have fun with deadlines. It's helpful to have someone else create a deadline to focus your attention on for any projects with open ends and where the potential for procrastination is very high. The fear of missing the deadline far outweighs any petty resistance thoughts about the perceived quality of the work. You'll do anything to ensure you don't look foolish in front of people you truly care about. Including, as it happens, delivering work that is well below your best. Of course, you only discover that you've delivered work that you wouldn't have found acceptable in hindsight. At which point, you realize that no one else noticed.

▶ Public pronouncements. If you're contemplating taking your first steps into a new project, one of the best ways of making sure it happens is to announce it. This is the mindset of the entrepreneur. Announce first; plan, build and deliver later. Richard Branson famously did this with his Virgin Cola brand. For years, people in his company had talked about producing their own cola but the company's collective resistance had always stalled the development in favour of other things. One day, Branson was at a press conference for something completely un-related and was asked what else the company had planned. 'This year, we're going to produce our own Cola!' Back in the office, he arrived to scenes of blind panic but frenetic activity. 'Did you hear what I just announced?!', he asked. He didn't need the answer.

GAMEIFICATION

Making a game out of your work can distract you from the resistance just long enough to overcome it. Gameification is a relatively new term and is certainly getting more sophisticated, but the principles of making your work a game have been around for a long time. Here are some of the main games we play at work:

▶ Sales Targets. No one wants to be a loser. So they push harder to meet that target and receive their winner's medal and some public praise.

▶ Appraisal Ratings and Performance Related Pay. The ultimate game, in that *all* of your work contributes towards one win or loss each year (or each quarter).

▶ Getting your inbox to zero. Yes, if you get obsessed with getting back to zero you know it'll be good for you, but you might not bother on those days where you're feeling over-whelmed. On our email training workshops, we give people small badges when they get their inbox to zero. This makes what is a serious process seem like a fun game, and you would seriously not believe the calibre of senior, senior people who could have any material possession in the world, but are sat in my training, clamouring for a badge!

▶ Ego-challenge. 'I bet you can't get an interview with that famous actress.' I bet you want to work harder trying to now, though.

POSITIVE *MOMENTUM HABITS*

Resistance is eventually beaten by momentum. But what if you could maintain and continue momentum anyway, without the need to create it just to silence the resistance? The truth is that sometimes we get into that positive momentum zone seemingly without effort, while at other times it feels near impossible

to get out of the starting blocks. There are a few habits that you can develop that will help drive positive momentum.

WORST *FIRST*

Start every day by doing the worst task on your list. It could be the biggest of your 'big rocks' or the thing you're least looking forward to. The sense of relief in having polished that one off before 10am is palpable. And everything else that day is of course, easier. It avoids all the resistance that can build and build if you continue to delay and procrastinate, finding yourself over-thinking that one big task throughout the day.

PAPER

If you need to get your brain in gear, give it permission to have thoughts and be creative. Surround yourself with paper, Post-it notes and nice pens and watch as good ideas flow out of you. This is a great tip if you're in a meeting where the group seems to have got stuck. Get some flipchart paper and Blu-Tack. Put up some sheets on the wall and give people Post-it notes to jot down their thoughts. It's one of those magical tricks for getting a group of people unstuck. It works equally well if you just don't know where to start. It feels easier to write down the possible structure of the report you're trying to write on a scrappy piece of paper than it does to commit those thoughts to a fresh Word document. So give your brain the permission it sometimes needs to have lots of bad ideas and from there the good ones will show up.

SHOW *UP*

So often when we think we're stuck, we just need to actually get to the starting line. Doing the first five minutes of a task is usually all that's needed to demystify it and get the ideas and actions flowing. So if you've been putting off reading that report, putting off working on your next big project, resolve to start. You should, of course, know the exact next physical thing that needs to be done, since that's how you're writing it on your Master Actions List. If you already know what you need to do, how hard can it be?! Go on, just show up for five minutes. You'll be surprised at what happens.

WARM UP

The dancer Twyla Tharp talks about one of her 'power habits' in the book *Mastering the Creative Habit*. As a dancer, her body needs to warm up. Therefore, her habit to ensure momentum and creativity is getting out of bed and downstairs to the waiting taxi, which takes her to the gym. No matter how rough she's feeling that morning, no matter how much she wants another half an hour in bed, the act of getting out of bed is the thing that ensures she warms up that morning. It in turn assures her that when the time comes to create, she's ready. Warming up sets the tone.

SHUT UP

Have you ever noticed that the people who spend a lot of time talking about their work are actually not getting anything done? Be the quiet assassin of the office, produce magic in the kind of volumes that others can only dream of. And once you're doing that, if you really want to talk about your work, you can be sure that others will be asking you about it.

COURAGEOUS CONVERSATIONS

If you're stuck in your thinking, or there's an awkward conflict that you have been avoiding, remember that courageous conversations will get things flowing again. If it feels awkward, you could even start your conversation with the words, 'You know, I think we need to have a courageous conversation.' Usually the other person will know exactly what it's going to be about. And you'll get some momentum back.

IN PRAISE OF ANTI-PERFECTION

Finally, let's talk about the idea of perfection. This might seem unorthodox as it's certainly not what you learned in school, but perfection is your enemy, not your friend. Avoid perfection at all costs as it can seriously stifle positive momentum. Perfection is generally a pointless waste of time. The last moments spent on something are rarely the best ones. Once your best and most productive time is spent, it's time to move on before perfectionism takes its grip. Do you want to ship a hundred new things out into the world or five perfect ones?

There's *always* more that you could give to something or more that you could do with something, but that doesn't mean you should try to. Move on to the other things that create impact. *If* there were only one task left to do before the world ended, you might decide to spend as much time as possible striving for perfection. Or you might decide to ship it earlier, then sit back with a beer and enjoy the fireworks.

Not only is striving for perfection often a pointless waste of time, but it allows resistance more time to develop its more sophisticated disguises. Our inner perfectionist is a voice that responds to resistance, but can also feed it too. Fiddling around with the spacing between paragraphs on a Word document is a sure-fire sign that you're letting your perfectionist win. Just get it out. Let people see it.

The value is never in the frills, it's in the substance. Remember Pareto's Law of 80–20 and from it, the idea that 20% of what you do creates 80% of the impact. I do a lot of work with boards of directors. The people who sit on boards are busy people with lots of things to do other than read the report you're preparing. Now ask yourself this honestly: does the board really want a 45-page perfect document that they'll have to pretend they've read when it comes to that point in the meeting – or do they really just want the salient points? The one-page executive summary is far more powerful than the perfect report. *If* they need to delve into the detail, they'll ask.

Sometimes we confuse care with perfection. 'Perfect' service in a restaurant isn't actually perfect, it's just done with such noticeable care. Care is to be celebrated. If someone knows you truly care about the outcome of what you're doing, they'll forgive imperfection. Ship it like you care, don't wait to make it perfect.

Therefore, as you strive for delivery, you might even like to strive for anti-perfection. Give yourself the personal permission to *be* imperfect and to produce imperfect work – that *still* counts. Let your work have the quality to result in amazing impact, but also produce it in such quantities that means more amazing impact still. Surely that should be what we strive for. Allow yourself the safe space to make mistakes and learn from them.

Indeed, there's glory in imperfection. We should celebrate accidents. Remember that over the centuries, accidents have led us to the discovery of the force of gravity, some of our most amazing pieces of music, new foods and recipes and a thousand things that fill our worlds, and our work, with wonder. Celebrate the fact that accidents can bring surprises, humour, colour and excitement. And celebrate the fact that it's only through these imperfections and the unpredictable that we remind ourselves that we're ultimately just humans after all. We're not superheroes, we're just Productivity Ninjas, doing our best.

And when imperfection has us questioning our ability and trying to convince ourselves that things aren't worth the hassle and we should ditch whatever we're doing for a quieter or easier life, we can just decide to focus instead on our many and varied successes and – *get this* – just stop beating ourselves up quite so much. We're human and it's those that expect everything to be perfect all the time that are the crazy ones, not us.

Yet importantly, the accidents and imperfections only serve as a contrast to prove how magical it can be when things go to plan and they remind us never to take it for granted that things always will. All that magic? All those amazing things that we made happen? All that energy and momentum and explosive productivity? Well, it wasn't magic at all, it just appeared so. And it was actually all quite easy – because of super *human* Ninja skills, not *superhuman* special powers.

Imperfection is the reminder that underneath it all, we're still remarkably and reassuringly human.

SO WHAT ARE YOU WAITING FOR? TIME TO DEVELOP YOUR OWN PLAYFUL, PRODUCTIVE MOMENTUM ...

I really hope you've enjoyed this book and I'd like to thank you for investing money, time and attention in what I've had to say. Before I go, I want to leave you with a confession. I used to be rubbish at all this stuff and even now after years of learning it and teaching it, knowing how much I've improved my own productivity, I know I can still do more. And before you ask for your money back and retreat for a guru, I did warn you of this at the very beginning. Don't get me wrong, I've got some great systems in place and I've worked hard at achieving a very high level of productivity. But I don't want you to put this book down thinking I'm any different to you. We're fellow travellers on the same journey because there's always new stuff to discover.

There's always more to learn, always opportunities to improve. Everything I've presented in this book is, I think, pretty much common sense. It's just less commonly applied than you might expect. You think *you* struggle with these things? Think about the people who aren't even self-aware enough to have bought a book and made a start!

So this is the moment that really counts.

The knowledge from the last few chapters is in the bank. Yours to keep. You can also go back and re-read bits of this tomorrow or next week or next month if you want to. It doesn't really matter if you do or not. Here's what's important:

WHAT ARE YOU GOING TO DO?

Let's make this so much more than an internally focused navel gaze at your own productivity bad habits. Let's make some change. All those exercises that you promised you'd go back and do later, all those great ideas you had about changes you can make to your own productivity habits, all the plans you were going to make tomorrow, well why not make a start right now? The big leap is from idea to practical action, so let's get started on creating the super Ninja that you want, hope and deserve to be. You don't need to start big, but you do need to start. Don't just sit nodding from the sidelines.

But more than this, let's make this an opportunity for you to change stuff, out there, in the world, too.

BECAUSE IT'S ALL POSSIBLE. ALL OF IT. **THE LIMIT ISN'T YOUR SKILLS OR YOUR TIME,** IT'S YOUR IMAGINATION.

You really can change the world. I know that sounds cheesy, but all of your heroes who have done that over the years were humans just like you, they just had the confidence to aim high. And when something went wrong, they got back up and used all their Zen-like Calm, Ruthlessness, Weapon-savviness, Stealth and Camouflage, Mindfulness, Unorthodoxy, Preparedness and Agility to start again. Persistent and brilliant always wins in the end.

Talk is cheap. Action is what counts.

We all have those mornings when despite the best of intentions we find ourselves stuck in a rut, unable to get going and start taking action. On those days, I put on my headphones and listen to Miles Davis's album, *Kind of Blue*. If you're a jazz fan (and even if you're not), you'll probably know that this album is considered one of the greatest albums of all time, regularly featured at the top of all of those critics' choice polls in books and magazines. It's a beautiful piece of music from start to finish and helps me to create the momentum I need.

I saw a documentary about the making of *Kind of Blue* a few years ago. I was amazed to find out that the entire album was recorded in just two short recording sessions, totalling no more than seven or eight hours. Those brief moments in time in the spring of 1959 produced a masterpiece that still has impact to this day – and yet the total time taken to record it was no longer than the hours available to you when you arrive at your desk first in the morning. Just seven or eight hours.

We're all capable of creating a masterpiece. Miles made it look easy and certainly made it look magical. It probably helped that Miles wasn't getting interrupted by emails as he played his solos. But the truth is just that he knew it was all about playful, productive momentum. He lined up great musicians and he made sure that everything was prepared – without being over-prepared of course. He encouraged his musicians to strive for impact, not perfection.

So when I hear *Kind of Blue*, it inspires me to get out of my morning fogginess and create the momentum to make things happen: by getting a team around me, by planning, by committing, by taking the decisive first steps and all the while doing my best to silence my own resistance. Once that playful, productive momentum is in the air, it's actually harder to stop things happening than it ever was getting things going, no matter how loudly my lizard brain is screaming. And of course, as a Productivity Ninja, I can keep all of that momentum under relaxed control.

It's amazing to think that as a result of this book, we could create a movement of Productivity Ninjas, spread across different industries, backgrounds, ages and roles, yet all intent on making positive change in the world, no matter how big or small. My plan with this book was to inspire people to become Productivity Ninjas and then inspire them to share their Ninja skills with others, to create a supportive community that celebrates and nurtures those that make things happen. So please lend this book to a friend, spread the word about the way of the Productivity Ninja, improve your own skills and help others do the same. You'll find Think Productive's contact details at the back of this book and I hope you'll keep in touch with us.

So that's what I'm going to do. How about you?

Are you a Ninja?

Unorthodoxy

Zen-like Calm

Ruthlessness

Agility

Weapon-savvy

Mindfulness

Stealth & Camouflage

Preparedness

A Ninja is not Superhuman

FIVE OTHER BOOKS YOU NEED TO READ!

The Seven Habits of Highly Effective People, Stephen Covey

Getting Things Done, David Allen

The War of Art, Stephen Pressfield

Meeting Together, Lois Graessle, George Gawlinski and Martin Farrell

Linchpin, Seth Godin

A word about products and perceived endorsements in this book

While I think it's by far the most useful way to go, one of the downsides of writing a book where you want to give practical advice about technology and tools is that it's out of date before it's even released, as the world of productivity software in particular moves so fast. Another downside is that there are many useful pieces of software and my job is often to pick just one, when in reality there are many good options. The Think Productive blog will occasionally run articles about new or interesting products coming on the market, so if you subscribe to us we'll do our best to keep you updated! And rest assured, my choices are always made based purely on experience and objectivity. I do not receive anything from any company recommended in this book in exchange for advertising their products.

Acknowledgements

Firstly, I want to thank you for buying this book. It's the result of me spending the last five years training myself and others to be more productive. During that time, I've received hundreds of emails back with tales of reduced time spent on email, improved meetings, life-changing moments and powerful impact created. It's been an amazing journey and I hope I have captured some of that here and provided something of value to you. If so, please do get in touch – I'd love to hear your stories. Likewise, as I said at the very beginning,

I don't believe there are all-knowing gurus and I'm still learning, so perhaps you've got something that really works for you that you didn't see included in the book? I'd be delighted if you could share it with me! My email address is graham@thinkproductive.co.uk. I'd love to hear from you!

There are so many people that have influenced my work and I want to thank them for what they've taught me. Many years ago I read Stephen Covey's *Seven Habits of Highly Effective People* and bits of that book have stuck with me ever since. David Allen's first book *Getting Things Done*, Sally McGhee's book *Take Back Your Life* and Merlin Mann's *Inbox Zero* talk have all been a big influence in helping me think about email, information and action in a different way. The work of Julia Cameron and Stephen Pressfield has encouraged me to express myself and overcome my own fear and resistance. Seth Godin has been an inspiration on similar themes and also generous at a critical point in the birth of this book, too.

Martin Farrell, Think Productive's 'Meetings Magician', is someone I'm proud to call a colleague and friend. Watching him create magic in meetings over the years has been inspirational. He also played an important role in the early development of Think Productive, helping to devise the CORD workflow model and co-delivering with me on some of our early workshops. His integrity, enthusiasm and wise counsel remain a constant source of support.

There are so many others whose contributions to the productivity 'space' are really worth acknowledging here as undoubted influences and I'm scared I'm going to miss someone obvious, but thanks to: Michael Sliwinski, Gina Trapani, Michael Hyatt, Leo Babauta, Laura Stack, Kevin Duncan, Tim Ferriss, Lois Graessle, Nancy Kline, Lee Cottier, Matthew Brown, Keith Bohanna, Stuart McKenzie, Russell Caird, Grace Marshall, Sharon Dale, Julia Richards, Wendy Smith, Bernadette McDonagh, Dawn O'Connor, Fokke Kooistra and Marcel van den Berg.

Thanks to my fantastic team of book reviewers and testers: Elena Boga, Sean Sankey, Natalie Reynolds, Charlotte Maytum, Kate Parsley, Lou Drake, Jen Lowthrop, Mark Fellows, Sharon Leonard, Rob and Sarah Geraghty, Jon Burgess, Lyss McDonald.

For fantastic and much-needed support and inspiration at different times in my journey: my editor Kate Hewson and the fantastic team of 'book ninjas' at Icon Books, Elloa Atkinson, Dr Rex Pogson, Lee Cottier, Lizzie Moore, Sneha Patel, Rob Wilson, Julia Slay, the whole Involve team, Max McLoughlin, Julia Poole, Marie Benton, Seyi Obakin, Paul Oginsky, Rasheed Ogunlaru, Allan Burrell, Chris Dubery, Adam Nichols, the SPW crew, Gareth Parker, Neil Smith, Mark Walsh, Claudia Pilgrim, Kathleen Cronin, Matt Hyde, Martin Farrell, Tom Wilcox, Jonathan Simmons, Amanda Prosser, Ian Ferriss, MT Rainey, Anne Moynihan, Ben Kernighan, Christopher Spence, Natalie Reynolds, Emma Serlin, Sophia Williams, Elena Boga, Lisa Brady, Marie-Anne Stucke, Charlene Campbell, Sam Davidson, Rachel Youngman, Anna Burton, Tony Wilson, Tom Wylie, Mum, Dad, Granny, Heather, Craig, Lyra Jo, Alex & Roscoe.

Finally to Chaz, partner-in-crime in work and life. I love you.

BUY A BOOK, CHANGE A LIFE

In reading *How to be a Productivity Ninja*, you are hopefully aware of the impact a good book can have.

Graham was the first Chairman of READ International and is now a founding ambassador for the charity. He is donating some of the royalties from sales of the e-book version of *How to be a Productivity Ninja* to READ International, meaning that for every e-book sold, real textbooks will find their way to schools in rural Tanzania!

Founded in 2006 by a group of passionate and visionary students, READ International harnesses the power of books and education to empower young people to change their lives and create futures free from poverty.

Graham's opening lines of this book are about changing the world as effortlessly as possible. By buying the e-book version of *How to be a Productivity Ninja*, not only will you develop effortless productivity in your own life, you'll also be helping to empower young people through education in rural Tanzania. And if you can, please also donate directly to READ International by visiting: **www.readinternational.org.uk**

It doesn't take much effort and it will seriously change lives.

HIRE GRAHAM TO SPEAK

Graham delivers a range of keynote talks and workshops for companies all around the world. To find out how to book Graham for your event, visit **www.grahamallcott.com** for more information, or drop us an email: **bookgraham@thinkproductive.co.uk**

CONTACT A PRODUCTIVITY NINJA NEAR YOU

think productive

You'll find details of all Think Productive's workshops, webinars and consultancy services over the page and at **www.thinkproductive.com** Email your nearest Think Productive office:

UK & Ireland –
hello@thinkproductive.co.uk

Australia –
hello@thinkproductive.com.au

Canada –
hello@thinkproductive.ca

Germany, France, Netherlands, Belgium & Luxembourg –
hallo@thinkproductive.nl

United States –
hello@thinkproductiveusa.com

BRING A PRODUCTIVITY NINJA TO YOUR OFFICE!

So you've become a Productivity Ninja, but what about Dave from accounts?! Perhaps we can help.

If you want to boost productivity in your organization, Think Productive runs a full range of in-house workshops to do exactly that. We started in the UK and are now making our way around the world, too:

GETTING YOUR INBOX TO ZERO

A 3-hour tour through Ninja email tips and tricks, complete with at-desk coaching so that participants finish the workshop with their inboxes actually at zero. Short, practical and dazzlingly effective. Also available as a full-day programme with 'Outlook Ninja'.

> *'Very satisfying. Love the approach!' – Julia Ewald, eBay*

EMAIL ETIQUETTE

Our Email Etiquette workshop focuses on good and bad email practice and teams leave having written an 'email manifesto' to help improve their email culture. Three hours later, watch the emails in your inbox get easier and easier to deal with as a result.

> *'Email has always annoyed me! This session brought these issues to the forefront of my mind and we were able to deal with them!' – Nick Matthews, Cardiff University Students' Union.*

STRESS LESS, ACHIEVE MORE

On this full-day workshop, we work both in the classroom and at desks to help people implement Think Productive's CORD workflow model, get their 'second brain' systems set up on computer or paper and fill several recycling bins full of old and useless paperwork. Energizing, clarity-inducing and fun, we regularly have people describe the day as 'Life-changing'!

'Very impressed. Actually the most productive and enjoyable course I've ever been on.' – Lisa Hutchinson, University of Bristol

MAKING MEETINGS MAGIC

A 3-hour workshop designed to transform the world of meetings! We cover good and bad meeting practices, the 40–20–40 continuum and a range of techniques. Coaching and group work focuses on both the individual and team issues with the aim of reducing the time everyone spends in meetings and making the meetings you do attend, well, magic!

'Really made us think about using our time for meetings more productively and in some cases had us questioning the need for a meeting at all!' – Alison Jenson, British Airways

HOW TO BE A PRODUCTIVITY NINJA

Ideal for conferences or team away days, this 1.5-hour talk is centred around the 9 characteristics of the Productivity Ninja as outlined in this book – and packed full of tips and tricks. It's also a great way to get a taste for our approach and explore which longer workshops might suit you best.

'Entertaining and packed with useful ideas. Extremely useful and thought-provoking.' – Heath Heatlie, GlaxoSmithKline

think productive

To find out about bringing our workshops to your company, email us: hello@thinkproductive.com

Join us on Facebook	Join us on LinkedIn	Follow us on Twitter
www.facebook.com/pages/ Think-Productive-Love- Your-Work	Think Productive – The Productivity Ninjas	@grahamallcott @thinkproductive